NEW YORK WRITING
from the
Penny Press to Melville

GOD IN THE STREET

NEW YORK WRITING
from the
Penny Press to Melville

GOD IN THE STREET

HANS BERGMANN

Temple University Press / Philadelphia

For Harriet
e,h

Temple University Press, Philadelphia 19122
Copyright © 1995 by Temple University. All rights reserved
Published 1995

⊗ The paper used in this book meets the requirements of the American National Standard for Information Sciences—Permanence of Paper for Printed Library Materials, ANSI Z39.48-1984

Text design by Adrianne Onderdonk Dudden

Library of Congress Cataloging-in-Publication Data
   Bergmann, Hans, 1941–
      God in the street : New York writing from the penny press to
   Melville / Hans Bergmann.
         p.   cm.
      Includes bibliographical references and index.
      ISBN 1-56639-357-4. — ISBN 1-56639-358-2 (pbk.)
         1. American literature—New York (N.Y.)—History and criticism.
      2. American literature—19th century—History and criticism.
      3. Melville, Herman, 1819–1891—Knowledge—New York (N.Y.)   4. New
      York (N.Y.)—Intellectual life—19th century.   5. City and town life
      in literature.   6. Cities and towns in literature.   7. New York
      (N.Y.)—In literature.   I. Title.
      PS255.N5B47   1995
      810.9'327471—dc20   95-6624

CONTENTS

ILLUSTRATIONS

ACKNOWLEDGMENTS

I am grateful to many people. When I got lost in writing this book I often turned directly to Herman Melville: not to the ghost but to the prose the living man left. Melville helped me again and again in my efforts to describe New York writing, and, as the book shows, I am grateful to him because his wonderful fiction is also literary historical explanation. Melville himself said "great geniuses are parts of the times; they themselves are the times; and possess a correspondent coloring." Melville was the genius of the times. He of course shares in no blame for my book's faults.

I would like to thank other people I don't know at all, each of whose scholarly work has made me work better and perhaps smarter; their names can be found in my notes, but I would like to mention here people whose writing is not directly about my topic and whose influence is great if not obvious: Donald Fanger, Alexander Welsh, John Berger, Jonathan Raban, and Richard Sennett. I am also happy to acknowledge my many Melville friends whose commitment in generation after generation to careful and exciting work—whether "old" historical or "new"—has been important to me always. I am grateful to the large institutions that gave me the time for my work—the National Endowment for the Humanities and George Mason University—and to many individuals in other institutions who unfailingly helped me get the materials I needed. I am particularly indebted to the staffs at the New York Public Library and the Library of Congress.

I thank those who read and advised about the manuscript with such care—my editor, Janet Francendese, and John Bryant, Lorna Irvine, Elizabeth Johns, Bob Madison, Dan McCall, and Debby Stuart—and to those who made extensive and repeated recommendations—Terry Comito, Harriet Bergmann, Deborah Kaplan, Barbara Melosh, and Eileen Sypher. I wish Terry were alive to celebrate the book's end: he would have known how. All these people made the book much better than it could have been without them. Here it is, people, and none of you is to blame either. Read it yet again if you can: it's better than it was because of you.

We incline to think that God cannot explain His own secrets, and that He would like a little information upon certain points Himself. We mortals astonish Him as much as He us. But it is this Being *of the matter; there lies the knot with which we choke ourselves. As soon as you say* Me, *a* God, *a* Nature, *so soon you jump off from your stool and hang from the beam. Yes, that word is the hangman. Take God out of the dictionary, and you would have Him in the street.*

Herman Melville to Nathaniel Hawthorne

GOD IN THE STREET

"Awake in his sleep, sure enough, ain't he?" said the cosmopolitan, again looking off in surprise.

Herman Melville
The Confidence-Man

Prologue: The Man in Cream-Colors

New York's Texts   I begin this book by saying that it ends with an unlikely argument. In my last chapter I show that Herman Melville's 1857 novel, *The Confidence-Man: His Masquerade*, which takes place entirely aboard a Mississippi steamboat, is a New York City story. What I mean is that Melville's last novel is written inside a discourse used about New York City in the period between 1833 and 1857. My book describes the formal practices of the discourse New York carried on about itself during those twenty-four years, from the time of the founding of the first cheap "penny" New York newspaper, the *Sun*, in 1833, through the publication of *The Confidence-Man* in 1857. The period begins when a "new," dramatically changing New York starts to be widely identified as an extraordinary subject and ends when the city has become firmly established as that subject. My book is one account of New York's becoming its own subject.

1

Not only *The Confidence-Man*'s setting but its indeterminacy and complexity make it seem a dubious final statement in a discourse about New York's becoming a subject. The reader's attention to Melville's novel is directed not to New York events, history, or sociology but to the sheer difficulties of deciding what is going on. The reader concentrates on the complexities of interpreting the book, and *The Confidence-Man*, like the biblical and secret narratives Frank Kermode describes, is "indeterminately studded with interpretations."[1] The wise reader understands enough not to linger long with any one interpretation but to emulate in thought the protean shifting of the Confidence-Man himself. I will argue that this effect on the reader marks the novel's place in New York discourse and identifies it as a New York book. Melville deploys the practices of the discourse and structures the novel on one key formal feature of the New York discourse—a narrative that describes encounters between ordinary individuals and extraordinary urban strangers, strangers who seem to *need* interpretation, even to insist on it.

The Confidence-Man's prologue is its first chapter, in which the "man in cream-colors" appears and writes quotations from 1 Corinthians on a slate ("Charity thinketh no evil," for example). The man, an apparent mute, seems to the crowd on the steamboat, as well as to the novel's readers, a character so extraordinary that he needs active interpretation. At a minimum we would like to know who he is, where he comes from, whether he preaches charity because he believes in it or whether he is softening up potential victims. But the man in cream colors and the prose that surrounds him do not allow us confidence in any single interpretation. The man in cream colors is mute, and yet he announces a book studded with interpretations.

The indeterminacy and complexity of *The Confidence-Man* are what some twentieth-century readers appreciate, and the conventional way of dealing with textual complexity is individual effort: we do "close reading" in an isolated struggle with the text until we understand it. The more difficult the text the more we want to think that it is individual, confined to itself, removed from its time and contexts: its complexities do not seem socially or historically significant. I think that as good and useful as individual close reading can be, better readings result when one comes to understand how even a complex text is a production of the conventions of its time and place. My recovery of New York discourse will not simplify Melville's complexities or turn hints into revelations, it will not make us able to say what or who the man in cream colors *is*, but it will make for more enlightened readings of all New York texts, including Melville's.

The New York discourse I describe in this book governs the form and content of a large set of texts published between 1833 and 1857. The texts are related because they all contain narratives of encounters between middle-class observers and a city that is so "new" and surprising as to require interpretation. They assume that there was once a knowable New York but that the new antebellum city is uncustomary, sensational, alien. The narratives describe encounters between observers and the city in many different ways. Some have observers encountering the whole of the city when they come upon a panoramic view of its vastness, as when they arrive at the top of a church steeple. Other narratives describe the observer taken on a tour of a series of sights of the city in which each new sight seems more sensational than the one before. Yet other narratives describe one-on-one encounters between a middle-class observer and an extraordinary individual (like Melville's man in cream colors) who belongs to the uncustomary city. All the discourse's narratives recount discoveries of the astonishing quotidian life of New York, and all are ways the contemporary urban culture had of trying to describe itself.

The New York observers come from many walks of life. The narrated encounter can occur between a newspaper journalist and the view from a church steeple, between a businessman and the denizens of notorious slum buildings, between a city visitor and the sights he sees when taken on a tour, between a charitable woman and a starving child, between a newspaper editor and a prostitute, between a minister and newsboys, between a physician and cholera victims, between a lawyer and a confidence man. The narratives occur in daily journalism, in popular religious writing, in popular fiction of several kinds, as well as in the work of Whitman and Melville. The texts are the apparently disconnected parts of the explosion of text that accompanies the conversion to a market society in the United States. Almanacs, cheap newspapers, story papers, popular novels, sensational nonfiction, and sentimental journalism were the *products* that New York publishing entrepreneurs offered the national and international reading market.

Market Society in New York The newspaper, magazine, and book business in New York shared in the enormous economic expansion of the antebellum period. Early twentieth-century historians accounted for New York's commercial success by citing Manhattan's favorable geography and the aggressive behavior of New York's elites: New York moved the goods and managed the money. In the years between 1840 and 1860, for example, American ocean steam tonnage increased six-fold, and New York's share of that total rose from 38 to 75 percent.[2] When in the 1840s it became clear that the railroad would soon supplant rivers and canals for internal trade, New York won that battle too (and here the geographic advantage was not so obvious) by making itself the major Atlantic terminus of the national railroad network. Wall Street financed the companies, the ships, the railroads, and the real estate by attracting American and international investors to the potential American profits, whether from western real estate or New York companies. The rewards for investing in and with New Yorkers continued through most of the antebellum period to attract people from around the world despite the risks made evident in the periodic financial panics (notably in 1837 and 1857) and in the oft-expressed outrage of Europeans at the flat loss of many of their American investments.[3]

During this period New York changed from a liberal mercantilist economy to an aggressive market economy. New Yorkers were not just traders and financiers: they owned small businesses that *made* things. We do not think of antebellum New York as a manufacturing center because we imagine such centers as dominated by a single industry and full of the thud and crash of machinery, like the prototypical Manchester or America's own Lowell. But even without a dominant industry, New York was during the antebellum period the most productive manufacturing city in the United States. Its production was carried on in "a metropolitan labyrinth of factories and tiny artisan establishments, central workrooms and outworkers' cellars, luxury firms and sweatwork strapping shops."[4] New Yorkers made clothes; New Yorkers made shoes; New Yorkers made furniture; New Yorkers made ships; New Yorkers made books and newspapers and magazines. The large number of these and other small businesses and the growth in their numbers had great consequences for social and political conditions in New York. The existence of small factories and artisan workshops helps explain what the large number of people who came to New York from Europe and from the rural United States were doing, how the "immigrant metropolis" was employed—when it was employed. Between 1815 and 1860, five and half million Europeans entered the United States. One-fifth of the entire population of Ireland, about one and a half million people, came between 1841 and 1855. A significant number of these immigrants stayed on in New York State and New York City: the 1855 New York State census showed that a quarter of the state's residents were foreign born while in the city almost one-half were foreign born. There was also significant immigration from the other sections of the United States, particularly from rural New England. In 1845 New York, with 361,000 persons, was still a small city on the world scale, approximately half the size of Paris. In 1860 greater New York, with over a million residents, was a world city and had caught up with Paris's own rapid growth in population.[5]

Living conditions were terrible for working and nonworking New Yorkers alike. In 1833 the first building designed to be a multifamily housing unit, a tenement, was built in New York, and by the Civil War over half the city's population, nearly five hundred thousand people, lived in eighteen thousand tenements. In 1856, one out of every twenty-nine New Yorkers died, a rate nearly double that of London at the time, and observers who had looked at conditions in London and New York were convinced that the Five Points neighborhood—just a short walk from City Hall—was worse than London's infamous Seven Dials or Whitechapel.[6] The Five Points became for New Yorkers and visiting Europeans alike the sign of the social horrors, and illicit excitements, of the new urban life. Living conditions for most New Yorkers were not as grim as those in the Points, but New York was a "modern" city with a large number of immigrants who were by the 1850s largely unskilled workers living on the edges of their employers' cycles of success and failure.

Literary History The study of discursive practice is complicated at best, and it might seem an unlikely way to add to the social history of the antebellum period, particularly when that history is now being painstakingly written by social historians. The historians themselves often have an understandable suspicion of contemporary texts that describe the material conditions of New York. They think the texts are tainted as evidence because they were written and published by people whose class interests distorted their understanding of their own time. The suspicions are well founded: the ideological analysis of discourse— the investigation of the relation between a set of texts and its social, historical, or political context—does not reveal material conditions directly.[7]

I think, however, as every historian primarily interested in writing must, that distortion is not obliteration. What is exciting about working with texts, as Roland Barthes explains, is that the bourgeois cultural product *needs* the energy of the "real" for its own force. For Barthes, careful interpretation could discover, for example, that a sentimental account of an urban newsboy contains, in however distorted a form, the elements of the "real" newsboy that gave the false picture its potency. Barthes argues that the specific study of forms "does not in any way contradict the necessary principles of totality and History. On the contrary: the more a system is specifically defined in its forms, the more amenable it is to historical criticism. . . . I shall say that a little formalism turns one away from History, but that a lot brings one back to it."[8] The actual can only exist in the corrupt and distorted form: that's all there is. The text is the product of the historical process, and it carries the evidence of that process with it. The census report or any other presumably objective data a historian might use is also a product of historical process, and it too contains the distortion that is not necessarily obliteration.

The dominant twentieth-century scholars of American literature were not interested in material conditions of production. They wanted to make the study of American literature respectable and important, and their method was to analyze certain writings in detail and assert that they were as complex as those of the English immortals. The creation of the reputation of five American antebellum writers—Ralph Waldo Emerson, Henry David Thoreau, Walt Whitman, Nathaniel Hawthorne, and Herman Melville—dominated the practice of scholars of United States literary culture in the mid-twentieth century. F. O.

Matthiessen's hugely influential *American Renaissance* (1941) told his time that the skills of the five were a sufficient claim to a transcendent excellence; their 1850s works were "America's . . . affirming its rightful heritage in the whole expanse of art and culture." If we have in Herman Melville a writer of Shakespeare's rank, then our long period of cultural exile is over and we have finally a literature that is distinct and self-contained and rises above the mass of subliterary efforts.[9]

The study of *regional* discursive practice, like New York's, had little to do with establishing the classics of American literature; their transcendence was not thought related to historical context. Two instructive books written after Matthiessen's *American Renaissance* do concentrate on antebellum New York literary culture: Van Wyck Brooks's *The Times of Melville and Whitman* (1947) and Perry Miller's *The Raven and the Whale* (1956). Both are learned and immensely helpful because Brooks and Miller were conversant with the works of many of the New York novelists, poets, and essayists active while Melville and Whitman were writing. Brooks tells the story of how New England culture moved to New York, transmitted by the poetry of Walt Whitman, the essays and novels of Brook Farm graduate George William Curtis, and the literary influence of Horace Greeley's *New York Tribune*. Brooks's wide reading forces his readers to recognize the richness of the New York literary culture of the period.

Perry Miller writes the history of New York's magazine "war" between the largely Whig writers associated with Lewis Gaylord Clark and the *Knickerbocker* magazine and the Democratic "Young American" writers associated with George and Evert A. Duyckinck's literary circle. The skirmishes were over personalities—particularly that of the novelist of New York City folklore, Cornelius Mathews—and over the "Americanness" of American literature. The Young Americans confronted the issue of the nation's sense of cultural inferiority head on and asserted with Whitman that "the United States themselves are . . . the greatest poem." The Whigs and the conservative *Knickerbocker* magazine took the more genial view that literature was a larger matter of participation in the international literary culture dominated by Charles Dickens.[10]

For Miller, literary history is an intellectual entertainment to be had once. There is only the *one* moment of amazement as the reader learns about Cornelius Mathews's self-aggrandizing speech at the February 1842 dinner for Charles Dickens at the City Hotel.[11] There is little sense in Miller or Brooks that anyone after them will ever need to read Mathews or Curtis, much less think seriously about their work. What energizes both scholars' narratives are their comic accounts of the minor writers—Brooks's shallow and tame George William Curtis or Miller's rude and inept Cornelius Mathews—men who never measured up to their aesthetic betters. Brooks and Miller provide a regional context for Melville (and to some extent Whitman and Poe) that is largely biographical, and although we are made to understand that the New York literary culture was important to Melville's career as he understood it, we are not to think it important to his art. We do not reconstruct a literary history from this analysis: we remember it to forget it again.

A comprehensive revisitation of the literary culture of the antebellum United States waited until two large studies appeared in the 1980s, Lawrence Buell's *New England Literary Culture* (1986) and David S. Reynolds's *Beneath the American Renaissance* (1988). Buell's book is important to me in that his starting point, like Miller's or Brooks's, is *region*, although he confines his remarks about the difference between New England and New York literary culture to an interesting note. Buell cites Perry Miller on New York as a haven for New England writers seeking a freer atmosphere and makes three brief generalizations about the cultural differences between New York and Boston: that New Englanders insisted more on the moral dimension of literary works; that their avant-garde was a Whig one while New York's was a (Locofoco) "Young America" Democratic one; and that in New York, literary activity was more openly recognized as a commercial pursuit than in fastidious New England.[12]

David Reynolds's book assumes a national literary culture, but because his methodology insists on the connection between the "literary" and the "subliterary" he does consider some regional discourses. Reynolds's title (with its allusion to Matthiessen's book) emphasizes that the classic texts are still on top, above the ground, but *Beneath the American Renaissance* embraces with wide arms the complex variety of antebellum literary history and finds in it an underground library of images and literary devices that were assimilated and transformed by Emerson,

Melville, Hawthorne, Thoreau, Whitman, Poe, and Dickinson when they created their major and transcendent works. Reynolds's premise is that the classic American texts are not self-sufficient but "open," the democratic meeting grounds of numerous idioms and voices from a wide variety of contemporary texts. The idioms and voices were, following the Bakhtinian conception, "relativized, or detached from single ideological meanings" and thus part of a carnival culture from which the major writers could draw. Each of the major texts of the American renaissance creatively reconstructs these freed socioliterary elements, and the result is a work of art that transforms and enlivens its materials through "fusion."[13]

Reynolds writes about socioliterary context but not the processes of ideological production (not even to the extent that Brooks or Miller did). Other "new Americanists" or "new historicists," on the other hand, have come to literary history because their methodology forces them to. Their interest in ideological analysis makes these scholars focus on the ideological system that produces the classic texts, and that in turn leads to an inclusion of the subliterary. The new methods have uncovered not only the underlying political categories of race, gender, and class in the themes and language of classic texts—as in the pieces collected in Sacvan Bercovitch and Myra Jehlen's *Ideology and Classic American Literature* (1986)—but they have forced a certain amount of attention again on literary history as a whole, on how popular writers and journalists and classic writers are part of the same ideological system.

I hope with John Bryant and many others that future literary histories of the United States will unite the best techniques of the old and the new historicists, combining the meticulous attention to particulars of biography, historical context, and text with an understanding of ideological production.[14] My book writes an old and new literary history of New York discourse, trying to document in detail the features of the New York discourse, in all its subliterary and literary forms, while at the same time suggesting the ideological function of that discourse.

I think with the new historicists that subliterary and literary texts are productions of ideology in the way that dramatic productions are productions of a playwright's text. The literary text does not passively reflect the class structure but rather comes of it, the way a dramatic production comes of its written text. The difference is that in the productions of ideology there is no preexisting, readable text: the ideological source is indwelling in its cultural production.[15] Some sets of cultural texts can be grouped as discourses, and all members of a particular discourse share formal elements and a congregated institutional power in the system of ideological production. "Ideology" is of course a term that has been endlessly defined and redefined. Sacvan Bercovitch's version is useful:

> An ideology . . . arises out of historical circumstances, and then re-presents these, symbolically and conceptually, as though they were natural, universal, and right—as though the ideals promulgated by a certain group or class . . . were not the product of history but the expression of self-evident truth. . . . Ideology transmutes history into myth so as to enable people to act in history.[16]

New York narratives of urban encounter in the antebellum period express the new middle class's effort to initiate and then continue its dominance despite the rapid and wide-ranging changes brought by its own success. The discourse contains ways of representing the threats to the simple comprehension of events that the new urban conditions presented, ways of asserting the continued plausibility of the power of the responsible Christian observer, and ways of representing the continued meaningfulness of the "other." If the meanings of the "other" are obscure or nonexistent, then one can have little confidence in interpretive systems, and confidence in interpretive systems is what makes for ideological perpetuation.

The New York encounter discourse can show us, if we look, some of the actual social and economic history that the ideology struggles to control and obscure. The narratives often treat the encounter in a way that shows the success of the middle-class observer at normalizing the alien and finding (often supernatural) "meaning" in it. Most interesting about many of the texts, and a clue to how complex productions of the discourse (like *The Confidence-Man*) can occur, is their representation of how close chaos and meaninglessness are. Often the encounter text provides a portrayal of an outright lapse in the middle-class individual's interpretive power. The gap, frequently only a momentary loss of confidence, is absolutely necessary to prove the power and adaptability of the operative ideological assumptions in overcoming the New York interpretive "problem." The gap itself shows us history and the class struggle. It is a brief instance of what Carolyn Porter calls a moment of historical crisis.

> Bourgeois man does not deny history, but rather is incapable of apprehending it at all, except in reified forms. Yet at moments of crisis, the contradictions inherent in bourgeois society surface, seem to break through the reified patina of the objectified world, revealing the incoherence of the rational systems by which its actual sensuous activity has been obscured, as well as the historically mediated nature of "objectivity."[17]

The antebellum New York texts, even in their sometimes graceless forms, enact the challenge to interpretation of daily events that the new urban realities posed, and many texts portray the moment of interpretive inadequacy, when the dramatized observer is, quite literally, "at a loss for words." The events and people the observer sees seem at first unspeakable—not interpretable within the usual rational and sentimental bourgeois systems. At those moments in the text, there is the chance of breaking through the "reified patina of the objectified world."

Herman Melville I do not share the view of many new historicists that an author can have no individual stamp on the discursive practice he or she participates in. I think an individual author *can* recognize the rules of the discourse he or she is in just as later readers can. But having knowledge of the requirements of a particular discourse does not mean that one can escape it. Even the self-conscious author is always subject to a discourse's authority because in order to be read and understood by a contemporary audience he or she must work within its rules. The author can, however, deploy the conventions so as to make the readers understand the conventions *as* conventions. This sort of author within a contemporary discourse is particularly valuable to the later historian of discourse, and the reader of my book will already have understood that Herman Melville is the contemporary expert I turn to frequently in my study of the antebellum discourse of New York. Melville, particularly in the period after *Moby-Dick* (1851), is a deployer of the complexities of New York discourse but also its self-conscious historian.

Because Herman Melville's works have continued to have such high prestige in twentieth-century American literary culture, the surviving records of his relations with his New York editors and publishers, with his friends and family, have been studied meticulously, and we now have better, and more accurate, knowledge of Melville's literary relations than Perry Miller had. In a large body of biographical, textual, and contextual research on Melville scholars, like Hershel Parker are trying to organize a study of the determinacy of the creative process—the force fields that surround the individual writer as he writes.[18] This research is invaluable to the new historicist because it shows that Melville was not only an active participant in late 1840s Young American literary culture, friend to Evert Duyckinck and Cornelius Mathews, but that his entire career was determined by the exigencies of the New York publishing business. His friends, his publishers, the men and women who published in the same magazines as he, were transforming New York's history into forms that tried to stabilize it, successfully interpret it. Melville was a New York writer working in the midst of the New York discourse.

I allude to a Melville sentence when I title my book *God in the Street*. I try thereby to acknowledge how important Melville is to this book and to use his phrase to specify one central theme of New York discourse. Melville wrote to Nathaniel Hawthorne in 1851 about his reaction to *The House of Seven Gables* and about the extent of God's knowledge:

> We incline to think that God cannot explain His own secrets, and that He would like a little information upon certain points Himself. We mortals astonish Him as much as He us. But it is this *Being* of the matter; there lies the knot with which we choke ourselves. As soon as you say *Me*, a *God*, a *Nature*, so soon you jump off from your stool and hang from the beam. Yes, that word is the hangman. Take God out of the dictionary, and you would have Him in the street.[19]

I will risk a reading of this part of Melville's letter. Melville is not perfectly clear: he is writing quickly in a private letter to a man he imagines will always understand him.[20] I presume that when Melville writes *"Being* of the matter" he means undivided being, simple existence that has nothing to do with knowing or thinking. That Being is the source of the problem of naming because it is with the attempt to *say* what Being is—*"Me," "God," "Nature"*—that the individual mind chokes on the knot. Making words and categories, naming, is a jump into individuation: the "word is the hangman" in the sense that it isolates the human individual, the namer, in a narcissistic self-reflection. Naming is suicidal for Melville because in giving words to something, one creates, the way Ahab does in *Moby-Dick,* an individual and arbitrary "truth" that permits action but makes no nearer approach to transcendent truth.

In the last sentence of the quotation—"Take God out of the dictionary, and you would have Him in the street"—I think Melville means that if God is not named, not made into a potential knowable, not in the dictionary, he would be "in the street," a part of the quotidian and ordinary life along with the modern crowd.

There are two possible consequences if God is in the "street" of ordinary life. In the first, God is much more available. This God in the street is a god who can be found in much more direct, emotional relationship with the humanity around him: his definition is not a matter of the dictionary but of intuitive feeling; he dwells in each person. In the second possibility, the one I think Melville has more in mind, the God in the street is the one who is so undifferentiated from the ordinary crowd, so silent, that we cannot find him. He has disappeared to humanity—something that, for all we know, God might choose to do anyway. It is like imagining Christ walking those stony Palestinian streets without revealing himself, with his eyes only on eternity and not on the Lazarus to be raised. The first, available God in the street is the sentimental and available god of feeling that nineteenth-century liberal Christianity is fond of imagining; the second and unavailable God in the street is the one that Melville writes about.

I realize that in saying that Melville is at the endpoint of my description of antebellum New York discourse I participate in the claim that Melville is our "great" author, the Titan who rises like his own Mount Greylock over the forgotten hundreds of foothills of our antebellum texts. I do claim a special place for Melville in my book, but I do so thinking that Melville does not rise above his times so much as he helps us understand them. Melville says it himself, in "Hawthorne and His Mosses," in describing (grandiosely, to be sure) how literary geniuses can be found among his contemporaries: "great geniuses are parts of the times; they themselves are the times; and possess a correspondent coloring."[21] Herman Melville's works "are the times," and it diminishes them to think them immutable "classics" that transcend their context. In Terry Eagleton's words, "valuable art comes into being not *despite* its historical limitations . . . but *by virtue of* them."[22] In my view, the *relation* between Melville's work and its historical discourse is the ground of its significance.

The four parts of my book describe the chronological development of New York discourse from 1833 to 1857. They also demonstrate how Herman Melville worked in and against the discourse from 1849 on. The discourse changes significantly during the whole period—it is never a fixed form—and my analyses will chart its forms at different points in the twenty-four years. Part One, "Panorama," describes narratives that sketch encounters with the whole of the city. I analyze the anecdotal forms and the cultural influence of penny newspapers; I describe the panoramic guidebooks that boosted the commercial city; I write about Walt Whitman's journalism and how his 1855 *Leaves of Grass* arose from the journalistic panoramic convention. All the panoramic accounts present the city as a topic for understanding: they assert that the everyday life of the new commercial culture is important and meaningful and that a "coming man," a new kind of culture hero, must be the one to interpret it in the name of the new mass public.

Part Two, " 'Dickens' Place,' " explains the huge formal influence Charles Dickens's writing had on the sentimental and sensational accounts of New York. I examine the many encounters with street children in narratives written by sentimental Christian observers, including those who by the late 1840s encountered not just "lost" children but dying ones. I show how Herman Melville takes the sentimental encounter with urban death and reworks it into a sight of untranscendable death in *Redburn* (1850). I explain how the accounts of visits to the Five Points neighborhood, which imitated Dickens's report of his visit there in *American Notes* (1842), tried to rationalize New York's hell and how Melville repeats and reworks that conventional visit in *Pierre* (1852).

Part Three, " 'Do You Not See the Reason for Yourself?' " asks the question that Bartleby asks the lawyer in Melville's New York story "Bartleby, the Scrivener." The remark underlines the interpretive isolation of the observer in the urban encounter that Melville unrelentingly portrays in the story. I discuss the importance of the sophisticated 1850s New York magazine *Putnam's* for the history of the New York lawyer's story; I write about "Bartleby" as a complex development of New York lawyers' stories and of liberal Christian theology.

Part Four, "Awake in Our Sleep?" asks whether the observer can be "awake" in the modern world, which seems a Babel of superficial dialogue. The first chapter describes the narratives of New York subliterary and literary culture that resulted in one version of the modern man, the confidence man, and the last chapter of the book describes how Herman Melville's *The Confidence-Man* is a history and meditation on "the moderns" and New York discourse itself. The indeterminacy of the "man in cream-colors" is revisited to demonstrate how sophisticated form arises out of its own historical materials.

PART ONE

PANORAMA

Writers must recognize that the life of intellect is going to be carried more and more in the weekly and daily papers. They hold the promise of great excellence, particularly for the condensed essay, narrative, criticism.

Margaret Fuller
Papers on Literature and Art

I

The Penny Press: Anecdotes of New York

Newspaper Culture   The discourse of New York City during the period 1833–57 is based on a narrative of an urban encounter between a representative middle-class person and the "new" New York. In this first part of my book I examine texts that enact encounters with the extraordinary city as a *whole*: they present verbal equivalents of the New York panoramic illustrations very popular in the same antebellum period. In this first chapter my texts are those created by the brash editors of the new "penny" newspapers in New York. These men announced in editorials and in what their papers covered that the city itself was the news. They asserted as well that they themselves were the new and necessary men, the heroic interpreters of the new urban culture.

The culture created by the emergent bourgeois class was foremost a "newspaper culture." Like European cities earlier in the century, antebellum New York defined itself to itself and the world largely by newspaper. The advent of the cheap newspaper in the nineteenth century in Paris and then in other cities and New York is the exact moment of the invention of *le quotidien* as an object of cultural attention. From that point on, the ordinary and daily is what we *assume*, and the newspaper is its medium. Walter Benjamin quotes Jean Villemessant, founder of *Le Figaro*: " 'To my readers,' he used to say, 'an attic fire in the Latin Quarter is more important than a revolution in Madrid.' "[1]

The newspaper is a metonym for modern life itself.

> In its routinized, quotidian recurrence, in its quintessential prosaicism, in its unrepentant commercialism, the newspaper almost seems to have been devised to represent the pattern of variation without change, the repetitiveness, autonomization, and commodification which . . . have marked fundamental patterns of our social existence.[2]

The invention of the cheap newspaper was the beginning of a disposable culture. The newspaper does not give us memorable story but information, and information does not long survive the moment in which it was new. It "lives only at that moment; it has to surrender to it completely and explain itself to it without losing any time."[3]

In the first third of the nineteenth century, New York was the newspaper capital of the United States, publishing about six dailies and six more weeklies and semiweeklies. Most successful of these papers were the *Commercial Advertiser*, the *Mercantile Advertiser*, the *Daily Advertiser*, the *Journal of Commerce*, and the *Courier and Enquirer*. As their names show these papers gave large amounts of space to commercial announcements and business news. James Watson Webb's *Courier and Enquirer* had a livelier tone than its ponderous competition, particularly after 1827 when Webb bought up the *Enquirer* and acquired thereby the clever journalists Mordecai M. Noah and James Gordon Bennett. Other papers, like the *Evening Post* edited by William Cullen Bryant, were primarily political papers. None of these papers gave the "news" as we now understand the term.[4]

In 1833 Benjamin H. Day's *New York Sun* changed the idea of the newspaper in New York. Day's innovation was to make his paper small in format, cheap, independent of party or mercantile patronage, and filled with what readers wanted, not what they needed. The paper was sold on the "London plan" to newspaper boys for sixty-seven cents for a hundred copies, and the boys aggressively resold their copies on the streets for a penny. The advertisement for boys in the first issue was headlined "To the Unemployed," and Bernard Flaherty, all of ten years old, was the first of the "unemployed" to sell the *Sun*. Day's idea was to forgo the stability of subscription lists and reach for the market just outside his office, the potential readers walking in the streets. Within four months the *Sun*'s circulation was four thousand, almost equaling the largest mercantile paper. In 1835 a new steam press increased the *Sun*'s printing capacity to twenty-two thousand copies, far larger than any daily paper in the United States and almost as large as the largest circulations in London.[5]

The *Sun*'s most important innovation was its coverage of everyday New York. Its news was the news of New York, with comparatively few commercial or political items. Like the newspaper sketch or "leaf" called a *feuilleton* in Paris, George Wisner's narratives and the *Sun*'s other anecdotes were rudimentary literary forms struggling toward a descriptive realism that could present the city's new effects in an entertaining way to the paper's readers. Each sketch is a narrated encounter with the city; collectively the sketches are the daily newspaper, an ever-reiterated panoramic description of New York.

Day's best-known early features were the humorous police-court anecdotes written by George W. Wisner. Wisner, imitating the *London Morning Herald*'s reporting on Bow Street court, was willing to get up early (court was at 4 A.M.) to cover the court and then write the brief narratives. His "funny" stories about the Irish lower class were an immediate hit.

> Margaret Thomas was drunk in the street—said she never would get drunk again "upon her honor." Committed, "upon honor."
>   William Luvoy got drunk because yesterday was so devilish warm. Drank 9 glasses of brandy and water and said he would be cursed if he wouldn't drink 9 more as quick as he could raise the money to buy it with. He would like to know what right the magis-

trate had to interfere with his private affairs. Fined $1—forgot his
pocketbook, and was sent over to Bridewell.

Bridget McMunn got drunk and threw a pitcher at Mr. Ellis, of
53 Ludlow st. Bridget said she was the mother of 3 little orphans—
God bless their dear souls—and if she went to prison they would
choke to death for the want of something to eat. Committed.[6]

Wisner's report does not seem so funny to us, nor would it seem so
funny just a decade or two later in New York, when the seriousness of
urban problems was even more in the public's view, but in 1834 the
style was an immediate hit and the beginning of the *news*.[7] The news
tells us about the immediate and the everyday, and at the same time it
tells us it disposes of it. The narrative persona is the satiric urban "expert" who is, despite his class, streetwise enough to know where the
police courts are and irreverent enough to crack jokes about drunks.
This police court reporter takes it upon himself to see what is going on
among the immigrant classes and presents the results of his encounter
with the (initially) inexplicable and unrecognizable "other." Implicitly
well educated and experienced, Wisner is alone among the savages and
places them within easily understandable, funny categories. He does
not linger to struggle with social analysis: it is as if the problem is not
serious enough to need explaining.

Another *Sun* innovation was to make up items that Day thought
would create a continuing desire for more papers in the public. The
most notorious faked story was Richard Adams Locke's "Moon Hoax"
in 1835. The paper printed a small article asserting that Sir John Her-
schel had invented a telescope that had discovered creatures living on
the moon and on subsequent days printed longer pieces, as if following
up on the original story. The interest was enormous. All the other
newspapers were taken in and became themselves eager for the latest
from the moon. Yale sent a delegation down to study the "documents"
from which the first article claimed authority. There was great fun and
great sales until Locke had a drink too many and slipped the truth to a
Journal of Commerce reporter. Even the revelations of the trick boosted
Sun sales, of course, and the condescending outrage of the educated
elites at the misuse of the media delighted the readership and helped
define the cheap newspaper as the irreverent opposition to cultural
dominance by the wealthy and established.[8]

The *Sun* was rapidly followed into the market. In the six years between 1834 and 1840, thirty-five penny dailies were issued in New York. Most lived only briefly, but others, particularly James Gordon Bennett's *New York Herald*, survived to outdo Day with his own idea. Michael Schudson contends that from the *Sun* on American newspapers started to "reflect, not the affairs of an elite in a small trading society, but the activities of an increasingly varied, urban, and middle-class society of trade, transportation and manufacturing." He thinks penny papers began in urban commercial centers and, more than anywhere else, in New York because they were needed to express and build the culture of a democratic market society. The papers articulated a radically new culture "which had no place for social or intellectual deference" and in which it became possible to think of " 'self-interest' as the mainspring of human behavior and . . . a motive to be admired."[9]

The Devil on Two Sticks: James Gordon Bennett James Gordon Bennett's *New York Herald* was the most untamed of the new papers. Bennett understood the principle of disposable news, had as much fun as Richard Adams Locke at being outrageous, and made clear in everything he wrote that the hero of the news narrative was the bold editor himself. *All* parts of the city were Bennett's beat: anything could be revealed in a flash by the revolving beacon of his panoramic attention; any urban mystery could be found out. The *Herald* reported on the city's variety and complexity, and its new sights—from the destitution of the Five Points slum neighborhood to the extravagance of the Astor House hotel—were sensations that the *Herald* worked and reworked for its public.

The *Herald* did become known and respected for the quality and seriousness of its news gathering, but violent death was often the heart of its New York news. In its first two weeks of publication the *Herald* carried accounts of three suicides, three murders, a fire that killed five persons, an accident in which a man blew off his head, descriptions of a guillotine execution in France, a riot in Philadelphia, and the execution of Major John André half a century before. To the lurid accounts of accident and crime the *Herald* soon attached investigative (and imaginative) narratives that reported the intimate details of the lives of the New York rich, exposing with undisguised delight the pretensions and excesses of heretofore inviolate elites. The *Herald* perfected the keyhole reporting that turned what had formerly been private event into public narrative.

Charles Dickens tells us what he thinks of the New York penny press of this early period when he has the eponymous hero of *Martin Chuzzlewit* (1844) arrive in New York harbor just as Dickens had two years before at the beginning of his United States tour. Martin experiences the United States first *as* New York newspaper. His ship is boarded and overrun by newsboys, and their shrill cries are the first voices he hears in the democratic country. Dickens re-creates New York newsboy speech and reorients it into an attack on the New York press as well as on the United States' brand of unprincipled democracy.

> "Here's the New York Sewer! Here's some of the twelfth thousand of to-day's Sewer, with the best accounts of the markets, and all the shipping news, and four whole columns of country correspondence, and a full account of the Ball at Mrs. White's last night, where all the beauty and fashion of New York was assembled; with the Sewer's own particulars of the private lives of all the ladies that was there! . . . Here's the Sewer, here's the Sewer! Here's the wide-awake Sewer; always on the lookout."[10]

The *Sewer*—remarkably like the *Herald*—is first of all proud of itself—its circulation figures, its fearlessness in exposure, its enterprise in getting "exclusives." Its primary story is the story of its own success. Most of all, the *Sewer* is "wide-awake." "Wide awake," an Americanism originating in the 1830s, is the most admired characteristic of the market-society American.

Bennett's writing in the *Herald* is so outrageous that Dickens's version hardly seems a parody. Bennett is always self-consciously creating a new "wide-awake" institution. The *Herald* is not merely a new newspaper, it is a new social organization, a new site where discourse occurs.

> What is to prevent a daily newspaper from being made the greatest organ of social life? Books have had their day—the theaters have had their day—the temple of religion has had its day. A newspaper can be made to take the lead of all these in the great movements of human thought, and of human civilization. A newspaper can send more souls to Heaven, and save more from Hell, than all the churches or chapels

in New York—besides making money at the same time. Let it be tried. (August 19, 1836)

The *Herald*'s claim is shocking, intentionally so. The unabashed focus on making money is amazing: we (if we belong to an older educated elite) do not want a great human institution to be so devoted to profit, or at least we do not want it to *say* it is. Even the typography—the newspaper dashes that Whitman was later to use in the 1855 "Song of Myself"—is shocking and casual, a sign of the editor's haste. Almost as stunning is the possibility that the editor is in some way joking, "putting us on," as we say now. But how can he joke about literature and religion?

Bennett's self-consciousness is the key to the tone and attitude of the early *Herald*. The tongue-in-cheek excess, the reckless daring, the outrageousness define the created persona of Bennett and his paper and are the most recognizable and exuberant characteristics of the beginnings of New York discourse. Bennett's own success was always his most important news story. He boasted that his brains were solely responsible for the *Herald*: "Shakespeare is the great genius of the drama—Scott of the novel—Milton and Byron of the poem—and I mean to be the genius of the daily newspaper press" (February 28, 1837). He was "the NAPOLEON of the newspaper press" (November 26, 1841) and compared himself at other times to Zoroaster, Confucius, Charlemagne, Homer, Herodotus, Alexander the Great, Caesar, Luther, and Byron.

Bennett is fully aware that he himself is the rising entrepreneurial hero of his newspaper. His own persona becomes one of the disposable commodities the paper sells. Here is Bennett in what is nominally a drama review in his September 2, 1836, issue:

Miss Clifton and Edwin Forrest will be the Luther and Calvin of the theatrical reformation. They are two great spirits, inhabiting majestic frames and fine limbs. They are producing, and will produce, the same revolution in the drama, that I am doing in literature and the daily press. The "loafers" must get out of the way in both cases. They season high, so do I. They make speeches which they laugh at "aside," so do I. We are all quacks together—but so was Shakespeare, so was Garrick, so was Kean, and why the devil should not we? This is a voluptuous city—of a voluptuous country. You must reach their souls through appetite and passion. Miss Clifton, Forrest, and I, will be the rage for three years—no more. Egad, let us "make hay while the sun shines."

Bennett knows he lives in a new time, that he has been temporarily empowered by a new medium to define himself as a culture hero. The "voluptuous" city is where everything for the moment seems possible. One can make money in information by playing to appetite and passion, and not only that, one can *tell* the paying readers that a lot of the information isn't serious—that it has no depth, that it can be thrown away the better to prepare for the next day's equally disposable information.

The Bennett created by the *Herald* glorified the hustle of the new market society, intentionally outraged the older privileged classes, and ambitiously took on the whole of the social life of the new city—from the sedate functions of its older elites to the poverty and crime of the Five Points. Most of all he tells his readers that his apparent vices will soon be seen as virtues. He will be the model New York man: "Accompanied with talent, independence, genius, and success, my vanity and egotism will in two years be deemed and taken for inspiration and virtue" (May 8, 1837).

Bennett most inflamed polite opinion by narrating urban encounters that revealed the religious, sexual, and social pretensions of the elites and by recounting those encounters in narratives whose language and implication were salacious. The outrage of respectable citizens and respectable newspapers organized itself into a "moral war" on Bennett by 1840: he and his paper were to be ostracized. A pamphlet published after the height of the moral war but claiming to be part it conveniently collects the most offensive passages from the *Herald*. Like nearly all criminal biographies and autobiographies, *The Life and Writings of James Gordon Bennett* (1844) certainly has an ambiguous status because its selections from the *Herald* make the pamphlet itself sensational reading. The picture of Bennett that serves as the frontispiece is cruel, making the most of Bennett's crossed eyes. Edgar Allan Poe identifies the pamphlet's editor in a letter to the *Columbia (South Carolina) Spy* as Thomas Low Nichols, a New York journalist known for his reform ideas.[11]

Nichols's selections reveal a Bennett acting like the devil Asmodeus in Lesage's *Le Diable boiteux* (1707). Asmodeus, originally a minor devil in Tobit, was Lesage's "devil on two sticks" who limped on his crutches across the roofs of Madrid to uncover the secrets of society dinner parties, sexual dalliance, betrayals, people starving in the gutter. Asmodeus had the panoramic knowledge of the whole that allowed him to show the hidden truths; he was the panoramic devil who showed people what they should not have longed so much to know. Lesage's book and character were revived in France in the nineteenth century, and American journalism and popular fiction imitate that revival.

Nichols's book reprints a March 7, 1836, *Herald* news account describing an Episcopal clergyman "of hitherto unimpeachable character" who is charged with "making love too suddenly—without due preparation,—to a lovely and accomplished widow, who lets out schoolrooms, takes in sewing, and owns a pair of fine eyes, and bust unmatchable in Broadway in its sunniest day."

> The reverend gentleman was . . . shown into the schoolroom, which was up stairs. He mounted the stairs with alacrity, entered the room, found the lovely widow alone, and immediately delivered his message, —then entered into conversation with her on some trivial subject, such as the weather—the snow—the long winter, &c., &c. The widow looked prettier than ever. Her black eyes burned with meaning, and the Reverend gentleman's very grey hair almost changed color, and turned brown with youth again. He could stand it no longer, but started up, and— * * * * * * ecstasy * * *
> * * * soft cheek * * * * * * * * clasped
> * * * * * * * * * * * * * * *
> * bust * * * * * * * * * * * *
> her * * * arms * * * * * screamed *
> * * * * * murder * * villain * * *
> unholy * * * * * rascal * * * * This was
> kept up for several minutes. At length she freed one of her hands, and commenced scratching and tearing at a furious rate. She then managed to get clear, and ran out of the room continuing her shouts and cries for some time.

The joke for the *Herald* is the clergyman's being overcome with illicit desire. What is offensive for polite opinion is the *Herald*'s delight in that as well as in what still offends us, a comic account of an attempted rape. The article is the outrageous production of a new journalistic principle that not only reports the quotidian but laughs at serious matters. Worse, the comic narrative leeringly suggests that the event is a synecdoche for the whole of elevated social life of the city. Good society is a sham.

Distinguished New Yorker and diarist Philip Hone hoped that the moral war against Bennett would ruin him: "Write him down, make respectable people withdraw their support from the vile sheet, so that it shall be considered disgraceful to read it, and the serpent will be rendered harmless."[12] Bennett on the other hand thinks that the members of the older elites like Hone are "loafers" (another New York Americanism new in his period). He makes their privacy public to expose their loaferishness, their hollow pretensions. People like Hone are not "wide-awake."

Hone and many others of his class were obviously reading the paper they hoped no one else would read, but historian Dan Schiller thinks that most *Herald* readers "must have been drawn from the ranks of artisans and mechanics."[13] The paper championed entrepreneurial equal rights, and the half of the population that was artisans and mechanics would have enjoyed its exposés of the elites. Michael Schudson claims nearly the opposite, finding that the money articles and the Wall Street reports mean that the *Herald* must have appealed to the bourgeois population. He contends that the "moral war" meant that Bennett had gained the middle-class audience he sought and that was what his competitors were worried about. I think the evidence shows that there was a wide audience—working and middle-class—for the *Herald* by the late 1840s.[14] Herman Melville was certainly one member of that audience: family tradition has it that he subscribed to the *Herald* because of the excellence of its shipping news. We do not know when after his taking up residence in New York in 1846 he began his subscription, but we have evidence that he ended a subscription to the *Herald* in 1854.[15]

Bennett covered the whole city, panoramically turning the *Herald*'s attention to all corners, but it was his coverage of one murder case that made urban encounter journalism notorious. Helen Jewett was a young and beautiful prostitute working at Rosina Townsend's luxurious brothel. Someone murdered her with a hatchet early Sunday morning April 10, 1836, and then set fire to her bed. The crime was sensational all on its own, but Bennett found a way to make it even more sensational by involving himself directly. On April 11, the *Herald* carried Bennett's own narrative of his visit to the scene of the crime. He entered the prostitute's room:

> What a sight burst upon me! There stood an elegant double mahogany bed, all covered with burnt pieces of linen, blankets, pillows black as cinders. I looked around for the object of my curiosity. On the carpet I saw a piece of linen sheet covering something as if carelessly flung over it.
> "Here," said the Police Officer, "here is the poor creature."
> He half uncovered the ghastly corpse. I could scarcely look at it for a second or two. Slowly I began to discover the lineaments of the corpse as one would the beauties of a statue of marble. It was the most remarkable sight I ever beheld—I never have and never expect to see such another. "My God," exclaimed I, "how like a statue! I can scarcely conceive that form to be a corpse." Not a vein was to be seen. The body looked as white—as full—as polished as the purest Parisian marble. The perfect figure—the exquisite limbs—the fine face—the full arms—the beautiful bust—all—all surpassed in every respect the Venus de Medicis according to the casts generally given of her.

Using a method we in the twentieth century understand well enough from our own print and television journalism, Bennett makes it seem as if it was *he* that discovered the crime in the first place. Bennett uncovers the ghastly crime with his intrepid visit to the scene and interprets it for us. He exploits the dead flesh of Jewett, but he does it as if he were acting in our name. In Bennett's account even the police are aware of the editor's representative status. When he went into Jewett's room, someone in the crowd asked why he was let in. An officer responded, "He is an editor—he is on public duty." Bennett's narrative creates us as readers who are aware that the new city presents events that are nearly inexplicable but who insist that the inexplicable be explained very quickly.

The *Herald* followed its original piece with story after story on Jewett's fall from virtue, on her diaries, on every detail of the trial of Richard P. Robinson for the crime. Robinson was acquitted and the mystery was never solved, but the *Herald* became the best-known newspaper in the city and the country.[16]

Twenty-four years later, in 1860, and after moderating its sensational methods somewhat, the *New York Herald* had a daily circulation of seventy-seven thousand and was the largest daily newspaper in the world.[17]

"Galvanize a New England Squash": Horace Greeley   Ralph Waldo Emerson was sure that penny paper circulation numbers were not measures of quality. In 1838 George Bancroft excitedly told Emerson that the *Boston Globe* had a circulation of thirty thousand, and since each copy was read by perhaps ten persons its editorial articles were reaching three hundred thousand persons! Emerson replied politely to Bancroft that if that were so he wished the articles could be better written. In his private journal he wrote more angrily, "What utter nonsense to name in *my* ear this *number*, as if that were anything. 3,000,000 such people as can read the Globe with interest are as yet in too crude a state of nonage to deserve any regard."[18] Emerson's disciple Henry David Thoreau wrote about Boston newspapers sixteen years later, but his opinions are much the same as Emerson's. The newspaper is "the only book which America has printed, and which America reads. . . . the people who read [it] are in the condition of the dog that returns to his vomit."[19]

Emerson and Thoreau, like many other well-remembered American writers of the antebellum period, defined themselves by opposing the popularity of the cultural products of the new urban middle class. In William Charvat's view, Emerson's 1837 speech "The American Scholar" should be read in the context of the Panic of 1837, an economic disaster that Emerson thought was caused by the overreaching greed of the grasping new class. The speech is for Charvat "essentially a plea to his own class to recapture cultural power and leadership by reforming its education and vitalizing its ideals."[20]

Emerson says in his speech that the American scholars he is addressing should take a specific interest in the quotidian. He demonstrates that he understands better than Philip Hone, for example, that ordinary life must become the *subject* of educated, elite attention. He proposes a new task for the American scholar:

What would we really know the meaning of? The meal in the firkin; the milk in the pan; the ballad in the street; the news of the boat; the glance of the eye; the form and gait of the body;—show me the ultimate reason of these matters;—show me the sublime presence of the highest spiritual cause lurking, as always it does lurk, in the suburbs and extremities of nature; let me see every trifle bristling with the polarity that ranges it instantly on an eternal law; and the shop, the plough, and the ledger, referred to the like cause by which light undulates and poets sing;—and the world lies no longer a dull miscellany and lumber room, but has form and order, there is no trifle; there is no puzzle; but one design unites and animates the farthest pinnacle and the lowest trench.[21]

Emerson asks the students to do battle for the quotidian life, draw it into their intellectual conceptions. They should use their talents to see the ultimate cause lurking not only in the firkin of the rural picturesque but even in the merchant's ledger. Emerson is a long way from sending the scholar to Helen Jewett's room, but he is imagining both a pacification effort and an appropriation. He longs for the vitality of the new market culture, but by recommending that the Harvard scholars range the everyday "on an eternal law," he tries to hurdle exactly the principle of the market culture that is most important—its disposability. Emerson's effort would make little difference to Benjamin H. Day and James Gordon Bennett, who already lived and reveled in the quotidian and were happily creating its recurring and routinized style. It did make a difference to one New Yorker, Walt Whitman, and to many young New Englanders like Margaret Fuller and George William Curtis who entered the New York publishing business in the 1840s.

The New Englanders did often praise one New York penny press editor, Horace Greeley of the *New York Tribune*. Greeley began the *Tribune* in 1841 in conscious contrast to Bennett's *Herald*, hoping to discover a respectable, family market for the penny paper and to profit from the moral war then raging against Bennett. Greeley announced in the *Log Cabin* that the *Tribune* would start on April 10:

"The Tribune" as its name imports, will labor to advance the interests of the People, and to promote their Moral, Social and Political well-being. The immoral and degrading Police Reports, Advertisements and other matter which have been allowed to disgrace the columns of our leading Penny Papers will be carefully excluded from this, and no exertion spared to render it worthy of the hearty approval of the virtuous and refined, and a welcome visitant at the family fireside.[22]

The first issue of the *Tribune* proudly announced its Whig principles at the same time it mourned the recent death of President Harrison, but it also took the space to attack Day's *New York Sun* and Bennett's *Herald*. (The *Herald* is "notoriously unprincipled and reckless.") On April 19, in an editorial on the newspaper press, Greeley defined his newspaper against the other two. He commented at length on the way the penny press had covered the trial and execution of a murderer in New Jersey: Greeley is shocked that there are those who are, for private gain, willing to "poison the fountains of public intelligence and to fan with destroying flames the hellish passions which now slumber in the bosom of society." The "minute publication of all this atrocious wickedness" results in hardened hearts, the blunting of the feelings of humanity, a "terrible pleasure" in thinking about what mistakes got the murderer caught. For the sake of "social security" Greeley wishes "a check might be put upon these infamous and baneful publications." Greeley had staked out his ground: the *Tribune* had the "higher duties" which it owed to the "best interests of humanity."

Bennett knew business competition when he saw it and responded in full cry on the next day, April 20.

> Horace Greeley is endeavoring, with tears in his eyes, to show that it is very naughty to publish reports of the trial, confessions and execution of [the murderer]. 'It makes one feel like a murderer,' says Greeley. No doubt he thinks it's equally naughty in us to publish a paper at all; and if we would stop "The Herald" he might condescend to thank us. 'A marvelously proper man.' Now this Horace Greeley, BA and ASS, is probably the most unmitigated blockhead connected with the newspaper press. Galvanize a New England squash, and it would make as capable an editor as Horace.

Bennett often gibed at Greeley's vegetative rural origins to show how far from a metropolitan editor and how much a rural creature the *Tribune*'s founder was. Bennett was attacking the New Englander for the quality that turned out to be the key part of Greeley's successful public image. Greeley dressed himself as the Yankee rustic—always wearing, as if unconsciously, an old light drab coat and a battered light-colored hat. Greeley kept alive in his clothing and abstracted shambling manner a memory of the moment of arrival, of the New Hampshire–born greenhorn lately from Vermont arriving in the big city. James Parton's fascinating 1855 *Life* has a frontispiece engraving of young Greeley with hickory stick with a bundle of clothes tied to it walking down a city street. Facing that engraving is another, of the contemporary *Tribune* editor, looking older and slightly more prosperous, but in his unfashionable light-colored surtout still distinctly an emblem of that original rustic (see pp. 34 and 35).[23]

The greenhorn experience—the one had on first arriving in the city—is often the key event in even a longtime city resident's account. Jonathan Raban describes the image of the immigrant:

> The greenhorn has everything to lose: his phylacteries, his innate convictions about the nature of the human community, even the language in which he thinks and feels. We relish his loss, his poignant sense of displacement. For he is the past we have all somehow survived: and he may tell us, in innocent or naive imitation, who we are now, because our present is his future. So city writing lavishes attention on the newcomer at that point of entrance: the greenhorn, at once the city's hero and its most vulnerable victim, is urban man at the crucial stage of emergence and transformation.[24]

Greeley represented in his person and his paper the moment of urban transformation, the moment of the hayseed's arrival in New York. Greeley acted or was a continuing greenhorn in memory of the high ideals of the "old" moral order, a promise that the ideals too, like the white-haired editor, could survive in the new city. Greeley's apparent lack of guile, his innocence, were acts of cultural power. His *sensations*, like Bennett's, were of the brave encounter with the city: the news was still New York, but Greeley's paper reiterated the first moments of urban arrival. Always implicit in the *Tribune*'s success was Greeley's own: the paper was a beacon of a fierce confidence in the educated individual's ability to encounter the city and comprehend and reform it.

Greeley brought meaning to the streets by importing New England culture, bringing it to market. In just the first week of the *Tribune*'s

"Young Greeley's Arrival in New York"

Frontispiece of James Parton's Life of Horace Greeley *(New York: Mason Brothers, 1855). From the author's collection.*

publication Greeley reprinted parts of seven essays from Emerson's 1841 *Essays* and surveyed the reviews of Emerson's book. This was the beginning of a long relationship between the *Tribune* and Emerson and the New England transcendentalists. Greeley saw it as his job to publish and promote them in New York. He once told an audience that he was a mere popularizer of the teachings of Emerson, humbly trying to "bring the diverging rays of [the moral truth of Transcendentalism] to

Horace Greeley the Editor

Frontispiece of James Parton's Life of Horace Greeley *(New York: Mason Brothers, 1855). From the author's collection.*

bear focally on the Practical Education of Man."[25] In the same first week of publication Greeley also reviewed the *Boston Quarterly Review* and the transcendental journal *The Dial*, copying two poems from the latter. The first week was also, despite the heavy political news of Harrison's death and coming elections, full of literary matter that was not New England: Greeley made New York literary friends by reviewing and extracting from the magazines *New-York Review, Metropolitan,*

Arcturus, and *Knickerbocker*. Still in the first week he extracted a section from Carlyle's *Heroes and Hero Worship* and began a long serialization of Charles Dickens's *Barnaby Rudge*. The *Tribune*, like the *Herald*, understood the cheap newspaper as a new medium for democracy, and it strove to adapt what Greeley thought was the best writing of England, New England, and New York for publication to the vast new audiences of New York.

Greeley supported socialist ideas, printing a regular column titled "Association" by the New Yorker Albert Brisbane, who had studied with Charles Fourier in Paris. The column popularized Fourierism in the United States and contributed to the design of the cooperative community at Brook Farm in West Roxbury, which was a crossroads for many New England intellectuals. Greeley supported Brook Farm, visited it, and eventually hired several of its former members. Charles A. Dana was managing editor of the *Tribune* from 1849 to 1862. Margaret Fuller wrote the literary reviews for the paper from 1844 to 1846 and also contributed articles on the city. After she left for Italy, the former leader of the Farm, George Ripley, became the chief reviewer. Brook Farm boarder George William Curtis wrote travel articles for the paper, publishing them very successfully separately as *Nile Notes of a Howadji* (1851), *The Howadji in Syria* (1852), and *Lotus Eating* (1852). James Parton's 1855 biography contains an engaging description of a day and night's work at the *Tribune* that shows how important Brook Farm veterans Dana and Ripley were to the paper in the 1850s. They worked with other highly talented writers like Solon Robinson, the agricultural editor, Bayard Taylor, a travel writer, James Pike, the Washington correspondent and political writer, F. J. Ottarson, the city editor, and George W. Snow, the commercial editor. Ripley called the movement of the New England intellectuals to New York a descent "from Utopia to Journalism." But it paid. These men clearly intended to gain access to a wide reading public composed of artisan and merchant and intellectual, all joined in making the practical best of the democracy.[26]

All the New England writers who moved to New York knew that working in journalism meant subjugating their own cherished romantic individuality. Margaret Fuller thought the newspaper held the "promise of great excellence." She thought of working for the newspapers as an erasure of the self, a conscious decision to use her talent for the benefit of others, and seemed to struggle to imagine a kind of writing that was selfless and yet serious. It should perforce confine itself to short forms, the "condensed essay" or the anecdote.[27]

Greeley had been convinced to take Fuller on as the *Tribune*'s reviewer, he says, by Mary Greeley's enthusiasm for Fuller's Boston "Conversations," some of which she had attended. Greeley found Fuller a little slow at even the short forms (he could, he tells us happily, easily write ten columns to her one), but he grew to admire her and her work. He gives tribute to "her wonderful range of capacities, of experiences, of sympathies, [which] seemed adapted to every condition and phase of humanity" and expressed itself best in her articles on poverty in New York City.[28]

The journalism of the time—as Fuller's own *Tribune* essays (unsigned, but always dramatically and distinctively marked with an asterisk) make clear enough—does not take away individual talent and style, even though it certainly encourages speed and attention to the ordinary. James Gordon Bennett and Horace Greeley were always highly individualized literary presences in their newspapers. But Fuller's experience working in New York for the market society opened her eyes to what was happening to people in the streets. The change Fuller made from being the wide-ranging intellectual in Boston, a specialist in *self*, to being a relatively modest interviewer of prostitutes in New York can be seen as a wholly liberating transition. For Fuller's biographer Bell Gale Chevigny, Greeley is the person and the *Tribune* is the paper that "root [Fuller] again in her time and place, and set her in action."[29]

Herman Melville knew the *Tribune* well: it was the most literary of the New York penny papers, and its reviews were important to him. His New York literary career had been well started by the widespread, friendly, and well-managed reception of *Typee* in 1846. Evert Duyckinck oversaw that reception and asked Margaret Fuller to review *Typee* for the *Tribune*. Her very favorable notice appeared on April 4, 1846. The newspaper often reviewed Melville in the next ten years, and Melville himself continued to be interested enough in Greeley to purchase his *Hints toward Reforms* in 1850.[30] Many readers of the 1857 *The Confidence-Man* think its "man in cream-colors" is a parody of Greeley's dress and facile preaching of charity and confidence.[31]

Greeley befriended many New York writers of the new generation, like George William Curtis and Melville, but he showed little veneration for one of New York's literary icons of the previous generation, James Fenimore Cooper. Greeley gave Cooper a rough education in media power. If Irving's Rip Van Winkle slept through the American Revolution to discover upon awakening that the country had gone from sleepy ease to unhappy political contentiousness, Cooper slept through the market society revolution while he was in Europe between 1826 and 1833. His objections when he returned were louder than Rip's. Cooper had the most trouble with the penny newspaper editors and quickly saw them, including the village intellectual Horace Greeley, as the chief villains of the new class and the new order.

Cooper's encounter with the press began with what he must have thought a simple problem with property rights in his ancestral home of Cooperstown, New York. Finding that the townspeople were trying to appropriate as town property land long owned by his family, Cooper sued to keep it. The Coopers had always allowed the public to use the land as a picnic place, but now Cooper could not allow that generosity to be translated into theft. The press objected strongly to his suit, asserting the rights of the people against the "aristocratic" landowner. The New York City newspapers had a delightful story and a lively enemy to engage and to help them define their freedoms. Cooper sued the papers, including the *Tribune*, for libel. Sensing the possibilities of a great story, Greeley himself went to Cooperstown to represent the *Tribune* in court and printed his own very funny first-person account of what had happened as fast as he got back into town. Cooper had won the suit but lost the media war. Naively, Cooper sued again. And Greeley wrote it up again.[32]

Cooper received his education in modern culture at the hands of the most intellectual of the penny press editors. Greeley always thought it part of his job to explain the commercial world to writers. He advised the transcendentalists in particular on how to make themselves popular, telling Thoreau, for example, in 1848, "You may write with an angel's pen, yet your writings have no mercantile, money value till you are known and talked of as an author."[33] Greeley wanted his imported culture to be wide-awake. He drew his sustenance from the vast public who knew him, who could recognize him on the street, who paid for his newspaper. Both Emerson and Thoreau noted with disapproval how Greeley was often surrounded by people.[34]

The *Tribune* was based, like its less respectable rivals, on the encounter with the panorama of the city, and it covered the city's variety, including its rapes and murders and suicides, although Greeley never admitted that his motives for reporting such events were anything but the highest, even when that was not the case. The *Tribune* represented reform values: it was a Whig paper that was antislavery, antiwar, antirum, antitobacco, antigrogshops, antibrothels, anti–gambling houses, and its encounters with the sensations of the city were designed to promote *reform*. The *Tribune* ran series of articles about the life of the city by "serious" journalists (like Fuller) who engaged themselves with the poverty and wealth of the new city. Often books were made out of the series. George G. Foster, "City Items" editor from 1844 through perhaps 1847,[35] developed the police-reporting form to a half-sensationalist, half-sociological art highly appropriate and profitable for the reformist newspaper. His 1848 series "New York in Slices" became a very successful book. The *Tribune*'s agricultural editor, Solon Robinson, made the *Tribune* mandatory reading throughout the rural United States for its advice on scientific farming. Occasionally Robinson also wrote sketches for the city editor's department, including the series that resulted in the 1854 *Hot Corn: Life Scenes in New York Illustrated*.[36] All of these series, some of which will be discussed later in this book, are based on the paradigm of the encounter between the middle-class observer and the extra-ordinary other of the new city.

The newspaper culture that evolved in New York was self-conscious, breezily unconcerned with older proprieties, and careless about the distinction between the public and the private. It promoted the entrepreneurial view by exhibiting the newspaper editor as the male cultural hero who is the "coming man," the species specially adapted to confront and explain the accelerating complexities and confusions of the city. He could be a sensationalist like Bennett or a reformer like Greeley, but the editor's ideological function was to be a model of adaptation. There *was*, the newspapers seemed to say, a problem in understanding the new and chaotic city, but the hero editors showed that there were men capable of encountering and explaining its panorama. These editors created and controlled new markets for literary production: they insisted on anecdotal forms and quotidian detail and helped change American literature.

The penny newspapers that, like the *Herald* and the *Tribune*, survived the intense competition were not only hugely successful in their hometown but eventually penetrated the national market as well. The *Tribune*'s *Weekly Tribune* reached out across America, and by 1860, when its thriving competitor the *Herald* was the largest daily paper in the world, the *Weekly Tribune* went to over two hundred thousand subscribers.[37] The New York newspapers sold the idea that New York *was* the news, and their national distribution meant that often the news of New York was the news for all.

Beneath the haze stirred up by the winds, the urban island, a sea in the middle of the sea, lifts up the skyscrapers over Wall Street, sinks down at Greenwich, then rises again to the crests of Midtown, quietly passes over Central Park and finally undulates off into the distance beyond Harlem. A wave of verticals. Its agitation is momentarily arrested by vision. The gigantic mass is immobilized before the eyes.

Michel de Certeau
The Practice of Everyday Life

2

Windows on the World:
Guides to New York

Panoramas   When tourists come to New York City they have in their mind's eye conventional images of the whole physical city. Primary among them is a view of the Manhattan skyline from a distance, a representation of New York as a silhouette of tall buildings rising up out of flat water. What tourists and New Yorkers alike imagine is the *panorama* of New York. They confront a view of New York rising startlingly up and filling the entire landscape. For the instant of the imaginative perception, the city seems all there is—the entire world. Any landscape beyond the city's rivers seems but dimly brushed in, a vague and featureless world subject to the random labeling of Saul Steinberg's famous *New Yorker* drawing—"Japan," "New Jersey."[1] High windows in Manhattan that look out on this view are, as the restaurant in the World Trade Center has it, "Windows on the World."

Over one hundred years before tourists and New Yorkers stared out of buildings that scrape the sky, earlier greenhorns (and New Yorkers) ascended the 280-foot tower above Latting's ice cream parlor and across from the 1853 Crystal Palace Exhibition. Paying customers could take a steam elevator part of the way, but the final ascent was by foot. Their climb earned them a view of the immense new city stretching out southward beneath them.[2] By 1853 the convention of picturing New York in panorama was well established in illustrations and prose descriptions, and the Latting tower cleverly adapted the convention into an attraction. The Crystal Palace Exhibition itself meant to demonstrate that New York in 1853 was a world city, equal to the European capitals. It was a vast display of American commerce and included even a celebration of the commerce generated by American authors. The exhibition hosted a "Complimentary Fruit and Floral Festival to Authors" and invited 650 of them.[3]

The word "panorama" did not exist until 1787, when English painter Robert Barker first used the term to describe his invention of 360-degree paintings. Barker's idea required a specially designed building in which the paying spectator could stand in the center of a circular space, turning around to see the whole of a 360-degree view hung on the surrounding walls. Barker acquired a site for exhibition on London's Leicester Square and opened for business to great success in 1794. Thomas Hornor followed Barker into the panoramic field by painting an immense and remarkably detailed 360-degree painting of 1821 London as seen from his tiny hut atop St. Paul's. Hornor got financing to build the Colosseum and showed the panorama on the walls of a big room that had a central tower with a steam elevator. The tower included a replica of Hornor's St. Paul's hut and thus provided a stunning representation and celebration of immense London while it evoked the courage and dedication of the panoramist.[4]

By the mid-nineteenth century the word "panorama" came to mean not only 360-degree views but also any scene taken from sufficiently far away to encompass the whole of a large subject. The word was used to describe paintings that were to be contrasted with *prospects*. Most often the *panorama* was a steeple or bird's-eye view of a city that stretched itself almost impossibly to include the whole of its vast subject. The United States adopted the European artistic and commercial techniques quickly, and New York became the American city most frequently represented. John A. Kouwenhoven's marvelous *Columbia Historical Portrait of New York* shows that in the 1840s and 1850s church-steeple and bird's-eye panoramas began to dominate all forms of New York illustration.[5]

In the illustrations of New York that come before the panorama the viewer is often made to see the city as a pastoral landscape in which the city is framed "in richer, darker tones . . . [by] a bucolic scene of grazing cattle, stacks of hay, tall trees, and open fields."[6] Other representations portray the city as a series of impressive buildings, each pictured separately. The 1851 "Souvenir of New York" drawn by J. Bornet and lithographed by C. Gildemeister (see p. 44) is an example of both kinds of representation put together. The central illustration, titled "View of New York from West Hoboken," presents a pastoral *prospect* with cows in the foreground and a party of walkers resting and pointing out the city as if it were a Catskill gorge. The view is framed in the elaborate landscape traditions drawn from Claude Lorrain and practiced by the New York artists who painted Hudson River landscapes. Trees frame the scene with leafy diagonals, softening the edge and forcing the eye inward to a calm, watery center. The relationships among foreground, middle ground, and background are carefully controlled: there are no abrupt shifts. Around the edges of "Souvenir" is another convention of New York representation—a series of individually portrayed significant buildings. Even here the natural landscape traditions are evident in the framing of the trees. Streets and people and the contexts of the buildings are not as important as the dignified individual building itself. The building is the (created) sign of wealth and order, a metonymy to suggest a whole city that is commercially successful and well regulated, all within the eternal natural system.

The "View of New York from West Hoboken" and the series of views of public buildings depend upon an observer who can "read" the scenes presented as showing that New York and its buildings are part of an eternal natural order. The walking party resting leisurely in the field, the women sitting with parasols against the sun, the man pointing out the major sights, represent an elite class with the education and time to appreciate the view: they imply the viewer of the lithograph itself. Like the implied author and the implied readers of Washington

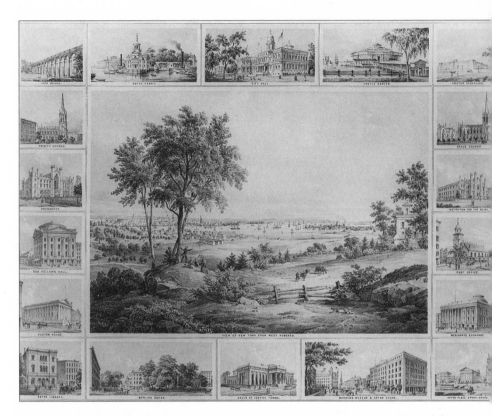

"Souvenir of New York"

Drawn by J. Bornet and drawn on stone by C. Gildemeister (New York: Nagel & Weingartner, 1851). Courtesy of the Library of Congress.

Irving and James Fenimore Cooper, the observer inside and outside the lithograph must read its meanings calmly. All is stable; the city is framed in the old conventions; it is part of natural time.

Both early representations, the landscape view from afar and the series of public buildings, are conventions that persist even during and after the dominance of the panorama. Guidebooks often display a series of public buildings, in part because the individual views make suitable illustrations throughout a book. In Ezekiel Porter Belden's *New York: Past, Present, and Future* (1849), for example, the twenty engravings show the "Aqueduct Bridge," "Bowling Green Fountain," "City Hall,"

"Trinity Church," and so on. Each engraving appears in the appropriate section of the book—"Government" or "Morals and Religion." Another 1849 guidebook, *The Picturesque Tourist*, is similar, as is Clarence Cook's series "New-York Daguerreotyped," which *Putnam's Monthly* offered its readers in February 1853 (although the series also has a fold-out panorama). The convention shows a great interest in New York and its impressive buildings, and we know that the interest comes because of the growth and change in the physical character and economic influence of the city, but the sights are treated as unchanging.[7] The pastoral urban illustration was rooted in nostalgia for a dignified and stable city. The new panoramic views of the 1840s, on the other hand, stripped the static pastoral from the illustration and pictured an unmediated encounter with the immediate, contemporary city.

Many of the new panoramic views were drawn from the viewpoints of New York church steeples in imitation of Thomas Hornor's view of London from St. Paul's steeple. One fine New York church steeple panorama is the 1849 "New York from the steeple of St. Paul's Church" drawn by J. W. Hill (see p. 46). This beautifully detailed view looks back east along Fulton Street toward North Dutch Church and south along Broadway to Trinity Church. It shows a good part of the city, but it foregrounds the center of the commercial and political life of the period, the intersection of Fulton and Broadway just below the viewpoint. The viewer sees Barnum's Museum across Broadway and Brady's Daguerreotype Studio on the near side of Broadway just south. Brady's skylight (needed to bring bright natural light into the studio) is visible steeply beneath the high viewpoint. All the store signs, the wagons, the omnibuses, the people are distinct as if in a perfect miniature world, and the viewer intently inspects the spectacle of commercial daily life.

The change from the pastoral panorama to the church-steeple panorama is a change to a different representation of time. The older framing imagery in which nature stood for eternal time is stripped away, and the panorama, like the penny press newspaper, presents the quotidian, the perfectly astonishing ordinary. All there is is there, and all there is is New York *now*. History, the sense of events in a social context that helps human beings understand and evaluate them, fades into the

"New York from the steeple of St. Paul's Church, looking East, South, and West"

Drawn by J. W. Hill, and engraved in aquatint by Henry Papprill (New York: H. I. Magarey, 1849). Courtesy of the Eno Collection, New York Public Library.

indistinct background as the bourgeois city celebrates itself. The city proposes itself as a continuing present.

When the viewpoint of the panorama lifts even higher than a church steeple, something different happens. The *whole* city is stretched out before the viewer from a physically impossible viewpoint. The 1856 Currier lithograph "City of New York" (see p. 47) is a good example, as is the fold-out panorama that *Putnam's Monthly* offered its readers in 1853 in preparation for the Crystal Palace Exhibition.[8] Often the point of view is high above the harbor off the southern tip of the island of Manhattan. We see the Battery, lower Broadway, and Trinity Church prominently in the foreground and the city stretching horizontally across the print from the Hudson to Corlear's Hook and vertically up to a vanishing point that is, in the early panoramas, as low as Fourteenth Street. High viewpoints looking south became popular by the

"City of New York"

Sketched and drawn on stone by C. Parsons (New York: Currier, 1856). Courtesy of the Library of Congress.

time of the exhibition and the Latting tower. They were visual testimony to the enormous growth of the city northward: between 1845 and 1860, almost as many people moved in above Fourteenth Street as had lived in the whole city in 1840—290,000.[9]

Because we twentieth-century viewers are used to the helicopter-borne movie camera swinging over New York City (or "Metropolis") to provide our own moving and high-viewpoint panoramas, the nineteenth-century high-viewpoint panoramas may seem stable and calm, but in comparison to the picturesque views of the city (p. 44) or even the panoramic church-steeple views, the high-viewpoint panoramas are alarming. They force the viewer into a sudden encounter with the immensity of the metropolis of the present moment. There is no story, only encounter: the historical past and nature seem to be irrelevant. The spectacle of the urban and commercial *today* is where meaning must be found, and the panorama makes clear that understanding such a complex immensity is not easy. But the panorama also insists that the whole city is explicable, comprehensible—just barely. The energy of the panoramist's imagination unites and integrates the city and interprets it as a single whole. Outside the city the landscape is a nearly complete blank, an empty background lightly sketched in. New York itself is the entire landscape.

John Bachmann's lithograph published in 1859, "New York and Environs" (see p. 49), is the most extraordinary view of New York during the period. Here is the bird's-eye view gone fish-eye. New York in this view is not simply a landscape by itself, filling up an otherwise blank world: the city is the world itself. The Navy Yard and Sandy Hook are the far edges of the globe; Broadway is the Greenwich meridian. The commercial and cultural centrality imagined in this conception is manifest: there is nothing but New York and nothing but contemporary New York. Bachmann's illustration, published just at the end of the antebellum period, is a remarkable step beyond the exuberant boosterism of panoramas of the early 1850s. Saul Steinberg's *New Yorker* cover illustration looking across the Hudson to "Japan" comes again to mind, and its self-deprecating humor reminds us that Bachmann's illustration may have been comically self-aware too. Bachmann so exaggerates the idea that New York windows are windows on the world, that quotidian New York is everything there is to know, that we cannot help thinking that he might intend a joke.

Guidebooks As Chapter 1 explains, penny newspaper editors like James Gordon Bennett and Horace Greeley invented a panoramic prose by printing anecdotes about the whole quotidian city. Book publishers took on the new city as well, providing hundreds of books about New York City in the antebellum period. Many of those books built into their narratives the anecdotal encounters characteristic of the journalistic descriptions. Although a narrative can of course never be panoramic in the way that an illustration is, guidebooks and popular nonfiction and fiction often used the visual terms "panorama" or "bird's-eye view"—sometimes as specifically as Cornelius Mathews did in his *A*

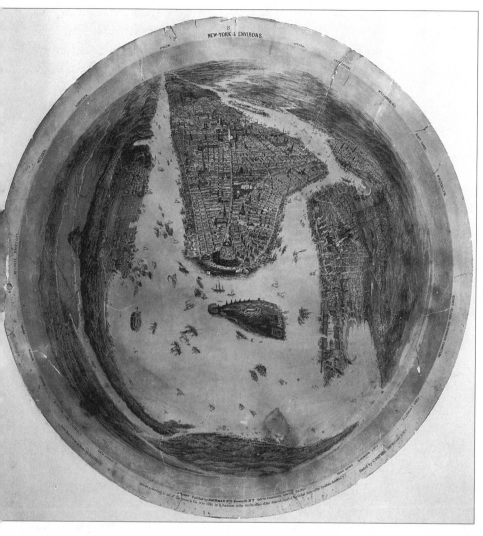

"New York & Environs"

Drawn on stone by Bachmann (New York: J. Bachmann, 1859). Courtesy of the Eno Collection, New York Public Library.

Pen-and-Ink Panorama of New York City (1853)—to describe a collection of anecdotes of the town written for Crystal Palace tourists.

Panoramic narratives often allude to, and try to mimic, the conventions of panoramic illustrations. A popular Broadway destination in the late 1840s for those who wanted to see a large view of New York was the new Trinity Church steeple, completed in 1846. Herman Melville, for example, climbed "to the top of Trinity church steeple" on February 28, 1848, and "had a fine view" of New York, according to his brother-in-law, Lemuel Shaw, Jr., who went up with him.[10] A reporter for the *New York Morning News* described the same view just after the new steeple opened. In "New York City and Environs from Trinity Tower," a long article published on March 21, 1846, the reporter gives us the giddy details of the climb to 250 feet above the pavement and then the shock of the view: "There beneath our feet, and stretching far away in every direction, lay one of the most beautiful and exciting spectacles ever looked upon. The vast and interminable city was spread out as upon a map before us." The reporter's enthusiastic prose works hard to imitate an illustration, and it verbalizes the illustration's visual paradox of the "interminable" city being wholly visible.

Longer narratives presenting the city often include a single description imitating a panoramic illustration, but they create a panorama in prose by relating a series of urban encounters between a single observer and parts of the city. This literary panoramic paradigm in New York narrative pervades many genres—guidebooks, journalism, "serious" journalism, charity-work reports, popular fiction, "serious" fiction—but determining which genre a narrative belongs to is difficult. Works of fiction contain passages that seem much like journalism while the nonfiction often contains obviously fictional stories. Panoramic narrative is often a mixed form in which "fact" and "fiction" intermingle unstably.

The most obviously panoramic narrative form was the factual guidebook. Guidebooks are by definition "tours of the town," and the antebellum New York guidebooks purportedly show the new immigrant, the tourist, the out-of-towner how to tour the city, what to see, what to watch out for. But like the illustrated panorama or Latting's tower, they have another important function—to boost the commercial city, to sell the new product. Melville describes the 1840s New York guidebooks in *Redburn* (1849).

> The New York guide-books are now vaunting of the magnitude of a town, whose future inhabitants, multitudinous as the pebbles on the beach, and girdled in with high walls and towers, flanking endless avenues of opulence and taste, will regard all our Broadways and Bowerys as but the paltry nucleus to their Nineveh. From far up the Hudson, beyond Harlem River, where the young saplings are now growing, that will overarch their lordly mansions with broad boughs, centuries old; they may send forth explorers to penetrate into the then obscure and smoky alleys of the Fifth Avenue and Fourteenth-street; and going still farther south, may exhume the present Doric Custom-house, and quote it as a proof that their high and mighty metropolis enjoyed a Hellenic antiquity.[11]

Melville takes the guidebook's enthusiastic imagination of the bustling city's expansion ever northward and twists it around into an unnerving, *Blade Runner*–like expedition back into the nucleus to exhume the past from its obscurity and darkness. Melville uses the language—"the obscure and smoky alleys"—ordinarily used for the heart of the slums to describe Fifth Avenue and Fourteenth Street and reverses the guidebook wisdom by implying that expansion will turn the formerly luxurious center of wealthy New York life into its grimy and dangerous slums.[12]

Most New York City guidebooks were, as Melville knew, thoughtless boosters of New York's commercial success, celebrators of its increased size and diversity. Belden's *New York—As It Is* or his *New York: Past, Present, and Future*, both published in the same year as *Redburn*, use the logic Melville amuses himself with.[13] Belden thinks the city's future is of continued, booming capitalist expansion: "New-York is doubtless determined to become the commercial emporium of the world." The vastly dissimilar elements that compose the population "are kept in a state of order and tranquillity," and the police make it "seldom . . . possible for a noted offender to remain undetected in the city." A visit to the "Tombs" prison, "this abode of the vicious[,] will convince the most incredulous of the activity of the police department as it regards offenders."[14] The ideological function of guidebooks like

Belden's is apparent: the city itself is the product that needs to be boosted if its merchants and manufacturers are to expand their markets.

But many New York guidebooks of the antebellum period are not as straightforward as Belden's, in part because talented writers were often hired to write them and in part because they overlap with other narrative forms. Asa Greene's *A Glance at New York* (1837) is divided into chapters that list some hard facts about different aspects of the city—"Population," "Hotels," "Theatres," "Hacks and Omnibuses" and so on—and follow the facts with amusing commentary. The book is guide and entertainment, full of what appears simple truth—there aren't enough hotels, the streets are in terrible condition, there are a great many criminals—and Greene's funny extensions, which show that we shouldn't take the facts so seriously: "the whole number [of dandies], after a careful estimate, is believed to be about 3000; or one to every hundred of the population." Greene also delights his audience with his reporting of New York's local speech: the dandies all say, when pleased, "shuperb!"[15]

Greene's novels, such as *The Perils of Pearl Street* (1834), are guide and ethnography as well as fiction. *Perils* tells the story of newly arrived William Hazard. Trying to become an honest merchant, Hazard is naive about the ways of New York business and therefore fails. He doesn't know about "drumming" for business (tricking out-of-town buyers into the store), "flying the kite" (where two fliers give each other bad checks, both hoping to find the funds before the banks exchange checks), or who "Peter Funk" is (a by-bidder at an auction but also a shape-shifting spirit of fraud). The book is a satiric parable but also a guidebook to the styles and languages of deceitful merchants.[16]

Later guidebooks also mix fact and fiction, providing entertainment with advice. George G. Foster's *Fifteen Minutes around New York* and Cornelius Mathews's *A Pen-and-Ink Panorama of New York City*, both published in 1853, are examples of the explicitly panoramic guidebooks sold to the tourists coming in for New York's grandest self-promotion scheme, the Crystal Palace Exhibition of 1853. Foster's narrator-guide races his readers around the city with lively anecdotes—"A General Dash at the Ferries," "A Plunge in the Swimming-Bath"—and the city is a panoramic whole of different types and sights. The anecdotes are often small fictions of urban encounter: they tell a (usually racy) story about each place on the tour. Mathews's equally breezy guide takes the reader on a trip around the town during which the reader tours the writer's opinions as well as the sights. We visit P. T. Barnum's Museum, a happy middle-class family, the New York Society Library, the seamstresses at work, and the Bowery. Like Greene and Foster, Mathews plays the insider's insider, the urban enthusiast sharing his knowledge of the variety and diversity of the new urban phenomena the 1853 exhibition was meant to call attention to. He encourages his readers to "take the city by surprise," seek it out at unusual times of the day. They should get to know "this very hurry-skurry, hum-drum, hodge-podge, harum-skarum City of New York." The guidebook they hold has given them a vision of the whole city, but they should understand that the city is "peculiar, variable, shifting."[17]

New York Flaneurs The structural principle that often makes guidebooks and more ambitious urban panoramic narratives hang together is the description of a walking tour of the whole city, or at least of its interesting or notorious parts: Wall Street, Broadway, or even "the dens of death" in the Five Points tenements. It is specifically a walking *visit*—a middle-class field trip—to the new city created by the middle-class market society. The implicit problem that starts the narrative into being is the same one that occasioned the panoramic illustration: how can the new city be accounted for, justified, interpreted?

I will use the term "flaneur" to describe some examples of the bourgeois walkers in nineteenth-century New York, although I mean my use of it to be wider than that made familiar by Walter Benjamin's comments on "Some Motifs in Baudelaire" (1939). Terry Eagleton, writing on Benjamin, thinks the touring flaneur is a "drifting relic," strolling "self-composedly through the city, loitering without intent, languid yet secretly vigilant." The flaneur is a "relic" in the sense that he is a premodern observer trying to make sense of the modern crowd. He walks at the edge of a distinction between premodern and modern. On his side is a presumably unified and coherent experience of the daily world; over the edge is discontinuous, ununified, chaotic "modern" experience. Eagleton continues:

His solitary dispossession reflects the commodity's existence as fragment (Benjamin speaks of the commodity as 'abandoned' in the crowd), and his meanderings are as magically free of physical traces as the commodity is absolved from the traces of its production. Yet at the same time his painstaking production of himself as 'personality', his genteel-amateur distaste for the industrial labour through which he glides, signifies the protest of a fading aura in the face of commodity production.[18]

Even the most ethnographical of the walking reports on New York speaks in the "genteel-amateur" voice Eagleton disparages. The "experts"—physicians, ministers, charity workers—have all-too-convenient opinions about the lower classes, and few think or write with enough awareness to see themselves as complicit in the structure of the class relationships they write about. I think, however, that many of the New York flaneurs I describe are more complicated than dandies at their ease.

As Dana Brand explains eloquently, versions of the flaneur predate commodity production, and using the figure to specify a particular moment for modernity's arrival is therefore a dubious practice. The nineteenth-century French and English narratives that American flaneurs used as models were themselves developments of long traditions in European urban description: they were often reactions to those traditions.[19]

In nineteenth-century France one literary imperative was to desecrate the formerly "sacred geography" of Paris. Paris could no longer be the place of the king, but when the Revolution beheaded him it also "obliterated a vital emblem of the city."[20] The new Paris, stripped of its royal names as well as its royalty, needed a new urban definition. Somewhat paradoxically the republicans turned to several influential eighteenth-century books for their inspiration, notably Lesage's *Le Diable boiteux* (1707), Montesquieu's *Les Lettres persanes* (1721), and the many works of Rétif de la Bretonne, like *Les Nuits de Paris* (1788–94). Images and characters from these books, particularly Lesage's minor devil "on two sticks," appear again and again in nineteenth-century French writing (and subsequently in American urban journalism and popular literature), even when the original satire has been replaced by the contrived ease of the flaneur.

Postrevolutionary attempts to describe Paris, to catch the newly uncatchable, also modeled themselves upon Louis Sébastien Mercier's *Le Tableau de Paris* (1781–88). Mercier had approached Paris not as the site for satire, as did Lesage, but as an enthnographer, and his nineteenth-century imitators wrote "literary guidebooks," collections of sketches on people, places, events, and institutions. Writers as diverse as Chateaubriand, Charles Nodier, Alphonse de Lamartine, Honoré de Balzac, Gérard de Nerval, Alexandre Dumas, and Victor Hugo all worked the paradigm.[21]

The bird's-eye view of the popular panorama becomes a device for French city novels, most famously in Hugo's "A Bird's Eye View of Paris" in *Notre-Dame de Paris* (1831) or "An Owl's View of Paris" in *Les Misérables* (1862). Writers like Hugo build upon the panoramic ethnographic base a complex art constructed of metonymy and synecdoche. The hero artist recreates the vantage point that was once the king's and restores the unity and human scale of the city "through exemplary (not 'typical') figures that give the city expression and definition. Rastignac, Quasimodo, Gavroache, Fréderic, Gervaise, Nana, and others are actors in revolutionary Paris as well as protagonists in novels."[22]

The novels of Eugène Sue, whose *Les Mystères de Paris* were first published in the *Journal de Débats* between June 9, 1842, and October 15, 1843, founded an international genre of fiction even before the serialization was complete. Translations into English and German appeared quickly, and an "extra" put out by the American story paper *New World* in 1843 shows the international excitement for Sue: *The Mysteries of Paris: Being the Last and Concluding Chapters of the Story Just Received from Paris and Wholly Omitted in the Harpers Edition!* Mysteries multiplied in translations, piracies, and imitations, and all major cities in Europe and the United States had mysteries written about them. One of the best known was G.W.M. Reynolds's *The Mysteries of London* (1845–48). The American imitations of Eugène Sue included Ned Buntline's (E.Z.C. Judson) *The Mysteries and Miseries of New York* (1848) and its sequels *The B'hoys of New York* and *The G'hals of New York* and George Lippard's many novels, including particularly *The Quaker City; or, The Monks of Monk Hall* (1845) and its sequel, *The Nazarene* (1846). Books in the "mysteries" tradition might be described as "panoramic" because they sometimes depend on touring notorious urban landmarks, but there is rarely a character at all like a flaneur. In fact, the "horrors" and "secrets" of the urban mysteries genre are often highly generalized "Gothic" ones.

As the speed with which Sue was translated and copied in Germany, England, and the United States indicates, the popular fiction market was not sharply separated by national borders or oceans. Sue himself acknowledges the influence of a very popular and much-imitated book of London walkabout satire, Pierce Egan's *Life in London* (1821). Egan's satire is based on his "rambles and sprees" with the book's illustrators, Robert and George Cruikshank. It itself is perhaps a vulgarization of eighteenth-century English books of walkabout satire like John Gay's *Trivia; or, The Art of Walking the Streets of London* (1716). Egan's Corinthian Tom is the London idler who invites his country cousin Jerry Hawthorn on a tour of the town. Tom and Jerry, along with Tom's friend Bob Logic, see the sights, and Jerry is instructed in all the languages and parts of London, from its street beggars, cock fights, and Newgate Prison to the opera and Bond Street. They enjoy the flaneur's London: their "metropolis is not a community or a place to do business so much as it is a spectacle to be consumed, a carnival of glamorous freedom where gentlemen can test the limits of experience before accepting those limits as the contours of their identity as gentlemen."[23]

Many nineteenth-century descriptions of life in London joined Egan's, and most had the name of the city in their titles.[24] Nearly all of these books are, like Egan's, panoramic in that they are narratives describing the city, or its most notorious parts, in the guise of a flaneur's visit or tour. Thackeray and Dickens were undoubtedly strongly influenced by Egan and his tradition when they began their popular writing careers. Dickens has many scenes that explicitly imitate panoramic illustration—in, for example, chapter 15 of *The Old Curiosity Shop* (1841–42), or in the "Town and Todgers's" chapter of *Martin Chuzzlewit* (1844), or in the final historical scene of *A Tale of Two Cities* (1859). Dickens also uses the conventions of panoramic narrative in his later, more socially committed, novels, like *Bleak House* (1852–53).

The change in Dickens's urban description from *Pickwick Papers* (1836–37) to, say, *Our Mutual Friend* (1864–65) reflects a change in urban journalism from the "satiric" to the "serious." "In *Pickwick* a bad smell was a bad smell, in *Our Mutual Friend* it is a problem."[25]

Dickens had repudiated satire to describe the city because of the actual horror of what he himself had seen during his visits and because of his reaction to the "serious" journalism of people like Edwin Chadwick in his *Report of the Sanitary Condition of the Labouring Classes of Great Britain* (1842) or Henry Mayhew in his influential series of newspaper articles published first in the *Morning Chronicle* in 1849–50 and collected as *London Labour and London Poor* (1851).[26] Dickens's influence on descriptions of New York in the 1840s and 1850s is enormous, as the next part of my book ("Dickens' Place") shows at length.

In New York penny newspapers constantly published encounters with different parts of the city, but by the late 1840s and early 1850s the papers increasingly carried long series of articles about New York. These series were like panoramic guidebooks in that they toured the city, and like the guidebooks they often mixed genres, containing both nonfiction journalism and fiction. Each installment was written in a rush to meet the newspaper's insatiable daily demand for prose, but the collection of installments together had a memorable identity that might entice the reader to buy the paper to read the next installment. The successful series could be published later as a book (often by the newspaper press itself), and more profits might accrue. In the series articles the newspaper editor was less likely to be the author, in part of course because by the late 1840s busy commercial men like Bennett and Greeley didn't have time for extended journalism. The series were instead written by a new kind of specialist in urban experience, a literate and thoughtful bourgeois who walked the streets, "knew" the city night and day. The reporter was engaged on a project, not simply a quick story, and the series of reports demonstrated the reporter's and the newspaper's sense of urban responsibility to investigate what was there. As always in New York encounter narratives, the primary assumption is that an explanation of the city is necessary, both for the New York reader and for the reader safely removed from the dangerous and exotic city.

The tone of the newspaper series on the city is often that of the genteel amateur Eagleton describes as characteristic of the flaneur because the reporter portrays himself or herself narratively as almost unexpectedly having come upon a topic. The first installment often embodies the reporter's surprise at some urban condition; and the implicit promise to investigate, to see all the truth, is what gives the subsequent installments their purpose. Each article is about a single part of the city, but all the installments taken together become the equivalent of a panorama of the whole. Like the flaneur the serious reporter has special knowledge but does not have what we would call expert or professional knowledge; unlike the flaneur's wandering his task has a social seriousness, or at least a pretended social seriousness, because it responds to the "problem" of the new city.

The *Tribune* made particularly successful use of the serial form, carrying series like "Labor in New York" (August 1845 through January 1846) and "The Dens of Death" (in June, July, and September 1850). The series were memorable examples of the *Tribune*'s uneasy combination of sensationalism and seriousness in its accounts of the city. Two very successful series were "New York in Slices" by the *Tribune*'s former "City Items" editor, George G. Foster, and "Hot Corn" by its agricultural editor, Solon Robinson. Foster's "Slices" was republished early in 1849 as the book *New York in Slices* in an edition of twenty thousand copies, according to an announcement in the *Tribune* of January 13, 1849.[27] Robinson's series became the 1854 best-seller *Hot Corn: Life Scenes in New York Illustrated*. *Hot Corn* "struck a popular chord and became famous. . . . and reached the phenomenal sale, for such a book, of fifty thousand copies."[28]

New York in Slices was one of several panoramic books Foster churned out in the late 1840s and early 1850s. In addition to *Slices* and the Crystal Palace Exhibition guidebook mentioned above, there is *New York by Gas-Light: With Here and There a Streak of Sunshine* (1850); a novel, *Celio; or, New York Above Ground and Under Ground* (1850); and *New York Naked* (1854). Grandiosely claiming that his work is socially beneficial because it exposes the underside of the new urban life, Foster believes that he, along with Cornelius Mathews, is an ethnographer of a great city, detailing its folk habits, its vices, its institutions, its variety of citizens. He compares himself explicitly to Thomas Mayhew and complains that Mayhew is both praised and printed in the very journals that damn him for sensationalism: "I do not think it too much to claim that the great movement of illuminating the depths of the moral and social degradation of life in a metropolis, owes something of its momentum to me."[29] Foster unabashedly makes the claim that his research is sociological in a book entitled *New York Naked*, which in fact is mostly pornographical.

Slices ran in the *Tribune* between July and October 1848, and its form is characteristic enough of Foster's usual panoramic method, although publication in the respectable journal moderated his salaciousness. All is quick; each section of the city has a short "slice" or chapter. First Broadway, then Chatham Street, Wall Street, The Tombs prison, the Five Points neighborhood, the gambling houses, the pawnbrokers' shops, the mock auction houses, intelligence (employment) offices, markets. Then people, treated rather like sights themselves: Bowery "b'hoys" (street slang for "boy" from the Irish pronunciation), firemen, needlewomen, the press. A special chapter devoted to "The Literary Soirees," a panorama of a literary gathering, lists the well-known writers or those the reader ought to know well. Here are Rufus Griswold, Cornelius Mathews, Evert Duyckinck (Herman Melville's friend), and Lewis Gaylord Clark (editor of the *Knickerbocker*). Elizabeth Oakes Smith, Fanny Osgood, Grace Greenwood, and Lydia Maria Child are all mentioned, as are Parke Godwin, Nathaniel Parker Willis, and Charles Fenno Hoffman. Slices follow on omnibuses, eating houses, dandies, "liquor groceries," immigrants, Sunday excursions, the theaters, oyster cellars, Sundays in New York, and newsboys.

Solon Robinson's *Tribune* series "Hot Corn" is also an example of mixed form and of the importance of the daily newspaper as the seed of that form. It begins with a straightforward journalistic piece that the *Tribune*'s agricultural editor first published in "City Items" for August 5, 1853. There Robinson tells of hearing a poor girl calling "hot corn" outside his window late at night and of appreciating for the first time that he must consider the meaning of a young girl's working alone on the streets. Despite its obviously factual and journalistic starting point, the later sensational and obviously fictional chapters in Robinson's series result in its being for one scholar the "very epitome of the form" of the urban sensational novel and therefore in her mind not worthy of attention as literature.[30] By this way of twentieth-century thinking, *Hot Corn* is not only bad literature but also bad journalism and bad sociology because its genres are mixed. This may be so, but I think that recognizing the mixing of genres in panoramic narrative is fundamental to understanding the complexities of antebellum urban representation.

The hugely successful journalist of the 1850s, "Fanny Fern" (Sara Payson Willis Parton), was also sometimes a New York panoramist in the sketches she wrote for the weekly *New York Ledger*. She was quite aware that her brief essays were like the French *feuilletons*, so much so that she titled her collections *Fern Leaves from Fanny's Portfolio* (1853, 1854). She did complain of the limitations of the flaneur mode for a woman.

> It is a great plague to be a woman. I think I've said that before, but it will bear repeating. Now the wharves are a great passion of mine; I like to sit on a pile of boards there, with my boots dangling over the water, and listen to the far-off 'heave-ho' of the sailors in their bright specks of red shirts, and see the vessels unload, with their foreign fruits, and dream away a delicious hour, imagining the places they came from; and I like to climb up the sides of ships, and poke around generally, just where Mrs. Grundy would lay her irritating hand on my arm and exclaim—'What will people think of you?'[31]

Parton is striking in her determination that women should share in the freedom of the streets, no matter what the representative of polite female society would say. She needs her own encounter with the streets, with their wide variety of sights, as the structuring principle for many of her sketches. We readers want to know what Fanny Fern thinks and Fanny Fern needs to see the culture around her.

Parton is the breezy inheritor of a distinguished and serious tradition of women's urban sketches established by Lydia Maria Child some ten years before. Child's influential short newspaper pieces were the *Letters from New York* written to the *Boston Courier* after Child started to live in New York. They were republished as two books in 1843 and in 1845. The series begins with the premise that a solitary individual living in New York (exiled by marriage to the fringes of civilization) can write back to Boston and describe it. The "great Babylon" is still the same, she thinks, a chiaroscuro where "Wealth dozes on French couches . . . while Poverty camps on the dirty pavement." But her conscience has made her newly careful about what she sees.

There *was* a time when all these things would have passed by me like the flitting figures of the magic lantern, or the changing scenery of a theatre, sufficient for the amusement of an hour. But now, I have lost the power of looking merely on the surface. Every thing seems to me to come from the Infinite, to be filled with the Infinite, to be tending toward the Infinite. Do I see crowds of men hastening to extinguish a fire? I see not merely uncouth garbs and fantastic, flickering lights of lurid hue, like a tramping troop of gnomes,—but straightaway my mind is filled with thoughts about mutual helpfulness, human sympathy, the common bond of brotherhood, and the mysteriously deep foundations on which society rests; or rather, on which it now reels and totters.[32]

Child rejects the flaneur role altogether. She knows that the new New York must be understood not just from its surfaces: she forces herself to realize that the vulgar market society cannot remain simply a passing show but that it exists permanently and must become an occasion for, in her terms, a witnessing of the ideal. The God of her clear, liberal Christian faith must be found in the street of quotidian life. The series of sketches that follow this initial observation range over the whole of the city; the reformist woman is perhaps a flaneur because she walks from docks to Five Points to the place where Mary Rogers was murdered. She is the genteel amateur, but the power of her knowledge that she must reorganize her thinking—her very theology—to take account of the new city is extraordinary and convincing. She knows that she must find, to use the terms of my book, that her God is in the street. Child is quite convinced he is there, in the ordinary details of the panorama.

New York minister Edwin Hubbell Chapin posed a similar moral problem in the "Lessons of the Street" chapter of his *Humanity and the City* (1854). Chapin too is flaneur as liberal Christian: "It is only the form of life that is transient and phenomenal; but the *Life* itself is here, also—here, in these flashing eyes, and heaving breasts, and active limbs. These conditions, however transient, involve the great interest of Humanity; and that lends the deepest significance to these conditions."[33] Child and Chapin were part of the new liberal religious culture that was attempting to construct a new Christology. They believed that all doctrines of Christ must start from and be grounded in humanly historical existence, and this left them with the formidable task of finding meaning and God in the midst of the New York crowd, in the passing figures of the panorama.

I will describe the relationship between the new liberal theology and urban narratives in greater detail in subsequent chapters, but clear enough here is that the New York walker in the city is by the late 1840s forced to confront the seriousness of the city's social ills. The walkers' narratives record the difficulties they have with interpreting what they see, with fitting it into their previous understandings of the world. The world before them seems initially contextless, inexplicable. In the phrase Poe quotes for his "Man of the Crowd," the crowd "lasst sich nicht lesen": it does not allow itself to be read. Foster or Robinson or Fern quickly succeed in reading the unreadable, but their initial difficulties pose the interpretive problems we associate with modernity and modern art. Contained within even the simplest journalistic account of a tour of antebellum New York are important questions about the relation between the individual perceiving mind and the new city outside it. How can the reflective bourgeois make connection with the crowd? What is the relationship between the conscience and the eye?[34]

Young Americans New York magazines also published panoramic narratives. The new magazines became important institutions of bourgeois culture in New York almost as quickly as did cheap newspapers. Many were explicitly urban, and all were intertwined with the booming (and busting) book-publishing industry based in the city. They paid particular attention to New York gossip and New York scenes and events, while still trying to be national magazines.[35]

The most powerful early New York magazine was the *Knicker-bocker*, founded in 1833 as an attempt to rival the great English journals like *Blackwood's*. Lewis Gaylord Clark became its editor and owner in 1834 and reigned over genteel urban literary society from that time until 1861. Hostile to the German and the transcendental, and particularly to the New England intellectuals, the magazine found its guiding spirit in Charles Dickens, whose morality and wholesomeness struck the right note for the conservative journal. Its writers, like Henry Cary ("John Waters"), were often businessmen, and the tone of the magazine suggested that there was still, as Perry Miller has it, "a species of merchant and banker who trailed behind him some clouds of eighteenth-century glory, who could make his way amid the [commercial] hubbub and yet secure a margin of leisure for reading, digesting good food, and for occasional evenings devoted to original composition."[36]

The *Knickerbocker* published flaneurs' sketches throughout the 1830s, first about London and then New York, as if sometime toward the end of the decade New York had earned the attention of the flaneur.[37] Between 1841 and 1844 the *Knickerbocker* carried the highly popular and urban New York "Quod Correspondence" by John Treat Irving, nephew of Washington Irving. The series resulted in two separately published and very successful books, *The Attorney; or, The Correspondence of John Quod* (1842) and *Harry Harson; or, The Benevolent Bachelor* (1844). The *Knickerbocker*'s best-known column was Lewis Gaylord Clark's "Editor's Table," with its literary and urbane gossip about New York. The editor's column in a magazine, still surviving in the "Talk of the Town" of *The New Yorker*, is panoramic form used to position a whole magazine. The magazine itself is the flaneur walking the city. The editor comments on the passing urban show: he knows about all the variety and scene of the city. He is the (literary) insider's insider, and buying his monthly or weekly guidebook makes the reader an insider too.

Opposing the formidable and Whiggish *Knickerbocker* were the magazines produced by the "Young Americans." These were the excitable literary members of the radical Jacksonian democrats called "Locofocos" after 1835. The leading members were Evert A. and George Duyckinck, William A. Jones, J. B. Auld, Russell Trevett, and later Cornelius Mathews. Herman Melville was adopted and promoted by this group in 1846 when Evert Duyckinck pushed Melville's *Typee* for Wiley and Putnam. Their chief organ was the political magazine edited by John L. O'Sullivan, the *Democratic Review*, and Young Americans also edited and wrote for the *New York Morning News*, a newspaper representing the center of the Tammany party.[38] The group held an urban point of view as firmly as did the *Knickerbocker*, but unlike the Whigs the Young Americans were literary nationalists: they wanted, most of all, a "home" literature. They strongly favored international copyright to protect the struggling American writer from being overwhelmed by "free" English competition.

The Young Americans' first attempt to counter the anglicism of the *Knickerbocker* was the magazine *Arcturus*, begun in December 1840 with Evert Duyckinck and William A. Jones in the lead. Its "The City Article" imitated Clark's "Table," but *Arcturus* carried the torch of American genius only until May 1842. Other briefly surviving Young American magazines were: the *Broadway Journal* (1845–46), edited by Charles F. Briggs and Edgar Allan Poe; *Yankee Doodle* (1846–47), a humor magazine edited by Cornelius Mathews; and the longer-lasting *Literary World* (1847–53), edited by Evert and George Duyckinck. The most significant late Young America magazine was *Putnam's Monthly* (1853–57), edited by Charles F. Briggs, assisted by Parke Godwin and George William Curtis.

All the Young America magazines carried panoramic commentary and fiction about New York. Charles F. Briggs's remarks in the first issue of the *Broadway Journal* (January 4, 1845) demonstrate how important New York was to his conception of the ability of American culture to compete internationally.

> Broadway is confessedly the finest street in the first city of the New World. It is the great artery through which flows the best blood of our system. All the elegance of our continent permeates through it . . . the most elegant shops in the City line its sides; the finest buildings are found there, and all fashions exhibit their first gloss upon its sidewalks. . . . It terminates at one end in the first square in the city [Union Square], doubtless in the Union, and at the other in the Battery, unrivalled for its entire beauty, by any marine parade in the world. . . . New York is fast becoming, if she be not already, America.[39]

Briggs's conceit that New York "is fast becoming" America is grandiose cultural boosterism not unlike that practiced by the city's merchants. The idea that the panorama of New York could be the part that stands for the whole, synecdoche for the continental nation, seems misguided to our century and a half's hindsight, but understanding that the Young Americans thought the literary culture of New York could become the culture of the nation is essential to understanding not just Briggs and Cornelius Mathews and Evert Duyckinck but also Walt Whitman and Herman Melville.

Briggs was a novelist well known and respected for his novels of

New York life. *The Adventures of Harry Franco* (1839) and *The Trippings of Tom Pepper* (1847) include panoramic accounts of the city, with Harry Franco, for example, wandering the commercial city in abject poverty, too poor, perhaps, to be the bourgeois flaneur but observing the brutality of conditions in the new city. Franco sees the sights but also the mind-numbing squalor of the Five Points, and he contemplates suicide in his failure to succeed in the city. Franco's first-person narration shows Briggs's point of view to be determinedly metropolitan but without the sensationalist voyeurism of a George G. Foster. Like Horace Greeley, who was editorially friendly to Briggs throughout the period, Briggs embraced the opulence of the commercial city enthusiastically and saw his role as creating a sophisticated literary culture for it.

Melville was a member of the Young American group after he started living and writing in the city in 1846. He began his career as one of a set of New York writers determined not only to create a sophisticated literary culture in New York but to make New York the center of all American culture. During 1847 Melville wrote for the Young American humor magazine *Yankee Doodle*, edited by Cornelius Mathews, publishing seven installments of "Authentic Anecdotes of 'Old Zack.' " He also wrote book reviews for the Duyckincks' *Literary World* between 1847 and 1850, including most significantly his recognition of Hawthorne's genius in his review of *Mosses from an Old Manse* (1846), published in two parts in August 1850 as "Hawthorne and His Mosses."

Melville's novel *White-Jacket* (1850), while not part of New York encounter discourse like the works of many Young Americans, structures itself on urban metaphor. Throughout the novel the narrator compares the world of the warship to a city: "a man-of-war is a city afloat," "a three-decker is a city on the sea."[40] The city is New York, and the conventions of New York guidebook description—promenaders on Broadway, Bowery boys running with their fire engine—become ways of explaining the ship: "the main-deck is generally filled with crowds of pedestrians, promenading up and down past the guns, like people taking the air in Broadway" (50); "Meantime, a loud cry is heard of 'Fire! fire! fire!' in the fore-top; and a regular engine, worked by a set of Bowery-boy tars, is forthwith set to playing streams of water aloft. And now it is 'Fire! fire! fire!' on the maindeck; and the entire ship is in as great a commotion as if a whole city ward were in a blaze" (67). One of the ship's corporals is "Leggs, [who had been] a turnkey attached to 'The Tombs' in New York" (306); the cook is "Old Coffee," who "often assured us that he had graduated at the New York Astor House" (58). *White-Jacket* even recalls a convention of slum description popularized by sensationalist novelists writing about the dangerous "Old Brewery" building in the Five Points neighborhood. The narrator says "a man of war resembles a three-story house in a suspicious part of town, with a basement of indefinite depth, and ugly-looking fellows gazing out at the windows" (75). The supposed deep basement is where the victims would be thrown.[41]

Cornelius Mathews, Melville's editor at *Yankee Doodle* and an intimate of Evert Duyckinck, became the central figure in Young American literary ambitions in the mid–1840s. Mathews uses the panoramic tour-of-the-town form in several of his books, but it was his *Big Abel and the Little Manhattan* (1845) that attempted to make panoramic description into serious fiction worthy of a New York and national culture. Perry Miller details how the book became the battleground between the two literary camps. Lewis Gaylord Clark of the *Knickerbocker* attacked it on its panoramic ground, calling it a "bald inventory," not a novel; the book required no thought "for the simple reason that it made no such demand upon the author who wrote it."[42]

Mathews tries to turn ethnographic description of New York life into fiction. The street boys Abel Henry Hudson, called "Big Abel," and Lankey Fogle, called "the Little Manhattan," are the central characters. The Little Manhattan is the descendant of Manhattanese, the supposed original Native American inhabitant, and represents those who were displaced by the Dutch. His friend Big Abel is the descendant of Henry Hudson and represents the newcomers. The two boys, working-class flaneurs themselves, set out on a tour of the city, "dividing" the town between them imaginatively, the "Indian" listing the items from nature and Big Abel those of urban culture: the Little Manhattan lists the trees and Big Abel the Astor House, and so on. Big Abel has the best of the division, as one might imagine: the Native American world is nearly gone. The plot and subplot all develop in the frame of a panorama of New York. We see newsboys and prostitutes and firemen and poor scholars and apple sellers and cart drivers and The Tombs prison and Sunday on the Battery and more. We learn the workday rituals, and we hear the special languages of the city. The Little Manhattan meets "fly-away boys" who say about him "He's in the big bellows tonight." The Little Manhattan orders a "Monongahela, hot-and-hot" at a road house. A "tip-top" restaurant is too "narrow" for Little Manhattan and Big Abel.

Mathews takes the stance of the flaneur in that he dabbles in the customs of others, and he participates in an ideology in glorifying the new city as it exists, in justifying its rowdy commercial self, in watching it with an attentive voyeurism that belongs to the bourgeoisie of the period. Like the writings of other flaneurs, *Big Abel and the Little Manhattan*'s attentive voyeurism obscures the nature of social relationships in the city at the same time as it provides some of the most interesting descriptions we have of contemporary Bowery life.[43]

At the end of the book Big Abel and Little Manhattan walk on the Banking House roof, and Big Abel takes panoramic control of what is clearly his city:

> as though it had been the very top and ridge of all the world. He called the company to look upon the city (his city, now . . .) spread below. Could any eye there take all in? Southward! Thick and dark, with houses; of all shapes, and heights, and schools. Westward! Another city back of that. East![44]

Like the viewer of the 1859 Bachmann lithograph, Big Abel imagines himself at the "top and ridge of all the world" and imagines that he, at this ecstatic moment, takes possession through perception. The reader is meant to feel some nostalgia for the lost natural order of life, but it is so distant in time as to be of small concern. For Mathews is arguing, along with other Young American writers, that New York's panorama *was* the world. By the mid–1850s this highly superficial conceit would seem comic even to Young Americans (as it possibly did to the panoramist Bachmann), and its absurdity underlies some of Melville's jokes in *The Confidence-Man*, but in 1845 Mathews and his promoters take it seriously. Broadway is a window to all that exists anywhere; Broadway is, as Mathews says, "a great sheet of glass, through which the whole world is visible as in a transparency."[45]

The direct trial of him who would be the greatest poet is today. [He must] flood himself with the immediate age as with vast oceanic tides.

Walt Whitman
1855 preface, Leaves of Grass

3

Walt Whitman:
Over the Roofs of the World

New York Journalist Walt Whitman always said that his poetry came from his life. He may have written the following biographical description himself.

In the first place he learned life—men, women and children; he went on equal terms with every one, he liked them and they him, and he knew them far better than they knew themselves. Then he became thoroughly conversant with the shops, houses, sidewalks, ferries, factories, taverns, gatherings, political meetings, carousings, etc. He was first the absorber of the sunlight, the free air and the open streets, and then of interiors. He knew the hospitals, poorhouses, prisons and their inmates. He passed freely in and about those parts of the city which are inhabited by the worst characters; he knew all their people, and many of them knew him; he learned to tolerate their squalor, vice and

69

ignorance. . . . Many of the worst of those characters became singularly attached to him. He knew and was sociable with the man that sold peanuts at the corner, and the old woman that dispensed coffee in the market.

The language of Richard Maurice Bucke's 1883 biography seems wholly Whitman's, and we know that Whitman revised the work.[1] The created Whitman of the passage is a man who has the freedom of the city. He walks in the "free" air and the "open" streets; he passes "freely" through its various locales. He can walk in any neighborhood and is "sociable" with the coffee woman. He is the flaneur extended into an imagined urban man entirely defined by his effort to absorb New York into himself. His eye and conscience unite in arrogantly seizing the city whole. This persona, this "Whitman," is a wonderful legend of urban identity that Walter Whitman built on the New York panoramic paradigm, and the paradigm shapes his journalism, poetry, and nonfiction through much of his career.

The dramatic change in newspaper publishing determined the path of Walt Whitman's early professional life. He learned the printing trade early in the 1830s just as other printers were founding the great urban dailies, like the *Sun* and *Herald*, and inventing bourgeois journalism. In the boom and bust of market-society newspapers Whitman did not succeed in attaching himself to a particular paper for long: he and his many similarly talented colleagues got paid work from a bewilderingly wide variety of brief attachments. New York newspapers rarely provided steady work, and journalists were part of the shifting workforce that served all the new entrepreneurial businesses.

In the beginning Whitman alternated between teaching and working for newspapers. In 1831–32 he was a printer's apprentice on the *Long Island Patriot*. From fall 1832 to May 1835 he worked as a compositor on the *Long Island Star*. From 1835 through 1838 he worked in printing offices in New York City and taught in various schools on Long Island. In 1838–39 Whitman edited his own weekly, the *Long Islander*, but by 1841 he was back in New York working as a printer at the *New World* and writing for several New York magazines: the *Democratic Review*, the *Broadway Journal*, *American Review*, and *Colum-*

bian Magazine. For about two months in the spring of 1842 he edited the *New York Aurora*, then the *Evening Tattler* for a few months. His temperance novel, *Franklin Evans; or, The Inebriate, "A Tale of the Times,"* was issued in a *New World* extra on November 23, 1842. In 1843 he edited *The Statesman* and then worked briefly for Moses Y. Beach, who bought the *New York Sun* from Day in 1838. In 1844 he edited the *New York Democrat* and then worked on the *Mirror*. In 1845 he returned to Brooklyn and contributed to the *Brooklyn Evening Star*, and then from 1846 until late January 1848 he was the editor of the *Brooklyn Eagle*. Traveling to New Orleans, he worked for almost three months for the *Crescent*. Back in Brooklyn he edited the *Freeman* for a year until September 11, 1849. In the early 1850s he operated a printing office and stationery store and was a building contractor and real estate speculator. In 1855 *Leaves of Grass* was first published. Later in that decade he was, from spring of 1857 to midsummer 1859, editor of the *Brooklyn Daily Times*.[2]

Working at so many papers through the 1840s and 1850s made Whitman an accomplished journalist. He published a large quantity of writing in the newspapers he edited ("editing" in both small and big papers meant writing for every issue, not just editorials but often large parts of the paper) and in newspapers and periodicals he freelanced for. The great majority of his writing is solid journalism and some of it is excellent, but it remains journalism seemingly not distinguishable from the work being done by many New York newspaper writers. The difference readers of Whitman's poetry perceive between his journalism and his first published book of poetry, *Leaves of Grass*, has led them to wonder how Whitman could have produced such a book without a sophisticated poetic apprenticeship. Ralph Waldo Emerson writes him after its publication to "greet [him] at the beginning of a great career" but he thinks it "must have had a long foreground somewhere, for such a start."[3] Emerson could hardly have imagined then that the "somewhere" was in the penny press he loathed.

Whitman, like George Wisner at the *Sun* and novelist George Lippard, worked several times as a police court reporter, the starting job in the new encounter journalism. In the *Brooklyn Eagle* for February 27, 1847, he goes for the Irish joke: "When brought up to the police office, [Andrew Ryan] formed the most perfect specimen of perpetual motion ever seen . . . being afflicted with a shaking that would have done credit to a western ague."[4] Ten years later, in "Scenes in a Police Justice's Court" that ran in the *Brooklyn Daily Times* in 1857, Whitman is more compassionate although he still finds comedy: "Life's drama is played there, on a miniature scale, and tears and laughter succeed each other just as they do on the larger stage." He describes Justice Cornwell's court—the policemen lolling in armchairs, the "Tomb Shysters of Gotham" (lawyers always on the lookout for a fee), and the rowdies who have been arrested for participating in a "free fight" in a porter house. Whitman sees the drunks both more scientifically and more sympathetically than he did ten years before.

> [There] sits a poor, brutalized Irishman, an habitual drunkard, who has been fetched up for beating his wife. The sodden wretch, with blinking, blood-shot eyes and matted hair, sits shaking and shivering with suffering at the unwonted privation of his morning dram. Next him sits an old woman denominated in the classic language of the police courts, a "Bummer," who has just gone off, probably from the same cause, into a fit that may be either hysterics or incipient delirium. The officer runs and brings a cup of water, and it is good to see that even here the spirit of womanly sympathy and kindness is not quite extinct, for two females who sit immediately behind the poor creature support her head and bathe it with a pitying care—true women and Good Samaritans they!

Whitman has diagnostic terms at his command—"habitual," "delirium"—that are characteristic of the seriousness of urban problems by 1857; he is, as always, careful to collect the authentic local word ("Bummer"); and he notes some of the charitable dynamics of women's culture. But the journalistic duty of the police-court form is to amuse, and Whitman obliges. Like Wisner's jokes, Whitman's are not so funny. "[S]omething rich" is occasioned by the "rows among the women, in which scratching and hair-pulling are the most prominent features. Most of these feminine rows occur in 'tenant houses' and cheap boarding establishments, and more merriment is sometimes to be extracted from these real-life affairs than from the most screaming farce."[5] Like all penny press editors and writers, Whitman could also be very high minded about the purposes of the penny newspaper. The key myth of the newspaper was that it was the medium of American democracy. Through its clarity and affordability the newspaper could educate the people to participate in their political destiny fully and intelligently. Whitman writes in the *New York Aurora*: "Among newspapers, the penny press is the same as common schools among seminaries of education. They carry light and knowledge in among those who most need it. They disperse the clouds of ignorance; and make the great body of people intelligent, capable, and worthy of performing the duties of republican freemen."[6] Editorial comments in the penny press like this one always sound like advertisements for the medium's self, brash boasting of a power not realized, self-conscious assertions of the clarifying power of knowledge of the ordinary. Jacksonian democracy asserted not only that the mass of people were the only source of legitimate power but that the principles of government were easy to understand, that they could be explained in a direct and uncomplicated way in the people's new medium.

The penny journalism imagined itself with great political power and threatened, as James Gordon Bennett did in his dangerous democratic way or Horace Greeley did in his cultivated republican way, to govern entirely. Here is Whitman in the *Brooklyn Eagle*:

> Where is, at this moment, the great medium or exponent of power, through which the civilized world is governed? Neither in the tactics or at the desks of statesmen, or in those engines of physical terror and force wherewith the game of war is now played. The *pen* is that medium of power—a little crispy goose quill, which, though its point can hardly pierce your sleeve of broadcloth, is able to make gaping wounds in mighty empires—to put the power of kings in jeopardy, or even chop off their heads—to sway the energy and will of congregated masses of men, as the huge winds roll the waves of the sea, lashing them to fury, and hurling destruction on every side![7]

Whitman is aware later in his life that the power of the daily paper is ephemeral. The old journalist sounds like Walter Benjamin when he tells Horace Traubel, "The newspaper is so fleeting . . . is so like a thing gone as quick as come: has no life, so to speak: its birth and death almost coterminous."[8]

In the 1840s, however, Whitman believed in the power of the press and specifically in its political power. He was politically active, participating vigorously in the sharp conflicts among different versions of New York democratic politics. He was a Free-Soiler and Barnburner, fired from his job at the *Eagle* because his radical ferocity did not please the owners of the Brooklyn paper. At the center of his politics was his belief that the unfettered American individual was the central actor in democracy and that the stage on which the radical democratic drama was to be played was the modern city.[9]

Whitman might have seen that the market-driven growth of the great cities was destroying the equality and freedoms of the working people he thought so essential to democracy, but the journalist participated in the same illusions as most of his contemporaries. In the 1840s he mistook the city's variety and hugeness, its "aggregates of people, riches, and enterprise,"[10] for unbounded opportunity for the forming of new and free men and women.

New York Words   From beginning to end, Whitman was influenced by the conventional journalistic images of the exciting and promising variety of the democratic city. The landscape of New York, its panorama, is often in Whitman's journalistic *feuilletons* that came before his *Leaves*. He writes about the sensational underside of New York, about the Bowery b'hoys, about the flow of people and sights on Broadway, and about the rich, new colloquial language of the city. He works and reworks the paradigm of encountering the city.

In his early temperance novel, *Franklin Evans* (1842), the city is the dangerous lure to alcohol for the naive country boy Franklin, and Broadway itself is the processional display of the market culture:

> How bright and happy every thing seemed! The shops were filled with the most beautiful and costly wares, and the large, clear glass of the shop-windows flashed in the brilliancy of the gas, which displayed their treasures to the passers-by. And the pave was filled with an eager and laughing crowd, jostling along, and each intent on some scheme of pleasure for the evening. I felt confused for a long time with the universal whirl.[11]

The novel contrasts, in the most ordinary way, the city and the country. The city symbolizes the possibility of individual, nonfamilial moral doom that threatens the greenhorn from the country. Drink itself is the perfect sign of degradation because it loosens one's loyalties to domestic family and threatens the already precarious membership in the middle class. The book participates in the conventions of popular reform literature, pretending to condemn the sins of the seductive city while at the same time exploring and celebrating those very things. Whitman gives a panoramic tour of the underside of the city and visits many of the locales that writers Charles F. Briggs, Cornelius Mathews, Ned Buntline, and George G. Foster did.[12] A Whitman story in the *Aurora*, "The Last of Lively Frank," also has the elements of the Asmodeus exposure. Whitman writes about the hidden New York: "If some potent magician could lift the veil which shrouds, in alleys, dark streets, garrets, and a thousand other habitations of want, the miseries that are every day going on among us—how would the spectacle distress and terrify the beholder!"[13]

Whitman wrote several series of urban sketches for newspapers, such as those for the *Long Island Democrat* ("Sun-Down Papers"), the *New Orleans Crescent* ("Sketches of the Sidewalks and Levees"), the *New York Leader* ("City Photographs"), the *Brooklyn Standard* ("Brooklyniana"), and *Life Illustrated* ("New York Dissected").[14] The series he wrote in 1855 and 1856 for Fowler and Wells's general-interest magazine, *Life Illustrated*, is an interesting example of this kind of work. It is perhaps unremarkable urban journalism except that the articles were written by Whitman *after* he published *Leaves of Grass*. Their publication shows that the poet could readily resume the panoramic journalistic style, using his poetic catalogue technique to evoke the splendor of New York's quotidian life. He wrote articles in *Life Illustrated* on "The Opera," "The Egyptian Museum," "Christmas at 'Grace' [Church]," and, under the specific series title "New York Dissected," six sketches: "New York Amuses Itself—the Fourth of July," "Wicked Architecture, Decent Homes for Working-Men," "The Slave Trade," "Broadway," "Street Yarn," and "Advice to Strangers." "New York Dissected" is in the panoramic style of journalism in which New York is "cut open" as it was in George G. Foster's popular "New York in Slices" series for the *Tribune*.

Like other ethnographic panoramists, Whitman was fascinated with the character of the Bowery b'hoy, whom he describes and defends. The poetic persona he creates for his *Leaves of Grass*, particularly in the poem later called "Song of Myself," owes something to the b'hoy as defined by bourgeois journalists. George G. Foster wrote about the character frequently, including a "slice" on him in *New York in Slices* (1849)[15] and defining him in a later piece this way:

> The governing sentiment, pride and passion of the b'hoy is indepen-
> dence—that he can do as he pleases and is able, under all circum-
> stances, to take care of himself. He abhors dependence, obligation, and
> exaggerates the feeling of self-reliance so much as to appear, on the
> surface, rude and boorish. But the appeal of helplessness or the cry of
> suffering unlocks his heart at once, whence all manner of good and
> tender and magnanimous qualities leap out. The b'hoy can stand any-
> thing but affectation—on that he has no mercy; and should he even
> find a fop or coxcomb in absolute distress, we fear his first impulse
> would be to laugh at him.[16]

Foster is quite aware that he is helping to define a folkloric type. He acknowledges the contribution Cornelius Mathews and Benjamin A. Baker made to recording the character. In Baker's play, *A Glance at New York in 1848*, the actor Frank S. Chanfrau made "Mose, the Bow-ery B'hoy" a popular New York type. Foster continues to think of Mose and Lize as "middle classes." Ned Buntline also writes about the characters in the sequels to *The Mysteries and Miseries of New York* (1848), *The B'hoys of New York* (1850), and *The G'hals of New York* (1850).

Sean Wilentz points out that the b'hoy character is in part bour-geois mythology of the lower middle classes. The b'hoy was not a mem-ber of a single body or ethnic group but "an updated version of still another metropolitan type, the youthful working-class dandy."[17] Whit-man is not as troubled as Wilentz by the figure's lack of social density and happily defends himself editorially. In the *Brooklyn Eagle* (January 7, 1847), for example, Whitman writes: "It is too common among su-percilious people to look on the Firemen as a turbulent noisy fold, b'hoys for a row and 'muss' only: this does the great body of them a prodigious injustice." Whitman also defended Mike Walsh, a United States congressman from New York and editor of *The Subterranean*, often viewed as the b'hoys' political leader.[18]

Walt Whitman

Frontispiece of Walt Whitman's Leaves of Grass *(Brooklyn: Walt Whitman, 1855).*
Courtesy of Roger Lathbury.

By 1852 Whitman had taken to dressing like a workingman in
flannels, open-throated work shirt, and high boots, in "self-conscious
contrast to the fashionable clothes he affected in the 1840s; the hat that
he was now cocking indoors and out as he pleased was not the fancy
one he had described in [an article in] the *Aurora* but the wide-brimmed
'wide-awake' which had caught his fancy of late."[19] He was of course
in costume as workingman, and the frontispiece engraving he used in
the first printing of *Leaves of Grass* portrays an ideal "Whitman" as the
new urban man, the flaneur gone native.

Whitman loved the language of the b'hoys, the slang of working

New York. In notes for a book he intended to write celebrating the English language he collects New York words as examples of the delights of American slang. In one two-page sequence he writes:

> Did he do it a purpose?
> That's so, easy enough
> That's a sick ticket
> Well I was looking for a man—about your size
> "go back"—"go back on him"
> He works on his own hook
> a good American word centurion
> Kosmos, noun masculine or feminine, a person who[se] scope of mind, or whose range in a particular science, includes all, the whole known universe

And two pages later, another sequence:

> "the New York Bowery boy—"Sa-a-a-y! What—á—t?"
> "So long"—(a delicious American—New York—idiomatic phrase at parting equivalent to "good bye" "adieu" &c.
> all right
> swim out
> cave in
> dry up
> switch off
> —git and git
> he is on that
> I am on that
> "hold up your head up"
> "Bully for you"
> a "nasty" man
> "that's rough"

A few pages later he also notes "lunatic 'looney.' " These are primarily words and expressions, like the "rowdy" and "beards" and "muss" and "rough" which he used in other writings, that originate in New York working-class language. Whitman, like the bourgeois ethnographer, collects the words for his delight and for his poetry. Interestingly, the New York journalist is fully aware of the international influences on his profession: he also writes down the useful French newspaper words "feuilleton" and "feuilletonist."[20]

Bringing slang words into his journalism was one thing, but Whitman's importing of New York slang into what purported to be serious poetry raised the ire of many reviewers. Charles Eliot Norton, writing in *Putnam's Monthly*, thinks the "writer's scorn for the wonted usages of good writing, extends to the vocabulary he adopts; words usually banished from polite society are here employed without reserve and with perfect indifference to their effect on the reader's mind."[21]

Charles A. Dana reviewed the 1855 *Leaves of Grass* for the *Tribune*. He gazes at the engraved daguerreotype (see p. 77) of the author that substitutes for his name on the title page.

> We may infer that he belongs to that exemplary class of society sometimes irreverently styled "loafers." He is therein represented in a garb, half sailor's, half workingman's, with no superfluous appendage of coat or waistcoat, a "wideawake" perched jauntily on his head, one hand in his pocket and the other on his hip, with a certain air of mild defiance, and an expression of pensive insolence in his face which seems to betoken a consciousness of his mission as the "coming man."[22]

The poet represented himself as the workingman he sometimes was but more as the bourgeois image of the workingman redefined as the sign of a new imaginative order in which ordinary men write poems about ordinary things and find them in transcendent meaning.

Whitman seems to have been a "loafer" in many senses of the New York word. One of his most striking qualities to people who knew him was that he didn't seem to work very hard despite the competitive demands of his journalistic craft. He was a "loafer" in a culture that highly valued the "wide-awake." In an article in the *Long Island Democrat* in which he wrote "how do I love a loafer!" and said that all great philosophers were loafers, he fantasized about a future "nation of loafers . . . an entire loafer kingdom."[23] He uses the noun "loafer" and the verb "loaf" happily about at least his imagined self, most notably in the fourth and fifth lines of the poem "Song of Myself": "I loafe and invite my soul, / I lean and loafe at my ease. . . . observing a spear of summer grass."

During the time Whitman worked for New York papers, his casual attitude was often a problem. The owners of the *New York Aurora* fired him from the editorial staff and accused him of "loaferism." He was for them "the laziest fellow who ever undertook to edit a city paper." Whitman's Brooklyn schoolmaster was amazed to learn in later years that his pupil had become a famous poet. He recalled him as good-natured but "clumsy and slovenly in appearance" and said kindly that Whitman's success went to show that "we need never be discouraged over anyone."[24]

Broadway Whitman loved the street. When Moncure D. Conway, at Emerson's suggestion, called upon Whitman a month or so after *Leaves of Grass* first appeared, he accompanied him on a walk through the city. "Nothing could surpass the blending of *insouciance* with active observation in his manner as we strolled along the streets. 'Look at that face!' he exclaimed once as we paused near the office of the *Herald*. I looked and beheld a boy of perhaps fifteen years, with certainly a hideous countenance, the face one-sided, and one eye almost hanging out of a villainous low forehead. He had a bundle under his arm. 'There,' said Walt, 'is a New York reptile. There's poison about his fangs, I think.'" The two watched the boy, and then Whitman called him over, and they found he was selling obscene books.[25] Whitman is the flaneur but he is actively engaged: he thinks that urban democratic consciousness begins with the experience of the street.[26]

It was perfectly conventional in New York journalism to think of Broadway as standing for the entirety of New York's (and perhaps even the world's) variety. Whitman developed the image of the street as representating of all of human life throughout his journalistic career, from early pieces like "Scenes and Sights of Broadway" in the *Brooklyn Evening Star* (February 20, 1846) and "Gayety of Americans" in the *Brooklyn Eagle* (September 23, 1846) through "Broadway" and "A Broadway Pageant" in *Leaves of Grass*.[27] He, like endless numbers of his journalistic contemporaries, used the figure of Broadway as a stream. Mathews, for example, called Broadway an "ever flowing wave," a "perfect Mississippi" of different human types.[28] Whitman, expanding that conventional image, depicts Broadway as a sea where the spire of Grace Church shows down on Broadway "like a ghostly lighthouse looming up over the porpoise-backs of the omnibuses, as they lift and dive in that unquiet sea, and over the tossing spray of ribbons and plumes that give back rainbows to the eye of him that gazes on the living waves."[29] The street is Whitman's symbol of democracy; it is his wellspring of types; it is his panoramic education.

In the "Broadway" sketch for the "New York Dissected" series in *Life Illustrated* Whitman concludes:

> Such is the procession of the street, to the outward eye. A dreamer would not fail to see spirits walking amid the crowd; devils busily whispering into scheming ears; the demons of falsehood, avarice, wrath, and impurity flitting hither and thither, and mingling eagerly their suggestions in the hot, seething atmosphere of human plots and devices; and angels, too, among or above the hurrying mass, seeking to lift some soul out of evil ways, or to guard it from imminent temptation.[30]

Ralph Waldo Emerson's influence on Whitman is visible here in his implicit distinction between the "outward eye" and the inner eye. But the problematic discontinuity between the inner eye and the outside world was not just a problem that Emerson set for antebellum thought. As we have seen, the panoramic journalism of the period posed the same problem for bourgeois walkers like Lydia Maria Child and Edwin Hubbell Chapin.

One discovery in the Broadway crowd is oneself. In Whitman's anonymously published "Street Yarn" for *Life Illustrated* he himself is there.

> Tall, large, rough-looking man, in a journeyman carpenter's uniform. Coarse, sanguine complexion; strong, bristly, grizzled beard; singular eyes, of a semi-transparent, indistinct light blue, and with that sleepy look that comes when the lid rests half way down over the pupil; careless, lounging gait. Walt Whitman, the sturdy, self-conscious microcosmic, prose-poetical author of that incongruous hash of mud and gold—"Leaves of Grass."[31]

This is standard insider journalistic joking, but like much of Whitman's journalism, like the engraved daguerreotype that is the frontispiece of *Leaves of Grass* and like the first poem in that book, it is an attempt to imagine the "coming man," a self-creation that advertises itself.

Whitman remembers Broadway in *Specimen Days and Collect*

(1882–83) in sections that were originally in the *New York Weekly Graphic* in 1874. The great street is still there, but the world he learned from for his *Leaves* is gone:

> The flush days of the old Broadway stage[coache]s, characteristic and copious, are over. The Yellow-birds, the Red-birds, the original Broadway, the Fourth avenue, the Knickerbocker, and a dozen others of twenty or thirty years ago, are all gone. And the men specially identified with them, and giving vitality and meaning to them—the drivers—a strange, natural, quick-eyed and wondrous race—(not only Rabelais and Cervantes would have gloated upon them, but Homer and Shakespere [*sic*] would)—how well I remember them, and must here give a word about them. How many hours, forenoons and afternoons—how many exhilarating night-times I have had—perhaps June or July, in cooler air—riding the whole length of Broadway, listening to some yarn, (and the most vivid yarns ever spun, and the rarest mimicry)—or perhaps I declaiming some stormy passage from Julius Caesar or Richard, (you could roar as loudly as you chose in that heavy, dense, uninterrupted street-bass.) Yes, I knew all the drivers then, Broadway Jack, Dressmaker, Balky Bill, George Storms, Old Elephant, his brother Young Elephant (who came afterward,) Tippy, Pop Rice, Big Frank, Yellow Joe, Pete Callahan, Patsy Dee, and dozens more . . .

He gives "those Broadway omnibus jaunts and drivers and declamations and escapades" credit for "the gestation of 'Leaves of Grass.' "[32] He expects the critics to laugh at this because he thinks that at this late date they still measure literature by the signs of classical education, by time spent in the past and not spent loafing on Broadway omnibuses.

Whitman came to think that his ethnographic collection of types and words and sights and his panoramic encounters with New York were not enough. He himself recognized that the laughing critics in his century and ours would want to know how it was that the journalist became the poet, how the hack became the United States' most original poet, and he therefore tries to explain in *A Backward Glance* (1889).

> After continued personal ambition and effort, as a young fellow, to enter with the rest into competition for the usual rewards, business, political, literary, etc.—to take part in the great *mêlée*, both for victory's prize itself and to do some good—After years of those aims and pursuits, I found myself remaining possess'd, at the age of thirty-one

to thirty-three [1850–52], with a special desire and conviction. . . . This was a feeling or ambition to articulate and faithfully express in literary or poetic form, and uncompromisingly, my own physical, emotional, moral, intellectual, and aesthetic Personality, in the midst of, and tallying, the momentous spirit and facts of its immediate days, and of current America—and to exploit that Personality, identified with place and date, in a far more candid and comprehensive sense than any hitherto poem or book.[33]

Whitman wanted his creations to be explicitly historical, to speak of his age. He wanted to be the *genius* of his age in the sense that Melville meant when he said "great geniuses are parts of the times; they themselves are the times."[34] As Whitman says in the 1855 preface to *Leaves of Grass*, the poet must "flood himself with the immediate age as with vast oceanic tides."[35]

The solution to this creative desire was not to turn away from the everyday, the immediate, which the penny newspapers covered and glorified, but to "give ultimate vivification to facts," because without vivification "reality would seem incomplete . . . and science, democracy, and life itself, finally in vain."[36] "Vivification" too, like so many of Whitman's words, is an Americanism. The involvement of the aesthetic personality in the facts of the time, the facts of the city, was not just to record and catalogue them, to put exclamation points after them in the style of the journalistic panoramists. It was instead to make them come alive by seeing that the facts are, as the "Song of Myself" persona has it, "letters from God dropped in the street" (l. 1279).

Panoramic Poet The 1855 *Leaves of Grass* opens with the engraved daguerreotype of the apparent author, a man portraying the devil-may-care workingman. The next page, the title page, lists no author, thus insisting that the reader pay attention to the engraved illustration of the author. The next page begins ten pages of prose printed in newspaper-like double columns. Whitman omitted what we now call the "1855 preface" from all subsequent editions, thus changing his book significantly. He later drastically changed the penny newspaper punctuation of the poem itself, moving away from the dash and ellipses to more traditional markers. The tone of the 1855 preface seems like a democratic penny press editorial boosting the United States and its free peoples: "The Americans of all nations at any time upon the earth have probably the fullest poetical nature. The United States themselves are essentially the greatest poem" (iii). But the prose soon begins to define the role and duties of the American poet, combining New England transcendentalist theory, particularly as expressed in Emerson's essay "The Poet," with a New York panoramic aesthetic. The poet is he who vivifies not just the urban sights of the new city but the entire American landscape and all its peoples. He "incarnates" the country's "geography and natural life and rivers and lakes" (iv). The poet *sees* the whole country as if on a map: he makes it equal; he is "the arbiter of the diverse and he is the key" (iv). His readers, the "folks," expect "of the poet to indicate more than the beauty and dignity which always attach to dumb real objects. . . . they expect him to indicate the path between reality and their souls" (v). The poet's task is to see everything, as in a panorama, and to vivify it. The poetic myth is that the poet, the maker, can unify all with words just as the panoramist did with illustration, but the facts now contain all the weight of God. All meaning is in the images of the country's landscape—urban and rural.

The poem proper begins with the unidentified persona loafing and inviting his soul. At this point city is negative and country is positive. His terror is urban—"Houses and rooms are full of perfumes . . . . the shelves are crowded with perfumes" (l. 6), and his salvation is rural— "The atmosphere is not a perfume . . . . it has no taste of the distillation . . . . it is odorless, / It is for my mouth forever . . . . I am in love with it" (ll. 9–10). The dailiness of modern life, the "trippers and askers" who surround him, his "dinner, dress, associates, looks, business, compliments, dues," are not the "Me myself"(ll. 57–65). The language is specifically Emersonian: the poet is saying that he must find his "Me myself" so as not to be overwhelmed by the "not me" in the new hectic life. Then he asserts a mystical union between the self and world that enables a new man to look at the world anew.

The persona then witnesses and sees and names, like the "loafer" walking his street. His "eyes settle the land" (l. 174). The beauty of the poetry is in the exactly rendered individual image, urban and rural. The witnesser sees all things. He sees:

> The blab of the pave . . . . the tires of carts and sluff of bootsoles and
> talk of the promenaders,

The heavy omnibus, the driver with his interrogating thumb, the
  clank of the shod horses on the granite floor,
The carnival of sleighs, the clinking and shouted jokes and pelts of
  snowballs;
The hurrahs for popular favorites . . . . the fury of roused mobs,
The flap of the curtained litter—the sick man inside, borne to the
  hospital,
The meeting of enemies, the sudden oath, the blows and fall,
The excited crowd—the policeman with his star quickly working his
  passage to the centre of the crowd,

(ll. 146–52)

as well as:

The big doors of the country-barn stand open and ready,
The dried grass of the harvest-time loads the slow-drawn wagon,
The clear light plays on the brown gray and green intertinged,
The armfuls are packed to the sagging mow.

(ll. 160–64)

The memorable sequence in the poem is the uninterrupted, long catalogue in the section of the poem later numbered fifteen where a whole
country is envisioned quickly. The list includes images from all the
regions of the United States—from opium eater and pavingman to
canal-boy and "squaw." All the people and all the landscape seem there,
panoramically seen by the persona. The man of many roles begins to
define an identity by seeing.

Soon the persona claims for himself the role of poet and names
himself as part of the crowd. He names himself using explicitly New
York words.

Walt Whitman, an American, one of the roughs, a kosmos,
Disorderly fleshy and sensual . . . . eating drinking and breeding,
No sentimentalist . . . . no stander above men and women or apart
  from them . . . . no more modest than immodest.

(ll. 499–501)

In later editions Whitman needs to annotate the New York origins
more specifically than the 1855 edition's language does: first he revises
to "Whitman am I, of mighty Manhattan" and finally to "Walt Whit-

man, a kosmos, of Manhattan the son." In 1855, the unexplanatory and fully democratic Walt is, as David Reynolds says, like a b'hoy: "swaggering, cocksure, indolent, wicked, acute, generous, and altogether lovable." Unlike the b'hoys, "he loafs and invites his *soul*, instead of inviting trouble, as the b'hoy was wont to do."[37]

"Walt Whitman" is different from the Bowery b'hoy in that he is one who sees and understands the poetic task of seeing. The poet self-created by section twenty-four is the panoramic man, the person who (like a gentle Asmodeus) sees into everything and can now not only witness it all but become it all. He walks the whole country as if it were Broadway, from the vantage point of both the ground ("afoot") and a balloon.

> My ties and ballasts leave me . . . . I travel . . . . I sail . . . . my elbows
> rest in the sea-gaps,
> I skirt the sierras . . . . my palms cover continents,
> I am afoot with my vision.
>
> (ll. 712–14)

Or, later:

> Where the pear-shaped balloon is floating aloft . . . . floating in it
> myself and looking composedly down.
>
> (l. 739)

Walt Whitman sweeps across the whole country, seeing the nation panoramically from aloft, even (briefly) the original city: "Approaching Manhattan, up by the long-stretching island," (l. 747). This imaginative panoramic flight is as astonishing as the Bachmann panorama that pictures New York as globe. Witnessing on such a grand scale results not just in the fusing organic perception of Emerson but in actual identification with what is seen.

Whitman is in no sense the flaneur who looks as if at goods in the shop window. The poet finally is the landscape he at first only saw, or, rather, he both sees and is. He himself sees and is the hero of the quotidian new world:

> I am the mashed fireman with breastbone broken . . . . tumbling walls
> buried me in their debris,

Heat and smoke I inspired . . . . I heard the yelling shouts of my
comrades,
I heard the distant click of their picks and shovels;
They have cleared the beams away . . . . they tenderly lift me forth.

I lie in the night air in my red shirt . . . . the pervading hush is for my
sake,
Painless after all I lie, exhausted but not so unhappy,
White and beautiful are the faces around me . . . . the heads are bared
of their fire-caps,
The kneeling crowd fades with the light of the torches.

(ll. 843–50)

The firemen, the men in red flannel, are the imagined heroes of the
present. They replace the ancient stories of deities.

Those ahold of fire-engines and hook-and-ladder ropes more to me
than the gods of the antique wars,
Minding their voices peal through the crash of destruction,
Their brawny limbs passing safe over charred laths . . . . their white
foreheads whole and unhurt out of the flames.

(ll. 1034–36)

The God that Walt Whitman finds is the God in the street.

Why should I wish to see God better than this day?
I see something of God each hour of the twenty-four, and each moment then,
In the faces of men and women I see God, and in my own face in the
glass;
I find letters from God dropped in the street, and every one is signed
by God's name.

(ll. 1276–79)

More even than that, "Whitman" is himself the street god, healing and
comforting the reader toward the end of the poem, extinguishing his
created self to become completely the objects he names and catalogues.
At the end of the poem he is the leaf of grass he began the poem by
observing: "If you want me again look for me under your bootsoles"
(l. 1330). The self that is in everything is also panoramically high above

the world of New York: "I sound my barbaric yawp over the roofs of the world" (l. 1323).

Roy Harvey Pearce writes that the history of American poetry is the history of an impulse toward antinomianism. It is a record of "a gradual but nonetheless revolutionary shift in the meaning of 'invention' . . . from the 'coming upon' something made and ordered by God, to 'making' and 'ordering'—transforming—something, anything, into that which manifests above all man's power to make and to order."[38] Whitman, as poet, is the god in the street himself. He has made the languages of meaning speak in the everyday urban idiom.

Leaves of Grass is a production of the ideology of the moment. It evokes the excitement, the acceptance of the everyday, the finding of the extraordinary in the everyday. It does that by using the discourse of New York encounter. It is the poem of the new order, although not many Americans fully understood that. Emerson is not far off when he calls the book a combination of the "Bhagavad Gita and the New-York *Tribune*."[39] Neither is Charles Eliot Norton when in his *Putnam's* review he calls the book "a compound of the New England Transcendentalist and New York rowdy."[40]

The New York feuilletonist "Fanny Fern" (Sara Payson Willis Parton), the maker of "leaves" like Whitman's, did understand, and she responded with great enthusiasm even though many male reviewers thought the book was not for "mixed" company. Parton first alludes to the poetic persona of Whitman in a column, "Peeps from under a Parasol," in the *New York Ledger*.

> And speaking of books, here comes Walt Whitman, author of 'Leaves of Grass,' which, by the way, I have not yet read. His shirt collar is turned off from his muscular throat, and his shoulders are thrown back as if even in that fine, ample chest of his, his lung had not sufficient play-room. Mark his voice! rich—deep—and clear, as a clarion note. In the most crowded thoroughfare, one would turn instinctively on hearing it, to seek out its owner.

To be greeted this way by the most popular writer in the United States is important, and to have that writer be a woman representing the contemporary sentimentalist point of view is more important still, but most interesting is that Parton understands enough to greet Whitman imaginatively on the street, in the crowd. Parton knew his real, rather than just his poetic, voice, but her panoramic greeting is carefully considered. She also wrote him a letter at about this time, telling him familiarly: "You are *delicious*! May my right hand wither if I don't tell the world before another week, what one woman thinks of you."[41]

Parton published her full review later in the *New York Ledger* (May 17, 1856) and specifically rejected the idea that the poem is not for woman's eyes, asserting it is wonderful *because* it is addressed to women as well as men. Against the charge of sensuality, Parton quotes passages and comments, "Sensual? The artist who would inflame paints you not nude Nature, but stealing virtue's veil, with artful artlessness now conceals, now exposes, the ripe and swelling proportions." She ends by offering Whitman her hand, and quoting him again: "The wife—and she is not one jot less than the husband, / The daughter—and she is just as good as the son, / The mother—and she is every bit as much as the father."[42]

Sara Parton revels in the "coming man," thinking that he can make meaning of the present historical instant. We see too that Whitman's 1855 book shows us the modern surface of thought; it advertises the presentness of the new city and the new culture. *Leaves of Grass* imagines, forcefully and beautifully, the meanings of the new culture and finds that God is in the ordinary street, available to all, or available to all with the gentle guidance of the loafing poet. *Leaves of Grass* is blind to the historical moment as a social product: Whitman sees men and women working, but he does not often see the context in which they work. The panoramic point of view of the early poems evades the reality and picks and chooses its way among the images bourgeois culture created of the city's people. It thinks that the present moment is a beginning and that the modern must trust the present.

The mature Whitman returned to New York and described it several times. Here he writes in *Democratic Vistas* (1871) about the city that started him:

> After an absence, I am now again (September 1870) in New York City and Brooklyn, on a few weeks' vacation. The splendor, picturesqueness, and oceanic amplitude and rush of these great cities, the unsurpassed situation, rivers and bay, sparkling sea-tides, costly and lofty

new buildings, facades of marble and iron, of original grandeur and elegance of design, with the masses of gay color, the preponderance of white and blue, the flags flying, the endless ships, the tumultuous streets, Broadway, the heavy, low, musical roar, hardly ever intermitted, even at night; the jobbers' houses, the rich shops, the wharves, the great Central Park, and the Brooklyn Park of hills (as I wander among them this beautiful fall weather, musing, watching, absorbing)—the assemblages of the citizens in their groups, conversations, trades, evening amusements, or along the by-quarters—these, I say, and the like of these, completely satisfy my senses of power, fullness, motion, etc., and give me, through such senses and appetites, and through my aesthetic conscience, a continued exaltation and absolute fulfillment.[43]

The aesthetic conscience is still at work and still inspired by the great, unitary variety of New York.

Whitman was, like Herman Melville, an eager early participant in the New York literary culture. He learned his journalistic skills in the newspapers of New York and created a New York poetry founded on panoramic encounter with the new city and on the announcement to the new New York of a "Walt Whitman" who was to articulate the eternal meanings of the encounter. The greater poems that came after this panoramic beginning feature the single observer more carefully picking his way through the sights before him, making and remaking them. After the first edition of *Leaves of Grass* Whitman remains a modern, the "coming man" in the sense that he must create like a god and make his world, but the major insights of an important poem such as "When Lilacs Last in the Dooryard Bloom'd" come from a sensibility not so confident that God's letters are dropped conveniently in the street.

PART TWO

"DICKENS' PLACE"

"They dies everywheres," said the boy. "They dies in their lodgings . . . and they dies down in Tom-all-Alone's in heaps. They dies more than they lives, according to what I see."

Charles Dickens
Bleak House

4

"Hot Corn!":
Encounters with Street Children

In the Footsteps of Little Nell   Walt Whitman describes leaving his *New York Aurora* office after twelve one night and finding a boy fast asleep on the steps of a building near Tammany Hall. The boy appears to be about eleven or twelve and is "very ragged and very dirty." A watchman tells Whitman that the child is a newsboy getting a few hours' sleep between having gone to the Chatham Theater and starting work in the morning. Whitman stoops over the boy and sees more than the rags: "The glare of the gas lamp near by, lighting up the sleeper's face, showed features by no means deficient in beauty and intelligence." Whitman lets the newsboy sleep on, quietly offers a "benison upon the slumbers and future lot of the poor devil," and walks on home. When he writes up the encounter for the *Aurora* (April 16, 1842), his narrative records the exact details of the street encounter and then goes on to

93

generalize about the freshness and innocence of all children—even ragged boys one finds on the street.

Like so many enlightened bourgeois people of his time, Whitman asserts that the beauty and native intelligence of children is something he and his contemporaries have newly discovered. The encounter with the poor child is always presented as revealing a wholly new insight— that poor children can be beautiful and intelligent. What Whitman means is that romantic conceptions of unsullied childhood (the child is "fresh from the hands of Him whose architecture is always perfect until desecrated by the conduct of the world," he writes) can be stretched to include the thousands of apparently homeless children—newsboys, hotcorn sellers, street sweepers—filling the streets of the city. When he thinks of individual children met singly on the street, he sees the child trailing clouds of glory and not the criminal urchin threatening peaceful urban existence.

Whitman explicitly credits Charles Dickens for the way he sees children.

> The great novelist of our day has shown a beautiful taste in selecting *children* for his heroes and heroines—if those two terms will apply. Previously, writers thought it was stooping too low; they considered the little people as too little for their pens. How true their notions of the subject were, bear witness poor Oliver, and crazed Barnaby, and pathetic Nell![1]

Little Nell of *The Old Curiosity Shop*, Oliver Twist, and later Jo in *Bleak House* become in the 1840s and 1850s bourgeois culture's models for understanding the solitary and apparently unparented child newly visible in the streets. I call this part of my book "Dickens' Place" after Pete Williams's Five Points dance hall, which became "Dickens' Place" after the novelist visited and wrote about it in *American Notes* (1842). Dickens's writing has a similar impact on New York urban narrative: after Dickens wrote about New York all narratives had him in mind. In this chapter I concentrate on sentimental encounters, first with children found working in the street and then with children dying in the street; in the next chapter I write about narratives describing the Five Points neighborhood.

The isolated child of the Dickensian novel has no parents, or certainly no proper and effective middle-class parents, and she evokes strong sympathy in readers whose cultural presumption is that families are the source of all well-being. The imagined future of the "lost" child is the same as her imagined past: she will rejoin the happy family she must have come from, even if it is in the very domesticated heaven of nineteenth-century liberal Christianity. Dickens also disconnects the street children from the city: they are merely *sojourners* there. Little Nell and her many literary descendants suffer in the city, are initially "lost" to the world they should belong to, but these children are not *made* by the city: they preexist it.[2] The urban narratives that rework Dickens's formula have a clear ideological purpose. Like all encounter narratives they confront the urban problem directly: the middle-class observer is perceptive and *sees* the city's problems embodied in the rag-ged child selling newspapers or hot corn. But at the same time as they confront reality they obscure the social relations that lie behind the child's condition.

American sentimental narratives of urban encounter remain fasci-nating in part because they do retain the trace of the original child. Writers like Lydia Maria Child were humane and thoughtful people who knew that the existence of street children was important to record and to contemplate. Child writes in her *Letters from New York* that

> the noisy discord of the street-cries gives no ear, no rest; and the weak voice of early childhood often makes the heart ache for the poor little wanderer, prolonging his task far into the hours of night. Sometimes, the harsh sounds are pleasantly varied by some feminine voice, pro-claiming in musical cadence, "Hot corn! hot corn!" with the poetic addition of "Lily white corn! Buy my lily white corn."

The very street cries are the signs, for Child, of the "lost," the "wan-derer." Another time she walks out, "for exercise merely," and meets "a little ragged urchin, about four years old, with a heap of newspapers. . . . The sweet voice of childhood was prematurely cracked into shrill-ness, by screaming street cries, at the top of his lungs; and he looked blue, cold, and disconsolate." Child then imagines the "miserable cel-lar" the newsboy must live in, the flogging he will receive because he has not brought home enough pence for his parent's grog, and years later the police office where he will be taken. "One tone like a mother's voice might have wholly changed his earthly destiny; one kind word of friendly counsel might have saved him." The true mother would have saved him "as if an angel, standing in the genial sunlight, had thrown to him one end of a garland . . . and drawn him safely out of the deep and tangled labyrinth, where false echoes and winding paths conspired to make him lose his way."[3] One needs little evidence other than such accounts of Child's encounters with street children to see the ideological force of domesticized Christianity, wherein the mother is intervening angel. Generous and thoughtful as Child is, and as helpful as is her call to Christian action, she reproduces the ideology of the narrative of encounter: the reader is not asked to think his or her way to an understanding of the boy's material condition, to cause and history (he belongs to a neighborhood, perhaps to a family), but away to the necessity for literal and metaphoric adoption.

Easily the best-known treatment of a New York encounter with a child was in Solon Robinson's "Hot Corn" series for the *Tribune*. In the first sketch of the series, Robinson describes an evening he spent at work at his desk, hearing now and then the familiar street cry: "Here's your nice Hot Corn, smoking hot, smoking hot, just from the pot!" At midnight, deciding to clear his mind with a walk in the park, Robinson encounters the crier and, because of his peculiar mood and the ghostly hour, consciously *hears* for the first time what he has heard without awareness all evening and many times before—the cry of Little Katy, the Hot Corn Girl. "I started, as though a spirit had given me a rap," and looking over an iron post at the edge of the park, Robinson discovers

> the owner of the hot corn cry, in the person of an emaciated little girl about twelve years old, whose dirty shawl was nearly the color of the rusty iron, and whose face, hands, and feet, naturally white and delicate, were grimed with dirt until nearly of the same color. There were two white streaks running down from the soft blue eyes, that told of the hot scalding tears that were coursing their way over that naturally beautiful face.[4]

The description is characteristically sentimental in directing our attention to Katy's "naturally white and delicate" features, her "naturally beautiful face," her dirty shawl. Robinson tells Little Katy (the adjective and name "Little" is one measure of Dickens's influence) to go home because it is so late. She answers that she cannot because her drunken mother will beat her if she comes back without having sold all the corn. Horrified, Robinson buys it from her.

The brief encounter opens a new world of experience—and narrative—for Robinson. He discovers the girl's abode at the Five Points; he investigates the neighborhood in the footsteps of Dickens; and he narrates his adventures for the *Tribune*'s readers. Robinson never doubts for a moment that it is solely intemperance (and the legality of saloons) that is responsible for the misery of those who live with Little Katy at the Five Points. "Hot Corn!" becomes a watchword, bidding all to eradicate intemperance. Robinson has journeyed among the savages and seen that the residents themselves are at fault. We are sympathetic to their children, who like Little Katy, are potentially like our own middle-class offspring.

What is remarkable about Robinson's *Hot Corn* is that the chapters in the series that follow the initial sketch about meeting Little Katy become progressively more sensational and, our good sense tells us, more fictional than the first sketch. After a beginning that contains the trace of the real encounter, the journalistic account borrows from popular sentimental fiction. The procedure, as is so often the case in encounter narratives, is for the narrator not to concern himself with genre boundaries but to work and rework all the variations on urban encounters. *Hot Corn* is a compendium of encounter narratives, tied loosely together with the thread that the narrator is a serious-minded flaneur walking the streets. ("Reader, walk with me," he says.)

Sara Parton, "Fanny Fern," writes a short sketch about "The Little Pauper" in her collection *Fern Leaves from Fanny's Portfolio*, much of which is about life in New York.

> It is only a little pauper. Never mind her. You see she knows her place and keeps close to the wall, as if she expected an oath or a blow. The cold winds are making merry with those thin rags. You see nothing of childhood's rounded symmetry in those shrunken limbs and pinched features. Push her one side,—she's used to it,—she won't complain; she can't remember that she ever heard a kind word in her life. She'd think you were mocking if you tried it. . . . There seems to be happiness enough in the world, but it never comes to her. Her little basket

is quite empty; and now, faint with hunger, she leans wearily against that shop window.[5]

This is sentimental popular prose in its most rococo form, a long remove from Lydia Maria Child's letters from New York a decade earlier. Parton's solution to the social problem she imagines is contained in the way in which she narrates the encounter with the innocent. Her satiric voice emphasizes the ease with which the callous observer could maintain emotional distance from the nameless child. Parton's imperative verbs tell us we can choose to "never mind her," even to "push her"; her misery has become routine both for her ("she won't complain") and for us (she's "only" a poor child). Any offer of kindness on our part would be futile and end in misunderstanding. Unlike Robinson's "Katy," her name is never known.

Even the trace of what the girl was doing, what she was working at, is minimized. If her basket held items for sale, its emptiness might signal success. If (possibly like the observer) she was shopping, she has failed at that because she leans against the window of the shop that presumably holds what she needs to stop her hunger. Parton's sentimentality softens the shock that we might have felt, that Robinson and Child did feel, and we see only what we knew already. The pauper is isolated, imaginatively up for adoption. We who are not callous and indifferent are to bring her in out of the isolation and feed her warm food and make her quickly one of us. She should hear kind words and become the rounded and happy child of middle-class fantasy.

Reverend Edwin Chapin, pastor of the Fourth Universalist Society in New York, was the 1850s' theologian of New York's streets. His *Moral Aspects of City Life* (1853) and *Humanity in the City* (1854) preach specifically on street encounters. Chapin expounds on what he thinks the relationship should be between the Christian and the streets. The city provides "lessons" for the moral self: "Wisdom . . . uttereth her voice in the streets."[6] The streets instruct: "the contrasts of human condition . . . that unfold themselves in the crowded street, may teach us our duty and our responsibility in lessening social inequality and need" (20). An "essential unity" lies beneath the phenomenal: "It is only the form of life that is transient and phenomenal; but the *Life* itself is here, also—here, in these flashing eyes, and heaving breasts, and active limbs." Urban encounters, however brief, "involve the great interest of Humanity; and that lends the deepest significance" to them (33). The people in the urban crowd are the same as "us" because beneath the merely phenomenal is the transcendent we should all recognize, despite the difficulties of seeing it through rags. Distant, panoramic vision is insufficient: "We must not stand so far apart from the crowd as to occupy the position of mere spectators, and regard these men and women as so many mechanical figures in a panorama" (35). Each "drop of that great stream is a conscious personality" (123).

The theological point that Chapin is making is essential to bourgeois Christianity. The *education* for faith, the parables, need not come from the Bible or from ancient history or traditional theology: they can come from the immediate, direct experience in the daily life of the Christian. Chapin thinks about the problem of the city in the way that his liberal Christian peers do. They were constructing a new Christology that accepted the view that all doctrines of Christ must start from and be grounded in historical human experience. The effort was to construct Christianity "from below" rather than "from above."[7] Chapin adapts these ideas to the modern city: one can meet God in the street. Chapin's most powerful image of the divinity hidden in the quotidian is the street child: "There, amidst the rush of gaiety; the busy, selfish whirl; half-naked, shivering, with her bare feet on the icy pavement, stands the little girl, with the shadow of an experience upon her that has made her preternaturally old, and it may be, driven the angel from her face" (20). Chapin's solution is unfortunately still familiar to us. His book evokes middle-class homes as the springs of contemporary social life, the cradles of modern Christianity. Society must find a way to establish such homes for urban children.

Elizabeth Oakes Smith's *Newsboy* (1854) is a novel, but like Solon Robinson's *Hot Corn* it has a journalistic starting point. The narrator leans out of her comfortable home:

> "And so your name is Bob, that means Robert," I said to the Newsboy one morning as I bought a daily paper at my window.
> "There ain't no Robert about it, nothing but Bob," he replied, and I saw he was vexed at my attempt to christen him. I saw he was proud of being only Bob, and I couldn't but feel it was a great thing to be

conscious of so much in ourselves, that we could afford to contemn birth, country, station and fortune. Then I began to reverence the Newsboy and to study his history, as I shall record it in these pages.[8]

The book that follows this encounter has more to do with sentimental convention than with a sociological history of the newsboys of New York, and yet the book seems to spring entirely from the force of the first encounter. Bob nearly sinks the book. Smith is so clearly interested in the meaning of the particular encounter, and then in newsboys and their customs, that she has at least some difficulty in allowing the senti-mental plot to overwhelm Bob.

Smith allows us to see that Bob has a more than momentary alien dignity, like a savage. He is not interested in the effort to *christen* him; he is not interested in birth, country, station, fortune. He rejects at first the explanatory tone of the upper bourgeois that instructs him in what his name really is. Bob is a cliché of independent newsboy life— spirited, full of lingo—but I think careful readers can sense his resis-tance to exactly the definition that the book will in fact paint over him. Bob's very opposition is the life energy of Smith's book, remembered long after Bob has become civilized, Christianized, and set up in a New York business.

Smith, a distinguished feminist, author of *The Sinless Child* (1842) and *Woman and Her Needs* (1851), says that the experience with Bob opened a new activity and she "visited the city, went from place to place, taking my eyes with me, and my heart also" (7). Bob is the guid-ing angel of her eye-opening tour: "Little by little, Bob . . . grew into my mind, not as a poor, forsaken, ignorant, neglected child, who ought to be taken up and sent to the Orphan Asylum, or asylum for vagrants, but as a great-soul'd boy, whose nobleness I dared not fathom, but which I could appreciate, the latchet of whose old, dilapidated shoes I was not worthy to unloose" (9). Like the Christian heroes, even the earthly incarnation of the Christian God, Bob can survive the (urban) wilderness because of his inner strength. Smith almost understands that the meaning of the street boy is more than she can account for with her Christian imagery. The particulars of her descriptions of the city, given in Bob's name, are often acute, although the sentimental often jumps on the perceptive halfway through a paragraph.

The second-hand clothes men in Chatham Street stood cross-legged in their doors, despairing of custom. Women with frouzly heads lolled over the counters, and gossipped [*sic*] with their neighbors. Children were sailing paper boats and hickory nut-shells in the gutters, shouting with delight as the little barques weathered the eddying current of the filthy stream. Poor things! born to fish in muddy waters; the first freightage of life consigned to an impure channel; but they boded nothing, and laughed and shouted, happy as the child whose dainty fingers touch only the filtered bath, and the delicate finger-glass. (80–81)

Smith also loves the new language of New York. Her book is full of ethnographic notation of newsboy and fireman talk. We hear, as we do in "ain't no Robert about it, nothing but Bob," that Smith has listened closely. She puts quotation marks around the language so that we know it is local and new to her: "posted up on the doings," "stiff upper lip," "mum's the word," "What in h——l is that to you?" "pickers," "stunner," "teeny," "gallus," "do the thing up brown," "scrimping," "blame me if it isn't," "Our gal made a spooney out of him." She often gives the language in dialogue, so the reader almost hears the spoken words. She observes, for example, the newsboys in their beloved theaters: " 'Carrots, give us a William' "; " 'Yoppy, none of that, or I'll pitch into you' " (32). Smith idealizes the boys at the theater. There is "no appearance of vice amongst them. . . . Nothing skulking, nothing mean, nothing vicious lurks in the aspect of the true Newsboy" (33).

Smith's novelistic solution to the problem of keeping the energy of the newsboy alive in her plot while still Christianizing Bob is to invest a new character, Flashy Jack, with the characteristics that she makes drop away from Bob. Jack remains the very embodiment of newsboyness; and although he doesn't change the way Bob does, we are allowed to see through his difficult personality to his good heart. In the meantime Bob is being recognized by the merchant class. The respectable merchant, Mr. Dinsmoor, learns by the example of Bob that there is good in the class of person he formerly thought just "a horde of miserable evil-doers, hunted down by the law, and entirely without the pale of human sympathies." He learns that in those people there reigns a "moral vitalism of the soul . . . in a sort of savage grandeur" (373). Dinsmoor learns to see the liberal Christian solution, cultural adoption.

Bob is taken up, converted, and finally becomes eligible for the hand of
Dinsmoor's daughter Imogen (519). The girl prefers another. At the
end Bob is "abroad," something like the second son in good families—
perfectly acceptable, but not in the main line.

Although not a novel, Charles Loring Brace's account of the founding of the Children's Aid Society is, like Smith's *Newsboy*, a powerful
example of the sentimental model's overwhelming of the energy and
life of the street children. In *The Dangerous Classes of New York* (1872),
a collection of pieces largely written in the 1850s, Brace enumerates the
causes of urban crime and finds that foreign birth, weakness of the
marriage tie, overcrowding, and alcohol are chief among them. "Foreign birth" means that the breaking of ties with the original country
has a bad moral effect: the immigrant has been separated from the
church and former cultural control without learning a new sort of cultural control in the new country. The weakness of the marriage tie
means that the home of the child becomes an unstable system with little
self-control: "The house becomes a kind of pandemonium, and the
girls rush desperately forth to the wild life of the streets, or the boys
gradually prefer the roaming existence of the little city-Arab to such
a quarrelsome home." Overcrowding too leads to pandemonium and
impurity, especially in girls. Alcohol leads to the same problems. In all,
the results of these social conditions for children is that they become
street children—newsboys, hot-corn girls, street sweepers.[9]

The narrative, unlike most I have described thus far, does not survive entirely on encounters. Brace is writing a history that aspires to
sociology: he will explain the social causes of crime; he will propose
social policy. Even in such an account, however, the encounter with the
boys and girls on the street is the key narrative form. Accounts of the
individual encounters give the book its life.[10] Most interesting is that
Brace, like Elizabeth Oakes Smith, loves the boys the way they are,
unchanged, even though he is going to try to change them. He too loves
New York words. He tells of the reaction that boys had to the "Boys'
Meetings" that ministers arranged in the late 1840s before the founding
of the Children's Aid Society.

The platform of the Boys' Meeting seemed to become a kind of chemi-
cal test of the gaseous element in the brethren's brains. One pungent

criticism we remember—on a pious and somewhat sentimental Sunday-school brother, who, in one of our meetings, had been putting forth vague and declamatory religious exhortation—is the words "*Gas*! *Gas*!" whispered with infinite contempt from one hard-faced young disciple to another. (80)

When the ministers ask, "My boys, what is the great end of man? When is he happiest? How would *you* feel happiest?" the boys respond, "When we'd plenty of hard cash, sir!" Again, "My *dear* boys, when your father and your mother forsake you, *who* will take you up?" The boys: "The Purlice, sir (very seriously), the Purlice!" (80–81). These are marvelous, almost unmatched, accounts of the confrontation between the sentimental classes and the realistic boys of the street, and Brace has the good sense not to stop himself from preferring the boys' colloquial materialism to his colleagues' gas.

He and those colleagues do found the Children's Aid Society. Their first circular, written in 1853, announces "As Christian men, we cannot look upon this great multitude of unhappy, deserted, and degraded boys and girls without feeling our responsibility to God for them." They have the same immortality as the rest of us, and they are growing up without homes. They peddle matches, or apples, or newspapers, gather bones and rags; the girls are cross-walk sweepers, apple-peddlers, and candy-sellers. But they must go: "We hope, too, especially to be the means of draining the city of these children, by communicating with farmers, manufacturers, or families in the country, who may have need of such for employment. . . . We design, in a word, to bring humane and kindly influences to bear on this forsaken class—to preach in various modes the gospel of Christ to the vagrant children of New York" (92–93). Brace and his associates combined the insight of people who had actually gone and looked at the terrible conditions with a sentimental regard for the middle-class home and came up with the astonishing social policy of "draining" the city of its children. The Society's program was an elaborately well-meant variant of what the police are always saying to Dickens's cross-walk sweeper Jo in *Bleak House*: "Move on."

Samuel Halliday was one of the missionaries to the poor for the American Female Guardian Association, and he published a first-person account of his encounters with the poor in *The Lost and Found; or, Life among the Poor* (1859). Like other books of its kind, Halliday's account is a mixture of statistics and sentimental stories. One story tells of his encounter with Mary Mullen, the "little street sweeper" always to be found at the corner of Beekman Street and Park Row. Halliday finds her and asks her to go with him. She refuses and begins to cry, but Halliday ignores the nine-year-old child's objections (such is the force of charitable conviction!) and takes her to see the mayor. The mayor is amused with her and places her in the charge of Halliday's Home for the Friendless. And then, significantly, Halliday takes her down the street to a photographer. He tells us that "her picture, with broom and dress as I found her, is quite striking" and that it comes to be widely distributed. He sees it in the homes of wealthy families, and the picture thus becomes an icon of New York charitable intervention, used as a parlor decoration to reward the bourgeois for imaginatively adopting poor children. At Halliday's Home they displayed it too, although they placed next to it another picture of Mary as she looked when she was sent off to "her pleasant country home."

Mary Mullen's first photograph was the basis of the engraving that Halliday uses as the frontispiece for his book (see p. 105). The existence and history of the use of Mary's photograph is evidence that men like Halliday understood so little of social context that it did not occur to them not to take a child against her will, or photograph her, or send her off to a Protestant family. The photograph and the engraving unambiguously give us a trace of the historical Mary. Mary lives through her representation with enormous presence. As Roland Barthes might say, her photograph's success in wealthy parlors is explicable because it carries within the force of the living Mary.[11]

In the Footsteps of Jo   Charity workers like Halliday and Brace think of drastic solutions in part because by the late 1840s and early 1850s New York was becoming a place of death. Children with the potential for a bourgeois adoptive future were dying regularly in the streets. Urban conditions were getting far worse for the poor, and Jo in *Bleak House*, who acts as a guide to death in the streets, seems to be as appropriate a model as Nell for the solitary urban child. New York newspaper accounts in the late 1840s concentrate more and more on the appalling deaths in the streets.

Mary Mullen

Frontispiece of Samuel B. Halliday, The Lost and Found; or, Life Among the Poor *(New York: Blakeman & Mason, 1859). From the author's collection.*

The *Evening Post* for December 13, 1846, reports that a German immigrant who hadn't found a job and had become a rag picker got sick and was finally cornered by poverty in a dank, cold cellar on Thirteenth Street. He died of starvation on a bed "consisting of a few shavings and his old rag bag being rolled up for a pillow." The *New York Sun* for March 17, 1847, reprints a *New York Express* reporter's account of a relief trip to the Old Brewery, where the reporter finds first an old Negro with no clothing and asthma, then a mass of rags that turns out to be a dying woman, then a girl with a baby in arms. The girl's mother had been dead a month. Showing just how much New York streets were imaginatively "Dickens' Place," the *Express* reporter writes, "The condition of Mr. Dickens's Little Nell, was perfect happiness, compared with the condition of the living, and yet dying orphan." The *New York Tribune* for March 31, 1847, reports that an Irish woman—a wife and mother—died in another damp, cold cellar on James Street. Her body was discovered "uncared for, in its rags on some wet straw scattered upon the floor in one corner, while the father and children were sick and moaning with hunger—all near the center of this great metropolis! Two of the children were near dying; in their abode, no fire, no food, no table, no shroud or coffin for their dead, no friends to console them!"[12]

The *New York Sun* for April 4, 1847, describes Bridget Sherry: "who arrived on Thursday last from Liverpool, was found in an alley on Saturday night with an infant 9 days old at her breast, in the utmost of destitution. Since her arrival she has been without food and shelter, each night sleeping in any retired alley she could find. She was taken to the 4th Ward Station yesterday. Yesterday the Coroner held an inquest on her offspring, it having died in her arms on Saturday night." Walt Whitman reported urban death extensively in the *Brooklyn Eagle*, and Thomas Brasher notes an item Whitman wrote on April 23, 1847, about an Irish couple found dying on a New York doorstep. The father held one dying child, and the mother held one already dead. "And this," concludes Whitman with the tone of surprise ever repeated in journalism long after there could have been surprise, "is a specimen of the pictures almost daily presented in that city!"[13]

Disease, particularly the cholera outbreaks in 1832 and 1849, made the poor and their deaths more noticeable and threatening. As one wealthy woman wrote to another during the 1832 epidemic: "No one notices the poor ordinarily. Those who frequently are to be found lying in the streets, are now picked up and taken to the hospitals—only on occasions such as this is the true extent of the misery of the City known."[14]

The 1849 outbreak was heavily reported in the newspapers, and it was reported specifically in encounter narratives. The packet ship *New York*, twenty-two days out of Le Havre, dropped anchor at quarantine late Friday night, December 1, 1848. Of her 331 steerage passengers, 7 had died of cholera during the voyage and others were sick. Before the New Year 60 immigrants were sick, and 30 had died. More frightening to New York was the half of those originally quarantined who had scaled the walls at Staten Island and made off for New York or New Jersey in small boats. The actual arrival of the disease in the city was detailed five months later in the newspaper accounts of visits by doctors to the rear basement of a house at 20 Orange Street, thirty yards from the Five Points intersection.

James Gilligan and four women lived at 20 Orange Street in a room ten or twelve feet square; they had no bed, no chair or table, only two empty barrels as furniture. Early Monday morning May 14, 1849, Dr. Herriot made his way to the cellar. When his eyes had become accustomed to the dark he discovered three bodies, Gilligan and two females, on the floor, covered only in rags. Two of the three died before the evening, and another resident took sick and died before the next morning. Dr. Seth Geer, the city's resident physician, was notified and visited the cellar too. The Board of Health was informed on the fifteenth that the victims had died of cholera. The epidemic spread rapidly. The city organized to clean the garbage and night soil from the streets, to move the pigs from the crowded neighborhoods, and to bury the dead more rapidly (bodies were often left in the streets for several days). Those who could afford to leave the city left, and by the end of July business had almost stopped in New York: hotels were empty, and railroad trains and steamships arrived without passengers. By the middle of August, however, the deaths had declined dramatically, and people began to come back to the city. Five thousand seventeen New Yorkers had died since cholera was discovered in Orange Street.[15]

The same worsening of urban conditions was going on in London in the 1840s, and Alexander Welsh finds that the effect on Dickens is profound. Dickens comes to think that "In the slums of the city . . . death is [no longer] the ironic and unexpected leveller of men of all classes and characters but the starvation that slowly and predictably overcomes those who do not have enough to eat."[16] And by *Bleak House* (1852) Dickens is defining the city as a vast necropolis. Death is everywhere, as Jo the street sweeper knows: " 'They dies everywheres. . . . They dies more than they lives, according to what *I* see.' "[17] Jo is an occasion for middle-class interest and sympathy, but he represents Dickens's perception that conditions are more severe and much more difficult to evade or remedy than they were a decade before. Jo belongs to the city in a way that previous Dickensian children did not. Jo lives most of his life alone, he brings terrible disease out of the city and gives it to the heroine of the novel, and he is much harder to bring into a middle-class home. He does die with the Lord's Prayer on his lips and with the charitable Woodcourt at his side, but the novelist looks at his death and threatens his audience: "Dead, your Majesty. Dead, my lords and gentlemen. Dead, Right Reverends and Wrong Reverends of every order. Dead, men and women, born with Heavenly compassion in your hearts. And dying thus around us every day." (572).

A reviewer of *Bleak House* in *Putnam's Monthly* specifically connects Jo to the street boys in New York: "Poor Joe [*sic*] . . . has already become a proverb. We read the deaths of a good many eminent men without an emotion . . . but we cannot withhold a tear when we read the death of poor Joe, and when he is 'moved on' for the last time we too are moved. . . . we weep over him and give him the sympathies which we withhold from the real Joes we encounter in our daily walks."[18] Jo is a proverb because he proposes the same principle, that street children are the sacred icons of bourgeois experience, but he also suggests that urban death is constant and hard to remedy. He does not overcome bourgeois explanation but he threatens its adequacy.

Herman Melville's *Redburn*   During the late spring and summer of 1849, during the height of the New York cholera epidemic, Herman Melville stayed in New York and composed both *Redburn* and *White-Jacket*. The speed with which he wrote the books and his private opinion that they were not good made him astonished that *Redburn*, in particular, was taken seriously by reviewers. When Melville arrived in London in November he read the fourteen-page review in *Blackwood's Edinburgh Magazine* and wrote in his journal: "saw Blackwood's long story about a short book . . . It's very comical . . . in treating the thing as real."[19] For Melville, the novel is not "real" because it does not struggle with the philosophical issues that made *Mardi* and then *Moby-Dick* so interesting to their author. For the *Blackwood's* reviewer and many readers since, the novel has been real enough in its treatment of a young hero who loses ground rather than gaining it in the usual way of the bildungsroman. *Redburn* is one of the most important of the reworkings of the New York encounter paradigm because in it the paradigm twists in upon itself. Confrontation with urban death in *Redburn* does not demonstrate how we sentimental souls can go on thinking the way we did. It demonstrates that we can only stand stunned before the untranscendable death in the city.

The first-person novel relates the adventures of young Redburn as he leaves upstate to go to New York City to find a ship to set out to sea as a sailor. He goes not solely out of the youthful spirit of adventure but also because of sad "disappointments in several plans which I had sketched for my future life" and because of "the necessity of doing something for myself."[20] He is already a "misanthrope," a "castaway," setting out angrily into a world that seems to him "cold, bitter cold as December, and bleak as its blasts" (10–13), and he takes as his only inheritance an old fowling gun. With that gun he nearly shoots the fashionably dressed ticket taker on the Hudson River boat because he can only act out of "demoniac feelings" (13) when challenged for his fare. But in New York he is suddenly less the misanthrope than the greenhorn and is tricked in his (highly conventional) urban encounters with a Jewish pawnbroker ("the hook-nosed man . . . ready to hook any thing that came along" [21]), who gives him only a dollar for the fowling gun, and with Captain Riga of the *Highlander*, who signs Redburn for three dollars a month (because he is a young "gentleman" and thus needs so little) to sail to Liverpool and return. He sails and has many conventional young sailor experiences, arrives in Liverpool and witnesses its horrific urban poverty, spends the night in a London gambling house, and returns to New York where he is tricked again by Captain Riga.

The world that opens to Redburn is one where space and time mean nothing. He cannot by means of travel distance himself from his starting condition, he cannot distance himself from New York, because the places he "discovers" just mirror the New York he knows. Liverpool, for example, is not the city of new adventure and a potential new self: it is New York all over again. The effect is of a book about the growth of a young man in which there is no growth, no change. *Redburn* is the opposite of the bildungsroman that it might seem to be because time has no meaning. There is no change.[21]

Even on board ship there is New York. The character Jackson is the key to the education of the young man, and he is a man of the city afloat. More than that he is a New Yorker.

> [Jackson] dressed a good deal like a Bowery boy; for he despised the ordinary sailor-rig; wearing a pair of great over-all blue trowsers, fastened with suspenders, and three red woolen shirts, one over the other; for he was subject to the rheumatism and was not in good health, he said; and he had a large white wool hat, with a broad rolling brim. He was a native of New York city, and had a good deal to say about *highbinders* and *rowdies*, whom he denounced as only good for the gallows; but I thought he looked a good deal like a *highbinder* himself. (56)

Jackson is not at all the happy Mose the fireman of New York popular tradition: he does not courageously save women from their burning houses by carrying them down fire ladders; he does not good-heartedly hang around with Big Lize; he is not the imagined happy working-class hero. If Jackson is a b'hoy like the Whitman who published the first *Leaves of Grass*, he is a very dangerous "coming man." He does not *save* anything; he destroys. He believes nothing:

> Though he had never attended churches, and knew nothing about Christianity; no more than a Malay pirate; and though he could not read a word, yet he was spontaneously an atheist and an infidel; and during the long night watches, would enter into arguments, to prove that there was nothing to be believed; nothing to be loved, and nothing worth living for . . . he seemed to run a muck at heaven and earth.

He was a Cain afloat; branded on his yellow brow with some inscrutable curse; and going about corrupting and searing every heart that
beat near him. (104–5)

Jackson curses the world that means nothing. He rages against it, a
precursor of Melville's Ahab in *Moby-Dick*. Redburn learns from this
b'hoy that the world sears when one encounters it. He learns even to
understand that Jackson's evil is perfectly quotidian. He compares Jackson to the great villains of historical record and thinks he is as "dignified . . . as [Tacitus] . . . even though he was a nameless vagabond
without an epitaph, and none, but I, narrate what he was"(276). Melville's development of the b'hoy encounter educates Redburn in the
necessity of trying to interpret and understand, just as the b'hoy encounters in the panoramic fiction by Cornelius Mathews and others do,
but unlike b'hoys in those other fictions Jackson is resistant to appropriation. Redburn finds no way to adopt him into his understanding: Jackson is forever a man of the city, a Cain.

In Liverpool Redburn has an urban encounter that reworks the
encounters with death in New York journalism of the terrible cholera
summer of 1849.

I heard a feeble wail, which seemed to come out of the earth. It was
but a strip of crooked side-walk where I stood; the dingy wall was on
every side, converting the mid-day into twilight; and not a soul was in
sight. I started, and could almost have run, when I heard that dismal
sound. It seemed the low, hopeless, endless wail of some one forever
lost. At last I advanced to an opening which communicated downward
with deep tiers of cellars beneath a crumbling old warehouse; and
there, some fifteen feet below the walk, crouching in nameless squalor,
with her head bowed over, was the figure of what had been a woman.
Her blue arms folded to her livid bosom two shrunken things like
children, that leaned toward her, one on each side. At first, I knew
not whether they were alive or dead. They made no sign; they did not
move or stir; but from the vault came that soul-sickening wail. . . .
They were dumb and next to dead with want. How they had
crawled into that den, I could not tell; but there they had crawled to
die. At that moment I never thought of relieving them; for death was
so stamped in their glazed and unimploring eyes, that I almost re-
garded them as already no more. I stood looking down on them, while
my whole soul swelled within me; and I asked myself, What right had

any body in the wide world to smile and be glad, when sights like this were to be seen? It was enough to turn the heart to gall; and make a man-hater of a Howard. For who were these ghosts that I saw? Were they not human beings? A woman and two girls? With eyes, and lips, and ears like any queen? with hearts which, though they did not bound with blood, yet beat with a dull, dead ache that was their life. (180–81)

Melville's language draws upon the conventional imagery of the journalistic encounter. He suggests the mythological parallels used by Dickens and so many others when he hints that Redburn is startled as if by a spirit and hears something from another world, a sound "from out of the earth," and that he then looks downward into the pit of hell, at someone "forever lost." But the allusions are deeply embedded and suppressed in favor of the immediacy, the stunning force of what the young man *sees* for himself. He sees human beings who are only barely human beings: a woman who is merely a "figure of what had been a woman," two shrunken things "*like* children."

If the conventional narratives of encounter with urban horror have some of the force of Melville's description, they ordinarily evade the full consequences of the confrontation by finding in the scene the possibilities of reform. Melville's narrative does not think change is possible. There is no thought of relieving the woman and the children: they are there to die in "nameless" squalor. The facts are not transcendable for Redburn or for Melville, and the encounter scene opens up to a vision of pervading urban death.

Redburn goes down to the family and makes the discovery that deepens the horror.

I tried to lift the woman's head; but, feeble as she was, she seemed bent upon holding it down. Observing her arms still clasped upon her bosom, and that something seemed hidden under the rags there, a thought crossed my mind, which impelled me forcibly to withdraw her hands for a moment; when I caught a glimpse of a meager little babe, the lower part of its body thrust into an old bonnet. Its face was dazzlingly white, even its squalor; but the closed eyes looked like balls of indigo. It must have been dead some hours. (183)

I have said that the child is the nineteenth century's image for what can be adopted into the bourgeois imagination, but the baby Redburn finds is untranscendably dead. Its eyes like balls of indigo are merely and only eyes like balls of indigo: the description leaves us at the scene—we can imagine nothing beyond it.

Redburn is not uncharitable—he does bring water, he tries to get the authorities to act—but his point of view is not reformist. The encounter does not prompt him to swamp the moment with the old formulas. For him the moment is open to something new: he simply sees and sees. When Redburn inspects the vault after the bodies have been efficiently removed, he realizes that we live in the house of the dead.

> Surrounded as we are by the wants and woes of our fellow-men, and yet given to follow our own pleasures, regardless of their pains, are we not like people sitting up with a corpse, and making merry in the house of the dead? (184)[22]

On the *Highlander*'s homeward voyage Melville improbably weighs the ship down with five hundred immigrants, and cholera breaks out just as it had on the packet ship *New York*. Many of the immigrants die, and Jackson too dies. On the main topsail he shouts "Haul out to windward!" and gives a "blasphemous cry." But "the wild words were hardly out of his mouth, when his hands dropped to his side, and the bellying sail was spattered with a torrent of blood from his lungs" (295). He falls straight into the sea and is seen no more.

Melville's *Redburn* does not try to attack and overwhelm the presumptions of the narratives that describe sentimental encounters with street children. Melville does not have a new interpretive system that would replace the imaginative adoptions of the sentimental observers. Melville uses the same encounter form as the New York discourse, he sets the interpretive problem in the same way, but he has his observer Redburn pause at the moment of shock in the conventional encounter, pause at the moment just before the usual explanations and rationalizations are meant to rush in. Redburn does not get beyond the pause: he considers the uninterpretable and cannot pass over into ready and convenient explanation. He does not, in the book as a whole, get anywhere because he fails to find, like the standard bildungsroman hero, an effective and convenient way to interpret the world he encounters. In *Redburn*, Melville presages his work to come, both the themes of *Pierre* in 1852 and the technique of "Bartleby, the Scrivener" in 1853.

You must descend to them; you must feel the blast of foul air as it meets your face on opening the door; you must grope in the dark, or hesitate until your eye becomes accustomed to the gloomy place, to enable you to find your way through the entry, over a broken floor, the boards of which are protected from your tread by a half inch of hard dirt; you must inhale the suffocating vapor of the sitting and sleeping rooms; and in the dark, damp, recess endeavor to find the inmates by the sound of their voices.

Dr. John Griscom
The Sanitary Condition of the Laboring Population of New York

5

Five Points:
Sketches of Hell

Dickens at the Old Brewery   Meeting solitary children late at night and finding Irish immigrants dying on the streets stunned contemporary New Yorkers. The illusion that the urban problem was a matter of a few lost children in need of middle-class adoption had blocked a widespread understanding that the new social order had created a large underclass. By the late 1840s many more people—reformers, charity workers, physicians, and tourists—came to think that neighborhoods like the Five Points where the poor lived were the source of the city's ills. Visiting the slums to verify this perception became an important and meaning-laden bourgeois activity. Uncovering New York slum life was the task of the individual visitor taking it upon him- or herself to go and look into a dance hall, a cellar apartment, an attic, a box under the stairs to find out how the other classes lived. The first-person narratives of the visits are in the panoramic tradition, and the Five Points was often a stop on the panoramic tour, but the Points encounter narrative was a special development of its own.

Over and over in the 1840s and 1850s, in the popular press and in fiction and nonfiction, the secrets of the Five Points neighborhood were discovered and "exposed" for the edification of middle-class New Yorkers. The Five Points was a convenient sign of the rapid change in social conditions in New York, an instance of the shockingly disordered lower-class life that seemed completely new to contemporary Americans. By the 1830s the Points were "fully developed as the American paradigm of urban crime and poverty,"[1] and yet in the mid-1850s there were still articles and books that described the discovery of the horrors of the Points. The neighborhood became over and over again New York's equivalent of London's Seven Dials or Whitechapel and added to the aspiring world city the perverse distinction of having a truly appalling neighborhood.

The original Five Points neighborhood formed around the place at which Cross, Anthony, Little Water, Orange, and Mulberry Streets came together at a small park called (with an irony noted many times) Paradise Square. The actual site no longer exists: Anthony Street was extended to Chatham Square and became the present Worth Street, Orange became Baxter, and Cross became Park. Little Water disappeared altogether. The present southwest corner of Columbus Park is where Paradise Square was. The term "Five Points" was used loosely to refer to the entire district near Paradise Square—that is, in the eastern section of the Sixth Ward, a short walk from City Hall. By 1840 the district was thought to be the most dismal neighborhood in the United States, and those who were experts in visiting poor neighborhoods in London and New York considered the Five Points worse than Seven Dials and Whitechapel and thought it the most densely populated neighborhood in the Western world.[2]

The infamous "Old Brewery" building became the architectural center of the Five Points horror in the imagination of the upper classes, and it was the most frequently cited example of the depravity that crowding and poverty and intemperance could produce (see p. 117). The Old Brewery was said (improbably) to have housed a thousand persons in the 1840s, seventy-five of them in a single room called the

"The Old Brewery at the Five Points, N.Y."

Lithograph by C. Parsons (New York: Endicott, 1852). Courtesy of the Eno Collection, New York Public Library.

"den of thieves." All the residents of the building were Irish or African American, as were indeed most of the inhabitants of the Points.[3] The intrepid editor of the *Sun* himself, Benjamin H. Day, visited the Five Points as early as 1834 and published a vivid account. He accompanied, in the manner of most such visits, a police officer, and found that "the colored, and some of the white tenants of the Five Points, are infinitely more degraded and debased" than the Indian or the Southern slave: "they endure literally, a hell of horrors, arising from their poverty and wickedness, such as few others on earth can suffer."[4]

The most influential Points narrative was the one Charles Dickens wrote for *American Notes*, his 1842 book about his visit to the United States. He was a veteran of visits to London prisons and dangerous neighborhoods and had written about them in magazines and newspapers as well as in his novels. His first *Sketches by Boz* (the subtitle of the collection was "Illustrative of Everyday Life and Everyday People") were little urban leaves that were immensely popular when they were published in 1836. Dickens's journalism and his novels were often praised for the qualities—a great variety and precision of character and setting—that we still think make his work extraordinary. Even his journalism seems to us to have an "observation so acute [that it] merges imperceptibly into creation."[5]

Dickens had been wildly and enthusiastically welcomed in the United States when he and his wife arrived in New York in early 1842. There was a festive dinner honoring him at New York's City Hotel on February 18, 1842 (at which Cornelius Mathews gave a speech on international copyright and praised the "wild barbaric splendor" of American literature). The United States did not think its generosity well repaid when it read Dickens's opinion of the country in *American Notes* (1842) and his novel *Martin Chuzzlewit* (1843–44), set in part in the United States.[6] The volcanic American reaction came because the novelist had portrayed the country in unflattering ways and because he had "discovered" scenes like those in the Points. Thomas Carlyle noted that in reaction to the novel, "All Yankee Doodle-dum blazed up like one universal soda bottle."[7] The insult was compounded because Dickens was so loved and respected in the United States.

In the beginning of his chapter on New York in *American Notes* Dickens comments breezily on the panoramic "stream" of life as viewed from the window of his expensive hotel on Broadway. Then he walks out into the throng and sees the variety of parasols and the foolishness of the "Byrons of desk and counter." He contrasts the "republican" pigs who have the freedom of the streets with the supremely elegant Broadway shops. He is the detached and satiric observer—noting all the contrasts of urban life around him, participating in the amiable panoramic convention. His description of the Five Points is quite different. He walks, with two policemen as his guides, away from the gaiety of Broadway into the reeking and inexplicable maze of the Points. All is confusion and darkness. The goal is a squalid tenement (unnamed, but perhaps the Old Brewery, the most obvious stop on the tour) and once arrived, Dickens undertakes to ascend its dangerous stairway. Each floor of the building reveals a new horror, the last at the top.

> Mount up these other stairs with no less caution (there are traps and pitfalls here, for those who are not so well escorted as ourselves) into the housetop; where the bare beams and rafters meet overhead, and calm night looks down through the crevices in the roof. Open the door of one of these cramped hutches full of sleeping negroes. Pah! . . . vapours issue forth that blind and suffocate. From every corner, as you glance about you in these dark retreats, some figure crawls half-awakened, as if the judgment-hour were near at hand, and every obscure grave were giving up its dead. Where dogs would howl to lie, women, and men, and boys slink off to sleep, forcing the dislodged rats to move away in quest of better lodgings.[8]

Dickens represents himself here as at once ordinary middle-class observer and the courageous class hero. Without any special qualifications other than his humanity and charity, he faces the dangerous mystery in order to expose it to us. He speaks to us in the imperative verb form, as if commanding us to share in his encounter: if you, reader, would know the Five Points, you "mount these stairs" with Dickens. His own first-person narration is hidden in the second person of the imperative, and the effect is to create a tone that is serious and intimate at once: it insists that we encounter along with our representative. In writing this way, Dickens is being the serious journalist who cannot remain detached and satiric about the nineteenth-century city but must confront it and say what he sees.[9] Through him we will learn how we might make meaning of what seems at first not to fit into our explanatory schemes at all.

In his interpretation of his experience, Dickens deftly arranges for us the powerful mythological parallels. The Old Brewery is a transhistorical sign of the Apocalypse. The inhabitants of the rooms are the dead rising from their graves; the sinful world is about to be judged. Or in the larger—and most obvious—mythological parallel of the journey, the trip to the Points is a visit to Hades: the reader looks directly at the inexplicable urban hell but holds on tight to the imperative guide Dickens, like Dante holding on to Virgil. Our Virgil has converted the immediate experience of a New York tenement into an event in the eternal and transcendent moral order: the local inexplicability becomes a transcendently explicable one. The effect of the trip is an implicit call to action, and the reader is meant to feel that "something must be done." Dickens reads the Five Points, interprets it, normalizes it into a bourgeois moral frame.

We can guess quite easily that Dickens was taken on what was becoming the standard tour of the poor and dangerous neighborhoods in New York, the very tour that his own account would make famous. He visited the New York City Prison, the "Egyptian Tombs" on Centre Street, where he found the conditions inhumane and appalling, and Pete Williams's dance hall—which featured wild interracial dancing and carousing (in large part, one thinks, choreographed for the entertainment of the slumming tourists).[10] The distinction of his visit to the dance hall caused that stop on the Points tour to be renamed "Dickens' Place."[11] George G. Foster devotes a chapter of *New York by Gas-Light* to the dance hall and always has Dickens in mind, making a typically extravagant assertion that his own highly colored description is more reportorial than Dickens's.

> Such is a brief description of Pete Williams and Dickens's Place. We trust that our readers will not draw 'oderous' comparisons between our humble and unpretending statement of facts and the elaborate and artistic picture of the place given by Dickens after a single visit. We both have written to the same end—to interest the reader: but while the great artist has summoned the aid of all his well-prepared colors to fascinate the imagination with harmonious hues, graceful proportions and startling contrasts, the unambitious reporter contents himself with sketching human nature as it is and as all may see it.[12]

After 1842, no journalist, novelist, charity worker, or clergyman writes about the Five Points without having Dickens's prose in mind. An example of Dickens's influence from the very year of publication of *American Notes* is Walt Whitman's use of a quotation from it as an epigraph to a chapter describing the Points in his melodramatic temperance novel, *Franklin Evans*, published as a *New World* extra on November 23, 1842. Twelve years later Solon Robinson writes, "Who that has lived long in this city, or read its history, particularly that portion of it written by Dickens, has not heard of the 'Old Brewery?'" The

Ladies of the Five Points Mission quote from *American Notes* in their 1854 book about their work and life at the Points and comment on the shame of what he reported.[13]

American accounts of visits to the Points repeated the mythological parallelism Dickens made popular. They were not particularly original: the slums are a hell on earth; the describer of the slums guides the reader, just as he or she was guided by the sturdy policemen; the experience of the visit is a call to change. In most narratives, as in Dickens's, the call is to reinforce or recontextualize one's long-held opinions rather than to remake them. Encounters with the Points abound in the collected journalism of the period, and among the more notable are those in the panoramic guidebooks and fiction by Robinson, Foster, and Mathews discussed earlier, as well as descriptions by Joel H. Ross and Samuel Iraneus Prime (editor of *Harper's* "Editor's Drawer" from 1853 on).[14] The many novels with Points encounters include those by Walt Whitman, Charles F. Briggs, John Treat Irving, Cornelius Mathews, Ned Buntline, and George Lippard. There were also encounter narratives in the books published by medical and charity workers, including those by Dr. John Griscom, the Ladies of the Five Points Mission, the American Female Guardian Society, and Charles Loring Brace.[15]

Most accounts—those in pamphlet novels, in serious novels, in journalism, in religious books, and in medical reports—were sensational. The encounter is replete with exotic *sensation* for the Points visitor and also provides (guilty) entertainment for the reader in witnessing poverty and debauchery while safely separated from filth and disease. George G. Foster stresses the bravery of the urban experts like Dickens and Mayhew—and himself.

> We do not believe that there is a city in Europe, where . . . a greater amount of degradation and suffering, licentiousness and crime, exists, than in this very proud and magnificent New York. Beneath the tall spires of its countless churches, and within the shadow of its commercial palaces and princely mansions, where life flows so brightly and so gaily, catching and reflecting every sunbeam as it dances across each cresting wave, rolls the deep, dark, sullen ocean of poverty, crime and despair. And he who must perform his duty to the times and to his race, must not hesitate to launch out fearlessly upon this gloomy sea,

but explore its profoundest recesses, and bring to light of day the horrid monsters that live and gender in its oozy depths. This work be
mine.[16]

Foster's imagery is conventional, however extreme his emphasis. Life
in the upper world is full of light and gaiety, a well-ordered stream of
mercantile existence, but *beneath* is the ocean of disorder, with monsters
engendering in its oozy depths. The disorder is sensational, both attracting and repelling, a chaos sometimes longed for and always feared
by the gainfully employed mechanics, clerks, small and large business
people—the widely defined middle class—trying to hold on to an idea
of order amidst the destabilizing city. Foster's insistence on his own
fearlessness and "duty to the times" seems silly given the slightness of
his work (in comparison to Mayhew!), but his boasts are exaggerations
of the attitude in all accounts of the mysteries of poor life. In the Points
narratives the visitor is the hero in a melodrama.

Again and again, no matter what its political, ethical, or aesthetic
intent, the Points narrative uses the Dickensian pattern. Here is Solon
Robinson's version of his walk through Cow Bay, a street just off Little
Water. Like Dickens more than a decade before, Robinson dramatizes
alcohol and race.

"If you would like to see [Cow Bay], saturate your handkerchief with
camphor, so that you can endure the horrid stench, and enter. Grope
your way through the long, dark, narrow passage—turn to your right,
up the dark and dangerous stairway; be careful where you place your
foot around the lower step, or in the corners of the broad stairs, for it
is more than shoe-mouth deep of steaming filth. Be careful, too, or
you may meet some one, . . . who in their drunken frenzy may thrust
you, for the very hatred of your better clothes, or the fear that you
have come to rescue them from their crazy loved dens of death, down,
headlong down, those filthy stairs. Up, up, winding up, five stories
high, now you are under the black smoky roof; turn to the left—take
care and not upset that seething pot of butcher's offal soup, that is
cooking upon a little furnace at the head of the stairs—open that
door—go in, if you can get in. Look; here is a negro and his wife
sitting upon the floor—where else could they sit, for there is no
chair—eating their supper off of the bottom of a pail. A broken brown
earthen jug holds water—perhaps not all water. Another negro and
his wife occupy another corner; a third sits in the window monopoliz-

ing all the air astir. In another corner, what do we see? A negro man and a stout, hearty, rather good looking young white woman."

"Not sleeping together?"

"No, not exactly that—there is no bed in the room—no chair—no table—no nothing—but rags, and dirt, and vermin, and degraded, rum-degraded human beings."[17]

Robinson includes all the important elements of the Points narrative: the imperative voice, the horrid stench, the darkness, the diseased airlessness, the Dickensian groping, and the ascent to the final interracial sex under the roof. Robinson repeats the encounter narrative again and again in his book, sometimes walking to see the horrors with Reverend Lewis Morris Pease, the Five Points missionary, as his guide.

One of the central features of Robinson's underworld is the same as that contained in descriptions of "Dickens' Place": African American men are cohabiting with white women (even "rather good looking young" ones). One definition of hell in the United States is that the races will mix there. The racist descriptions of African Americans in the Old Brewery and at "Dickens' Place" is a significant and pervasive feature of the Points narratives. Here is Foster in *New York by Gas-Light* on African American men:

> They associate upon at least equal terms with the men and women of the parish, and many of them are regarded as desirable companions and lovers by the "girls." They most of them have either white wives or white mistresses, and sometimes both; and their influence in the community is commanding. But they are savage, sullen, reckless dogs, and are continually promoting some "muss" or other, which not unfrequently leads to absolute riot.

He goes on to say how the "woolly-heads" can be "kept in tolerable subjection" if the police aim their clubs not at the head, "but the SHIN." Foster thinks all this is very funny.[18]

Middle-class hatred of the African Americans at the Points, its undisguised vehemence and violence, is an obvious marker of the intense bourgeois fear that a whole underclass was boiling in chaos and disorder beneath the surface of modern urban life, constantly threatening to break out and destroy the ordered society. Concern for the "lost"—the young middle-class drunkard, the street walker from good family—is often an expression of the fear of economic descent, of losing bourgeois status through loss of financial status. The existence of a "hell" imagines safety from that fear: we are never going to be like that, no matter what, and if a formerly respectable person somehow ends up at the Points, with African Americans, she is morally doomed. In the American Female Guardian Society's book *Wrecks and Rescues* (1859), for example, the decline of "the Broadway Belle," Julia Darley, is accelerated because "she has been herding with the lowest creatures to be found in the kennels of this city; black and white indiscriminately!"[19] Perhaps one American newspaper's reaction to Dickens's *American Notes* indicates the racial attitude best. The paper is so upset with Dickens that it angrily collapses the author with the people he describes: the paper finds Dickens "fit to associate only with the dancing monkeys and mulatto girls of Five Points."[20]

Even a man as distinguished as Dr. John Griscom could share in the paradigm and give room to racist interpretations of poverty. His *The Sanitary Condition of the Laboring Population of New York* (1845), highly influenced by Edwin Chadwick's *Report of the Sanitary Condition of the Labouring Population of Great Britain* (1842), begins with first-person accounts by physicians who have visited the poor. Dr. John A. Swett, Dr. Stephen Wood, Dr. B. W. McCready all write in the encounter paradigm I have described, and Dr. Wood makes it a point to show that the unclean inhabitants of the Points are most often Negroes and that he thinks their race the problem.[21]

The logic of the encounter narrative taught Dickens and Dr. Wood that the source of urban disease and disorder was *visible* with the individual visit: hell itself was visible. The narrative power of the educated single observer means that the problem at the Points can be understood by a man who is brave enough to go there and thoughtful enough to think through what it means. No research other than the visit is necessary: the intrepid observer can see the reason for himself.

Mysteries of New York All of the Points narratives participate in a wide taste in Western culture for "mysteries," descriptions of the social and sexual depravity hidden "beneath" ordinary society. This taste becomes most developed in the mid-nineteenth century in the popular literature of the "urban Gothic." Between Ann Radcliffe's *The Mysteries* *of Udolpho* (1794) and Eugène Sue's *Les Mystères de Paris* (1842–43) or G.W.M. Reynolds's *The Mysteries of London* (1845–48), "secrets became entangled with an idea of city life."[22] By the middle of the 1840s, the urban mysteries formula was spreading to many parts of Europe and to the United States, with many popular novelists imitating primarily Eugène Sue. Many of the American sensationalist narratives in the Sue tradition, like those by George Lippard and Buntline, use the Points encounter. These novelists write urban Gothic popular literature, and the actual locales they use, like the Old Brewery or The Tombs, become more the items in an urban Gothic inventory of effects than accurate topographical sites.

However remote the action of books like Lippard's *The Empire City: New York by Night and Day* (1849) or its sequel *New York: Its Upper Ten and Lower Million* (1853) seems from the actual sites and facts of New York life, these books and others like them are expressions of contemporary urban society. The mysteries books base themselves on a central conspiracy in the city that oppresses working- and lower-middle-class people. The controller of the conspiracy, the secret boss, is often a debased and depraved aristocratic figure reminiscent of the solitary Gothic madman.[23] The people who enact his wishes are low criminals and tricked or compromised members of the classes in between. The novels imagine a city in which economic control is secretly still in the hands of the "aristocratic" elites. The victims of the secret system are the members of the skilled working class (the "mechanics," in the term of the day) and also the small owners.

The novelists in the mysteries tradition were often converted to versions of radical politics. As Peter Brooks notes, Eugène Sue began *Les Mystères de Paris* "with the vaguest of ideological orientations" and emerged from it a declared socialist.[24] He became a deputy from a Parisian working-class district during the Second Republic. In England, G.W.M. Reynolds became a Chartist in 1848, apparently converting to the cause during a spontaneous speech at the Chartist demonstration at Trafalgar Square.[25]

In New York, the most extraordinary participation of a popular novelist in working-class politics was Ned Buntline's involvement in the nativist Astor Place riot in 1849. English Shakespearean actor Charles Macready had been touring the country, often appearing in the same cities at the same time as his American rival Edwin Forrest. Buntline enflamed the contest in his journal, *Ned Buntline's Own*, screaming that people should give Macready what their ancestors had given the redcoats at Lexington. When Macready opened *Macbeth* in New York at the Astor Place Opera House, the house was filled with b'hoys throwing things—eggs, oranges, rotten apples—and shouting "Down with the codfish aristocracy!" "Huzza for native talent!" They sang when the witches chanted, and Bill Wilson, trainer for the prizefighter Yankee Sullivan, threw a chair from the gallery. More chairs made Macready stop his performance, and the b'hoys marched out victorious. Real trouble came three days later, on May 10, when Macready played *Macbeth* again, in response to a petition from New York's leading citizens (Washington Irving's name headed the published list; Herman Melville signed). Again, Buntline's nativists organized. Despite massive police protection, a crowd of ten thousand formed outside the theater and pelted the building with paving stones. Ned Buntline, sword in hand, incited riot in the streets ("Workingmen, shall Americans or English rule?"), and for a time it looked as if the rioters, many dressed in firemen's uniforms, would burn the aristocracy in their theater. The militia was called out and after much confusion finally fired into the crowd. Newspapers reported that 34 were killed and 141 wounded. Ned Buntline was arrested.[26]

One of George G. Foster's descriptions of "Dickens' Place" has b'hoys and other working men there, and the dancers are "wild with excitement, like Ned Buntline at Astor Place."[27] At other times Foster is more sympathetic to working men and women, praising Mike Walsh, for example. His political ideas vary widely, but at their heart is a Fourieristic fantasy popular in New York during the period. Foster's novel *Celio; or, New York Above Ground and Under Ground* (1850) ends with a socialist pastoral when the gang leader, Captain Earnest, turns out to have entered into criminality and low life "solely for the purpose of testing and carrying out my theory of the nature of man and the false organization of society" (!) and finally uses the profits of violent crime to set up Mr. Bunch, Screech Owl, Dandy Jake, and others in a huge edifice in a pleasant spot by the Connecticut River. There the thugs are to live in their Fourierist phalanstery and labor happily in communal workshops.[28] This concocted suburban socialism was promoted even by Whigs like Horace Greeley, whose *Tribune* promoted Fourier and experiments like Brook Farm throughout the 1840s.

Another well-known popular writer who worked in urban sensations was George Lippard. He supported the labor agrarianism of the National Reform Association and the Industrial Congress and went on to found a working-class secret society, the Brotherhood of the Union. For David S. Reynolds, Lippard was an artist "both speaking *for* and speaking *from* American working-class culture." Michael Denning teases out the ideology of Lippard's novels more carefully, finding that the "mysteries of the city was a form imposed upon its mechanic readers, not a species of working class fiction."[29]

Denning parallels his analysis of Lippard with Karl Marx's criticism of Eugène Sue in *The Holy Family*. He points out that for Marx workers in Sue are "represented through bourgeois eyes . . . as passive victims or active villains, to be moralized or punished." Marx thinks that the interest in the poor, in their mysteries, is yet another disempowerment of the workers because the controlling consciousness of Sue's fiction is bourgeois, however friendly Sue felt toward the poor of Paris. Sue's hero is Rodolphe, the nobleman in disguise, who controls the moral action of the book. " 'The whole of Rodolphe's character,' Marx writes, 'is finally summed up in the "pure" hypocrisy by which he manages to see and make others see the *outburst of his evil passions* as *outbursts against the passions of the wicked.*' " Denning shows that Lippard, like Sue, is fascinated with the superman acting in the city—in, for example, the characters of magician-scientist Ravoni in *The Quaker City* and Paul Mount Laurel in *The Nazarene*. Denning raises a further complexity by showing that although Lippard's work is essentially bourgeois, his *audience* is working class.[30] Denning follows Dan Schiller's arguments about the penny press, and I find it harder than Schiller or Denning to assume that we know exactly what the audience was, despite the protestations *inside* the works that they were reaching working-class audiences. Part of the difficulty is that many members of what the nineteenth century called working class were in fact skilled small owners, small bourgeois, worried as much about unskilled immigrants as about the power of capital.[31]

Dickens is as present in Lippard and other American mysteries writers as Sue. The wholesale acceptance of Dickens as bourgeois icon makes it hard to remember that at first his writing seemed almost as sensational and lurid as what G.W.M. Reynolds or Buntline or Lippard produced later, and in fact even *Bleak House* (1852–53) is still a mysteries-of-the-city plot, although not with the same grisly effects as, say, *Oliver Twist* (1837). Prime Minister Melbourne could get through only a few chapters of *Oliver Twist*: "It is all among workhouses and pickpockets and coffinmakers. . . . I do not like those things; I wish to avoid them. I do not like them in reality and therefore do not like to see them represented." Despite Melbourne, Dickens became the great urban artist of his time, and his success is a tribute to his ability to appropriate material from less respectable traditions, like those of the Newgate novel, and transform it "in the direction of circumspectness and propriety of language and allusion."[32] George Lippard is very different from Dickens. He *is* more sensational, far less acceptable to polite opinion, and it is probably true that mechanics were more apt to read him. But the bizarre excesses of the "subversive imagination" that David Reynolds thinks of as "thoroughly, indelibly American"[33] in Lippard have some origins in Dickens, particularly in *The Old Curiosity Shop* and the book Melbourne couldn't read, *Oliver Twist*.

The central evil character in *The Old Curiosity Shop*, Quilp, is the model for many urban villains in the mysteries tradition in the United States—Lippard's Devil-Bug, for example. The disorder, the chaos, that seems to rule the underworld of the city is made explicable by the existence of a single controller who rules the evil space. These villains are *peeping* devils, like Lesage's devil on two sticks. Dickens perfects the character of the all-seeing urban man, whether it is Quilp actually peeping through keyholes at young women or Tulkinghorn brilliantly interpreting all the clues and invading all the privacies of *Bleak House*. The knowledge the villains possess is at first financial and has to do with complex bourgeois paperwork, but that knowledge ultimately enables demonic behavior within the modern context. The villains occupy a special panoramic position from which they can view the personal secrets of the modern city, prying into the lives of bourgeois and artisan alike. They are ubiquitous devils, able to appear almost everywhere at any time, suggesting their capacities are almost supernatural.

The failure of a respectable middle-class character to understand the urban complexities is a staple of the sensational novel. An interesting example is in Ned Buntline's huge and widely popular *The Mysteries and Miseries of New York: A Story of Real Life* (1848). The sprawling book opens with a crooked intelligence office (employment agency) telling the elegant confidence man, Frank Hennock, that Peter Precise, a retired soap maker of great wealth, wants a secretary. Transformed into a threadbare poet who sentimentalizes the poor, Hennock gets the job, and he and the intellectually thirsty Precise talk and talk in the soap maker's elegant townhouse. Precise does not believe Hennock's descriptions of the horrible poverty that exists just a few blocks away, and Hennock gets him to agree to tour the Five Points.

At the Points, Precise sees a soup house, the Old Brewery, and "Dickens' Place." What is remarkable about Precise's encounters is that although Precise is "green," he is not a naive country youth: he is a man of fifty-five who has lived in New York City and is experienced in business, a successful and practical man. Yet nothing in that experience has prepared him for what he sees in his own city. He is nearly broken by what Hennock shows him: "Can all this *be*, in a Christian city?" He has never even imagined any of the poverty before, even though his townhouse is not so far away. He has never seen The Tombs prison. At the soup house he makes the mistake of trying to give gold to a man who does not have even a penny for soup. He is nearly torn apart by a mob until Hennock (who understands such things) throws another coin to the other side of the room, drawing the mob away from Precise. Later he, like Dickens and so many others, ascends the stairs of the Old Brewery and is overwhelmed by the stench and stunned at the hopelessness of the disease. Precise insists on getting a doctor to come immediately. On the way home, they stop in at "Dickens' Place" and witness the debauchery. Precise is psychologically overwhelmed by his experiences—and by this time Hennock has lifted Precise's wallet and five hundred dollars.[34]

Confidence-man Hennock does not work alone: he is part of a conspiracy whose energies are devoted to bilking honest, well-to-do and charitable people of their money. The conspiracy presents the victim with such a shock to his or her ordinary expectations that he or she is overwhelmed for a moment, unable to understand what to think and so forced to do something the swindler wants. At the very moment of the gap in understanding, the money vanishes. The narrative pretends to exist for its readers as warning: "read this and do not do likewise" or "you should do something about these conditions." It suggests that the interpretive models bourgeois people operate with will need to be modified in order to cope successfully with the new tests to them. Charity must continue but it must be a careful charity; conditions are more difficult than we had guessed, but, most importantly, reform in consciousness, not reform in politics, is what is necessary.

The opponent of the confidence men and the lower criminals and all the conspiracies is, in the mysteries tradition, a kind of detective, a person like Dickens's Bucket or Foster's Captain Earnest, who operates in disguise amongst the criminals but holds on to middle-class values. He is the special agent of the middle class who works like the superman Rodolphe that Marx describes and condemns in *Les Mystères de Paris.* Like the peeping devils, these heroes are ubiquitous, able to appear, as Jo says of Dickens's Bucket, "in all manner of places, all at wunst."[35] Superman himself as well as other twentieth-century superheroes are late incarnations of the mysteries-tradition underground heroes. Batman, familiar with the night, is the nobleman in disguise working in the interest of the honest middle classes, and he can fix the apparently overwhelming problems of the city while still reaffirming the existing cultural system. No revolution in understanding is necessary. Only the extravagant excesses of the system—the alliances between old aristocracies and new low criminals—need to be pruned away.

Herman Melville's *Pierre* Herman Melville picks up the conventional imagery of the Points encounter in his novel *Pierre; or, The Ambiguities* (1852). The youthful American aristocrat, Pierre Glendinning, has taken on "Truth" and decided to devote his life to Isabel, the woman his mother would not acknowledge but who he thinks is his illegitimate half-sister. Like the knight of old, Pierre seeks the ideal and leaves his country estate with Isabel and quests for truth in the nineteenth-century city. In *Pierre* the "city" is perhaps recognizably New York with its "great Oronoco thoroughfare"—Broadway, we assume—and the "large, open triangular space, built round with the stateliest public erections"—City Hall Park—but the omission of the actual New York place-names is apparently intended to make readers understand Pierre's city as a *mythic* urban place that is the appropriate site of the destruction of youth's idealistic enthusiasms.[36]

On the night of their arrival in this city, Pierre encounters a prostitute, and his response to the encounter is framed and underlined by Melville's parody of urban narratives.

> "I say, my pretty one! Dear! Dear! young man! Oh, love, you are in a vast hurry, ain't you? Can't you stop a bit, now, my dear: do—there's a sweet fellow."
>
> Pierre turned; and in the flashing, sinister, evil cross-lights of a druggist's window, his eye caught the person of a wonderfully beautifully-featured girl; scarlet-cheeked, glaringly-arrayed, and of a figure all natural grace but unnatural vivacity. Her whole form, however, was horribly lit by the green and yellow rays from the druggist's.
>
> "My God!" shuddered Pierre, hurrying forward, "the town's first welcome to youth!" (237).

Melville's comedy is to have his narrative voice itself adopt the melodramatic language of the urban Gothic. The scene gives us in brief the "unnatural" intensity of the Gothic, the glaring colors of the clichéd urban underworld, and the supposed intensity of the hero's encounter with mythic evil. Like the hero of Whitman's *Franklin Evans* or of Melville's own *Redburn*, Pierre enters a melodrama at the same time as he enters New York, but in *Pierre* Melville makes sure that his readers understand that the language parodies itself. The reader realizes that the encounter and its description show how hollow the conventions are and how little Pierre understands because he can only think inside the clichés of the city arrival.

The prostitute's advice, it turns out, is quite right: Pierre is in all too "vast" a hurry. He should "stop a bit" to see what nontruth has to offer—to listen, for example, to the prostitute. This is made clearer at the Watch House, where Pierre's party of refugees for Truth stops while Pierre seeks out his cousin Glen. Rebuffed by the elegant New York dandy Glen, Pierre returns to the Watch House, where all has changed.

> The before decent, drowsy place, now fairly reeked with all things unseemly. Hardly possible was it to tell what conceivable cause or occasion had, in the comparatively short absence of Pierre, collected

such a base congregation. In indescribable disorder, frantic, diseased-looking men and women of all colors, and in all imaginable flaunting, immodest, grotesque, and shattered dresses, were leaping, yelling, and cursing around him. The torn Madras handkerchiefs of negresses, and the red gowns of yellow girls, hanging in tatters from their naked bosoms, mixed with the rent dresses of deep-rouged white women, and the split coats, checkered vests, and protruding shirts of pale, or whiskered, or haggard, or mustached fellows of all nations, some of whom seemed scared from their beds, and others seemingly arrested in the midst of some crazy and wanton dance. On all sides, were heard drunken male and female voices, in English, French, Spanish, and Portuguese, interlarded now and then, with the foulest of all human lingoes, that dialect of sin and death, known as the Cant language, or the Flash.

The Watch House is a Babel of voices, an Apocalypse of massed peoples of all kinds: "The thieves'-quarters, and all the brothels, Lock-and-Sin hospitals for incurables, and infirmaries and infernoes of hell seemed to have made one combined sortie, and poured out upon earth through the vile vomitory of some unmentionable cellar" (240–41).

The passage is Melville's parody of the Points descriptions of his time. It concentrates and jumbles together all the elements of the descriptions of the Points as Hades. The crowd is in total disorder, as if in a "crazy and wanton dance" like the racially mixed and naked dancers at "Dickens' Place." The men and women have no control: their sexuality and drunkenness and criminality are all visible, and their speech is a Babel of many languages, including—as if the most melodramatic of all—"the foulest of all human lingoes, that dialect of sin and death, known as the Cant language, or the Flash." The diseased-looking men and women are like the dead rising from Hell, "scared from their beds," or, in Dickens's words from *American Notes*, "as if the judgment-hour were near at hand, and every obscure grave were giving up its dead."[37]

Melville's description of the chaos, the swirling combinations of peoples, the incomplete and tattered clothing, are a kind of urban clothes philosophy retailored from Thomas Carlyle's *Sartor Resartus*. These clothes do not cover the inexplicable essences of the mad assemblage: they emphasize the chaos. Melville doesn't just mix the races but all of humanity. The young Pierre is completely unprepared to comprehend this spectacle because of his "imperfect and casual city experiences" (241), but he *assumes* (like Dickens) that he is confronting a moral horror, a hell, and smashes his way through the crowd and rescues Isabel and Delly, her maid, just as Delly is being stripped of her clothes. The city Pierre sees is one where there is Right and Wrong.

What his "Dickens' Place" scene could teach the uneducable Pierre is that humanity is a patchwork affair, a tattered assemblage in which the whole cloth of "Truth" cannot be found. The Fool for Truth is one who lives inside the melodramas of his own making. Pierre learns some of the painful "ambiguities" of the title, but he dies a murderer and suicide in New York's City Prison, The Tombs. Pierre's naïveté enables Melville to describe the conventional Points encounter even as his satire shows us the inadequacy of Pierre's shallowly conventional response to that encounter. As Melville's later works, particularly "Bartleby" and *The Confidence-Man*, make even more apparent, Melville practices in the New York discourse and is its historian and critic as well: we understand the discourse better because of the way Melville uses it.

PART THREE

"DO YOU NOT SEE THE REASON FOR YOURSELF?"

What my own astonished eyes saw of Bartleby, that *is all I know of him.*

Herman Melville
"Bartleby, the Scrivener"

6

Putnam's and New York Stories

Melville's New Career Any reader of Herman Melville's "Bartleby, the Scrivener: A Story of Wall Street," first published in *Putnam's Monthly* in November and December 1853, knows that the story's unusually narrow field of vision controls his or her reading. The lawyer/narrator's own reading of the events is immured within the walls of his law office, just as Bartleby himself is walled in that office and in himself. Character, narrator, and reader all look at "dead" walls and cannot see beyond the ordinary office life they enclose.

Bartleby is the unspeaking prophet who has made us see that the walls are there. Like the walls themselves, Bartleby does not acknowledge humanity. He has only one flicker of interest in the lawyer, and that is when he responds to his question about why he has stopped writing as well as proofreading. Bartleby "indifferently" replies with another question: "Do you not see the reason for yourself?"[1] The lawyer thinks for a moment that he *has* understood a reason—the scrivener's eyes are bad and he therefore cannot write—but we, and soon the lawyer, know that Bartleby's indifferent question simply emphasizes the interpreter's isolation: if we are to see reasons for Bartleby, it must be for ourselves.

What the New York lawyer's "own astonished eyes" (13) see marks the bounds of our knowledge. He knows no more than he sees; he imagines little more than he knows. His story gives us an illustration of daily life in which he and his clerks are the entire scene: they fill the picture to the edges of the frame. There is nothing outside the frame except blank walls. We readers must see, and can only see, the isolated office world, and it seems complete and full. We think nothing could be added to the balanced office—Nippers grinding and gnashing before a stomach-calming lunch, and then Turkey enflamed in the afternoon by the drinks at the same lunch—but Bartleby *is* added to the picture, and he silently expands until he fills the picture out to the frame himself. Even then the story does not seem the interpretive puzzle that it is: the lawyer's narration is so straightforward, the scene so local, the office events so ordinary, and even Bartleby (at first) so unexotic, that we do not imagine having any difficulty interpreting it. Offices are ordinary parts of our lives. We understand them, and even the unusual things that happen in them must be decipherable. But thanks to Melville's design, we are soon thrown from our interpretive confidence into an interpretive isolation and frustration almost as complete as the lawyer's, and we struggle to make our own astonished eyes see and understand as we read the lawyer's words. Readers have stumbled along by themselves since the story was published, one interpreting the story this way, the other that.[2]

We struggle because the movement from simple reading to interpretation is very difficult in "Bartleby." We can only see the possible themes in the vaguest ways; our generalizations are uneasy. Melville achieves these destabilizing effects through constriction of the scene and point of view, through an extraordinary intensification of the techniques of the New York discourse. He shows an ease and economy and clarity that might not have been expected from a writer experienced in the complex digressions of *Moby-Dick* (1851) or the contortions of tone in *Pierre* (1852). The surface of the story is unruffled by grand themes and speculative philosophy: "Bartleby" is a straightforward story of quotidian New York.

In writing "Bartleby" in this restricted mode, Melville was probably reacting in part to the severity of the criticisms of *Pierre*, including those by Fitz-James O'Brien in the very magazine that was soon to publish "Bartleby." As part of their effort to treat American literature seriously and accord it the critical respect it deserved, the editors of *Putnam's Monthly* had run O'Brien's "Our Young Authors—Melville" in the February 1853 issue, nine months before "Bartleby" began. O'Brien's comments in the most sophisticated of New York magazines could not have been encouraging to Melville. The critique would have been painful if only because O'Brien, unlike many contemporary reviewers, had read Melville's books carefully. He sees Melville's novelistic career as descending into a mad self-indulgence that reaches its nadir in *Pierre*, a book in which, O'Brien thinks, Melville has lost all aesthetic rein on his ideas: "Thought staggers through each page like one poisoned. Language is drunken and reeling. Style is antipodical, and marches on its head." O'Brien's criticism is interesting because it is high-minded in comparison to other contemporary reaction to *Pierre*, which questioned Melville's morality and sanity for taking up topics like incest and murder (and the Five Points) in serious fiction.[3] O'Brien concludes hoping that stylistic reform is still possible: "let [Melville] diet himself for a year or two on Addison, and avoid Sir Thomas Browne, and there is little doubt that he will make a notch on the American pine."[4]

I think it remarkable that the magazine that published O'Brien's attack on Melville's style went on to publish not only "Bartleby" at the end of 1853 but seven other pieces before 1856—"The Encantadas," "The Two Temples," "The Lightning-Rod Man," "The Bell Tower," "Benito Cereno," "I and My Chimney," and "Israel Potter." The last was published separately as the book *Israel Potter* in 1855, and all except "The Two Temples" and "I and My Chimney" appeared (along with a new title story, "The Piazza") as *The Piazza Tales* in 1856.

During this period Melville also placed short pieces at *Harper's*, issued by the publishers of the unsuccessful *Pierre*. The magazine had printed a chapter of *Moby-Dick*, "The Town-Ho's Story," in October 1851, in conjunction with the house's publication of the novel, and from

1853 on it published eight short stories: "Cock-A-Doodle-Doo," "Poor Man's Pudding and Rich Man's Crumbs," "The Happy Failure," "The Fiddler," "The Paradise of Bachelors and the Tartarus of Maids," "Jimmy Rose," " 'Gees," and "The Apple Tree Table."

Melville's success in getting these short works published in *Harper's* and *Putnam's* as well as collecting the *Putnam's* pieces in two separately published books suggests to me a modest but notable recovery in critical fortune for the author whose career seemed wrecked by the critical reaction to *Pierre*. His success is a tribute to Melville's resilience and creative energy and also reflects well on the magazine editors who had faith enough in his work to continue publishing him in magazines they edited or were influential in. George William Curtis is particularly important in Melville's magazine career because he was interested in Melville's work from the beginning of his own career and because of his influence as an associate editor of *Putnam's* and as the popular "Easy Chair" columnist for *Harper's*.[5] I think we should be grateful for Melville's perseverance and for the editors' perception (however flawed) because Melville's short pieces of the period are a great achievement, some of the most interesting works in the English language. I can only repeat Warner Berthoff's view that the recovery of these works would have occasioned high excitement even if they had been the *only* Melville works known.[6]

The "Charming *Putnam*"   "Bartleby, the Scrivener: A Story of Wall Street" was very much a New York story, and the tastes and standards of the prestigious New York magazine that published it influence its content and shape. *Putnam's* had begun publication in January of 1853. George Palmer Putnam was apparently himself the original projector of the magazine, but he convinced a talented group of New Yorkers to run it. Charles F. Briggs was the first editor, and he was closely associated with George W. Curtis and Parke Godwin. Putnam wanted to publish a monthly that would carry only American fiction and nonfiction, in explicit and self-conscious contrast to the highly successful magazine of the competing New York publishing house, *Harper's Monthly*, that depended heavily on the serialization of English novels.

The first number of *Putnam's* makes explicit the connection between the new magazine and literary nationalism: "The genius of the old world is affluent; we owe much to it, and we hope to owe more. But we have no less faith in the opulence of our own resources."[7] *Putnam's* was fighting the stiff competition to the American cultural product appearing monthly in *Harper's*. That magazine had begun publication in 1850 without even planning to *pay* for the British product it transferred to its pages, but even when the success of the magazine made it advisable to compensate the most famous British authors, it was still very difficult for an American author to make it to market. Just as *Putnam's* began, *Harper's* was carrying Dickens's *Bleak House* and followed it up immediately with Thackeray's *The Newcombes*.[8]

Putnam's confident expectations, as well as its financial imagery of an American "opulence," were New York's latest transformation of Ralph Waldo Emerson's call, in "The American Scholar," for American young men to stop listening to "the courtly muses of Europe" and remake themselves. Publisher Putnam, editor Briggs, and associate editor Curtis were themselves transformed New Englanders and combined an admiration for New England intellectual culture with their enthusiasm for New York. They thought they were founding a magazine that would assemble not only New England and New York literary culture but all American regional literary cultures into a national voice capable of articulating the cultivation of the nation—and of resisting British cultural dominance. Like many New Yorkers after them, they saw no contradiction in localizing that national voice in New York. It seemed obvious to Briggs and Curtis that to appreciate and understand their national literary culture Americans would have to learn about life in New York. The nation would have to encounter New York.

Charles F. Briggs, as we have seen, was a Nantucketer who had made his reputation with the story of New York encounters. His well-known collections of earlier *Knickerbocker* pieces, *The Adventures of Harry Franco: A Tale of the Great Panic* (1839) and *The Trippings of Tom Pepper* (1847–50), were panoramic celebrations of the new urban culture at the same time as they aspired to an urban realism and seriousness that other panoramists (like George G. Foster) didn't have time for.[9] Briggs's manifesto in the first issue of the *Broadway Journal* in 1845 had announced without embarrassment that New York *was* the nation.

In *Putnam's* Briggs had the well-funded journal that would broadcast Young American goals in far more genteel fashion than had his *Broadway Journal*. The magazine's assumption of cultural sophistication replaced most of the vulgar metropolitan boosterism of the earlier Young American magazines. Since New York was the center of intellectual culture, its leading magazine could include writings by Americans of all regions— Henry David Thoreau, James Fenimore Cooper, Henry Wadsworth Longfellow, James Russell Lowell, John P. Kennedy, Richard Henry Stoddard, Charles Eliot Norton, Henry James, Sr., Fitz-James O'Brien, and Henry W. Herbert ("Frank Forester"), Donald G. Mitchell, and Herman Melville—while at the same time strongly featuring life in New York in nonfiction, fiction, and engravings. *Putnam's* under Briggs seemed at first a true replacement for the deteriorating *Knickerbocker*, a metropolitan and sophisticated journal only implied in the earlier democratic competitors of the venerable Whig magazine. Briggs made the magazine, in Thomas Bender's words, "a panoply of visual icons and social forms that represented the city to itself and to the nation."[10]

One of Briggs's principal associates at *Putnam's* was George William Curtis, and he too was formed in New England. Born in Providence, George and his brother Burrill had heard Emerson speak on the "Over-Soul" in Mr. Hartshorn's classroom and had also met Margaret Fuller, then teaching in Providence. The boys moved with their family to New York in 1839 and three years later began an extraordinary, grandly leisured, eight years of education—at Brook Farm, then living in Concord (George helped build Thoreau's cabin), and then four years in Europe. While abroad, George Curtis wrote, like Fuller, for the *Tribune*, and after he returned to New York in the summer of 1850 he contributed occasional music and art criticism to Greeley's paper and assembled the travel pieces into the highly successful books *Nile Notes of a Howadji* (1851) and *The Howadji in Syria* (1852). Greeley was feeding the continuing American appetite for travel books, and Curtis's lush and risqué descriptions of life in the East complemented other successful *Tribune* travel articles, like Bayard Taylor's two collected series, *Views Afoot; or, Europe Seen with Knapsack and Staff* (1846) and *El Dorado; or, Adventures in the Path of Empire* (1850).

From the beginning of his publishing career, Curtis had Melville very much in mind. He alludes in *Nile Notes* to Melville's own dreamy

Mardi (1849) and makes it clear that the Howadji's very successful book was heavily influenced by Melville's not so successful one:

> The sky was cloudless and burningly rosy. To what devote the delicious day? . . . Yet the Howadji looked along the shelves and the book was found, and in the hot heart of noon he had drifted far into the dreamy depths of Herman Melville's Mardi. Lost in the rich romance of Pacific reverie, he felt all around him the radiant rustling of Yillah's hair, but could not own that Polynesian peace was profounder than his own Nubian silence.[11]

Curtis collected another *Tribune* series—this time of travel from New York to summer resorts—into *Lotus-Eating: A Summer Book* (1852), illustrated by his friend the landscape painter John F. Kensett.[12] In *Lotus-Eating* Curtis imagines himself for a moment to be the Herman Melville of *Typee* (1846) as his boat touches Lake George's (Polynesian?) shore: "For that moment I was a South Sea Islander, a Typeean, a Herman Melville, and down the ruined steps I ran to catch a moonlight glimpse of Fayaway, but saw only the rippling brilliance of the rapidly fading boat."[13] Here Fayaway and Melville are used as they often were—to remember Fayaway without her clothes.

Lotus-Eating, despite its apparently frivolous subject but true to its title, is thick with educated allusion. Curtis frequently compares the American resorts and scenery unfavorably with their European counterparts. The Hudson, for example, is not quite the Rhine, for one cannot "float at evening or morning along its shores, following the wildest whim of fancy, with Uhland in one pocket and a *flasche* of Rüdesheimer in the other, dozing away the noon in the coolest corner of some old ruin, and dreaming of Ariadne as you drift, sighing, beneath the moonlighted vineyards" (22). Curtis was always, in Van Wyck Brooks's apt phrase, "the sugared Transcendentalist,"[14] substituting a collegiate idyll of cosmopolitan and leisured intellectual life for the desperate intensity of his friends in Concord.

Curtis begins in his travel books, particularly in *Lotus-Eating*, the definition of a new educated class, one that has the credibility of its intellectual New England origins but deploys its New York commercial wealth into a cosmopolitan sophistication. The jibes at vulgar New Yorkers on holiday in *Lotus-Eating* look forward to the popular social satire that Curtis did for *Putnam's* in "The Potiphar Papers." In Saratoga, for example, Curtis comments on "the crisp courtesy of the New Yorker, elegant in dress, exclusive in association, a pallid ghost of Paris—without its easy elegance, its *bonhomie*, its gracious *savoir faire*, without the *spirituel* sparkle of its conversation, and its natural and elastic grace of style" (114–15). By showing what is missing in the nouveau upper bourgeois New Yorker, Curtis identifies his own social and intellectual ideal. Bonhomie and "*spirituel* sparkle" should mark the cultural leadership of a new class. Curtis wants the hollowness and vulgarity of the new wealth put in its place by a sophisticated new elite.

The *Putnam's* Curtis joined was one attempt at cultural control by the new American elite that Curtis defines. He was finally of more consequence at *Putnam's* than even Briggs because of a complicated sequence of editorial changes occasioned by financial problems in George P. Putnam's larger business. In December 1854, after *Putnam's* had had almost two years of editorially and financially successful publication, Putnam tried to save desperately needed cash by replacing the editors with Frederick Beecher Perkins and himself. Soon after, in April 1855, he sold the whole magazine to Joshua Dix and Arthur Edwards, a publishing house with Frederick Law Olmsted as one of its partners. Olmsted needed experienced help, and he finally convinced George Curtis and Charles A. Dana, managing editor of the *Tribune*, to be the secret editors of *Putnam's*. The reasons secrecy was necessary are unclear, but we know from letters that Curtis was interested in limiting his responsibility because he knew (from watching his friend Briggs) the amount of work a whole editorship demanded, and perhaps Olmsted and Dix wanted Dana's role suppressed because they didn't want the magazine to seem another *Tribune* product.[15]

The *Tribune*'s influence must have been obvious to many contemporaries even without Dana's role being known. Many contributors to *Putnam's* had been associated with the paper. *Tribune* regulars like art critic Clarence Cook, travel writers Bayard Taylor and Curtis, and review editor George Ripley all wrote for *Putnam's*, as did Horace Greeley himself. Greeley supported the magazine warmly in the *Tribune*, and Greeley was praised in *Putnam's*.[16]

The influence of the *Tribune* at *Putnam's* is remarkable, and, since both Dana and Curtis were Brook Farmers, it shows how successfully the younger generation of New England intellectuals participated in the formulation of 1850s New York literary culture. They produced a restructured *Putnam's* that had what many thought its best issues, but they also started losing the magazine's national audience, in part because the Republican cause started taking up more and more of each issue. Curtis, to his eternal regret, was induced to invest in the firm and then even sank some of his father-in-law's money in the failing business. Collapse and financial disaster came in August 1857, and *Putnam's* ended its brief and brilliant career.

Putnam's featured New York explicitly at the same time as it tried to reach the national audience. The first issue began a series of heavily illustrated articles by Clarence Cook called "New-York Daguerreo-typed." In the panoramic mode the articles toured the city, writing about and illustrating extensively (for example) "Educational Institutions of New York," "New York Church Architecture," or "Art-Manu-factures." As these titles indicate, the *Putnam's* panoramic articles differ in tone from earlier panoramic journalism in that they tour an established and sophisticated world city busily producing first-rate education, art, and architecture. The magazine was not, however, above boosting the 1853 Crystal Palace Exhibition with a richly illustrated article.[17] Beginning in January of 1856 Curtis wrote a monthly column called "The World of New York." Its prose toured the city, gave the "talk of the town," and offered comments on the greatness of New York. In July 1856 Curtis writes that New York outshines all American cities and that no one could find fault with the "growth of our city toward a cosmopolitan rank."[18] Curtis goes on to compare New York to Vienna, Berlin, and London. In the spring of 1857 he starts a column of humorous notes called "Putnam's Kaleidascope" (spelled just that way) that subsequently gives way to "Our Window," by which the author proposed to "sit, month by month, and watch all that passes." A New York window looks out on everything: the sophisticated New York editor is a flaneur while calmly sitting at his desk.

Curtis's principal fictional contributions to the magazine were also explicitly New York stories, a series of satirical thrusts at New York society he later collected as *Potiphar Papers* (1853) and a group of contemplative and sentimental pieces put together into *Prue and I* (1856). The Potiphar series was an outgrowth of Curtis's satires on nouveau society in *Lotus-Eating*, and it was an enormous success with at least the New York readers of *Putnam's*. It began with "Our Best Society" in February 1853, an article that attacks the "rampant vulgarity" of New York society. It thinks the "fast" world of dancing masters, décolleté girls, and ignorant young fops is a sign of decadence. New York has degenerated from the time of the sturdy capitalists who made the money that makes the new decadence possible. Curtis (as in *Lotus-Eating*) has transatlantic comparison in mind: "In London, and Paris, and Vienna, and Rome, all the really eminent men and women help make up the mass of society. A party is not a mere ball, but it is a congress of the wit, beauty, and fame of the capital. It is worth while to dress, if you shall meet Macaulay."[19] The article is so much direct lament that it seems, in the book version, an awkward introduction to the lively satiric representations of the "best society" that follow. Curtis does identify a stylistic inspiration by praising Thackeray's *Vanity Fair* as a portrait of superficial society. Curtis was Thackeray's friend and entertained him when he was in New York, and Thackeray was in turn an influential friend of *Putnam's*. Longfellow heard Thackeray say at a dinner in London that he thought *Putnam's* was the best magazine in the world, and "was better than *Blackwood* is or ever was!"[20] Curtis would probably have been the first to admit that the satiric pieces in *Potiphar* are thin stuff next to *Vanity Fair*. Curtis's dinners for Thackeray at the Century Club must have been better tributes. George Templeton Strong remarked to his diary that Curtis was a "nice, pleasant, amiable, superficial, genial Epicurian."[21]

Potiphar is an encounter with high society adrift in its ignorance. Wealth concentrates on putting its servants in livery, even though the old capitalist Potiphar understands that "no genuine American would ever ask another to assume a menial badge." It is a society whose manly values have been overwhelmed by socially ambitious women who lavishly overfurnish houses and work in concert with trivial ministers like the Reverend Cream Cheese. The hero of the later sketches is the philosopher emissary for the government of Sennaar, Mr. Kurz Pacha. Pacha is the bachelor cosmopolitan who wanders the earth for his country and philosophizes and makes fun of the plutocracy to their faces. The Potiphar set does not understand his jokes, but Pacha is more conscientious than a simple jokester. He tries hard, for example, to

explain to Mr. Potiphar that the excess in his household is not consonant with the stout business principles that made the money in the first
place. Pacha, like Curtis, is well traveled and knowledgeable, easy and
convivial, educated and well spoken—the ideal, in short, of a true best
society. He is the ambassador from the country of Good Sense.[22]

Curtis's other extensive *Putnam's* series was collected as *Prue and I.*
Leon H. Vincent describes it well: "*Prue and I* is a book of the sort Zola
used to hate—literature which 'consoles with the lies of the imagination.' . . . It is the idyll of contented obscurity, the poetic side of humble
life."[23] The narrator is a bookkeeper devoted to his plain life: he finds
complete satisfaction in a happy marriage and a rich imaginative life.
His wealth, his chateaux, his elaborate dinners are all creations of the
imagination and better than the real thing: "I am the guest who, for
the small price of invisibility, drinks only the best wines, and talks only
to the most agreeable people."[24] He tours the city in panoramic fashion,
peeping into carriages and windows and creating whole worlds from
the small details he sees. He "owns" the panorama because he controls
everything in his imagination. He is happiest at home with his wife,
and their existence is a vision of unruffled male privilege, where the
privilege is not wealth but dreamy speculation. *Prue and I* is a completely domesticized narrative panorama, with the encounter with the
city tamed because the city exists only as starting point for soothing,
occasionally melancholy, meditation. Zola would hate it because the
book in fact sees nothing. Asmodeus, the crippled old devil, has settled
down to genteel suppers by the fire.

In one *Prue and I* sketch, "Sea from Shore," the solitary clerk Titbottom has been seen "with . . . Bartleby, the scrivener" (85). The sketch
was first published in *Putnam's* in July 1854, six months after "Bartleby"
appeared. Bartleby and Titbottom "rather clubbed their loneliness than
made society for each other." Curtis is cutely having his New York
fictional world allude to Melville's, reminding his in-crowd readers of
Putnam's as venue for both, and showing us that "Bartleby" was enough
of a hit to be alluded to in this way. Curtis is also defining for us the
idiom in which *he*, a *Putnam's* editor, thinks "Bartleby" falls. Bartleby
and Titbottom are signs of the irremediable solitude that one encounters in the city. One sees people truly alone, people without any sort of
relationship like the one that "Prue and I" have. They are seen not as

victims of a particular social condition but as reminders of the *sentimental* in life, of what Curtis later calls "that mood of nameless regret and longing, which underlies all human happiness" (111). One of the most important of male privileges is melancholy, the dreamy perception of a not unpleasing sadness in the world.[25]

Putnam's and Curtis soon found in Republicanism a cause with greater dignity than simple *savoir faire* or male sentimental melancholy. In its first year of publication Parke Godwin attacked Franklin Pierce in "Our New President" (September 1853) and gained considerable notoriety, but by the troubled summer of 1856 *Putnam's* had become as activist as the *Tribune*. Godwin, and presumably Dana and Curtis, helped the magazine define an emerging New York political attitude on the issues that led the nation to Civil War. Godwin's "Our American Despotism" (on slavery), "Kansas—It Must Be Free," and "The Two Forms of Society—Which?" were fierce, calling the old political leaders "the flatulent old hacks, the queasy and prurient old bawds, who have so long had control of the old parties."[26] During the presidential campaign of 1856 Curtis himself became a leading propagandist for the Republican cause. The Republican party was itself in part a cultural product of the same educated elite of transformed New Englanders like Greeley and Briggs and Curtis that founded the *Tribune* and *Putnam's*. Curtis was instrumental in reinterpreting Emerson's "The American Scholar" for the 1850s undergraduate scholar, for the potential young Republican. His version, "The Duty of the American Scholar to Politics and the Times," given first at Wesleyan, made an analogy between the heroics at Thermopylae and the opportunities for bloody action in Kansas:

> And to-day, as the scholar meditates that deed [at Thermopylae], the air that steals in at his window darkens his study and suffocates him as he reads. Drifting across a continent, and blighting the harvests that gild it with plenty from the Atlantic to the Mississippi, a black cloud obscures the page that records an old crime, and compels him to know that freedom always has its Thermopylae, and that his Thermopylae is called Kansas.

Curtis did not imagine for those young men mild outdoor chores in Concord or leisurely cosmopolitan tours of Europe. Perhaps he can be forgiven for not imagining the scale of the slaughter.

Curtis's August 5 speech at Wesleyan was reprinted in the *Tribune* for August 16 and then separately as a pamphlet that sold in very large numbers. Charles Eliot Norton, Curtis's friend and literary executor, remembers at the end of the century that the speech brought Curtis "into prominence as a leader of public opinion." It "helped to define the political ideals, and to confirm the political principles of the educated youth of the land."[27] Kansas had allowed Curtis to discover high seriousness: he had cause and party and a *voice*: he remade himself from the "sugared Transcendentalist" to New York Republican.

The *Putnam's* Henry James remembered reading as a young man was the milder magazine. James recalled his "very young pleasure" in "the prose, as mild and easy as an Indian summer in the woods," of Donald G. Mitchell, Melville, and Curtis as he read their fiction in "the charming *Putnam*" of "the early fifties."[28] It is hard to think of "Bartleby" or "The Encantadas" as "mild and easy" prose, but Melville's *Putnam's* stories were not just popular with the young Henry James. Many reviews of the magazine attest to the contemporary critical success of his stories. When, for example, the *American Publisher's Circular and Literary Gazette* praised Melville's collection of *Putnam's* pieces, *The Piazza Tales*, in 1856, it said Melville's tales "were, in no small degree, instrumental in raising [*Putnam's*] to its present proud position—the best of all American monthlies."[29]

"Bartleby" and Lawyers' Stories   "Bartleby" is recognizably in a New York tradition of stories in which lawyers narrate their first-person encounters with extraordinary, isolated characters from the urban streets. In part the lawyers' stories use the narrative form that Washington Irving made immensely popular. A convivial man, often a bachelor, narrates a tale full of speculative interest, like Irving's "The Legend of Sleepy Hollow." The narrator *frames* the story; he narrates from a position outside the narrative proper, and his genial character is important. Knickerbocker's own sleepy speculation, the softness of the romantic eye, is contrasted with the acquisitive emotion of the aggressive capitalist—comically portrayed as Crane inside the story and as a dim-witted listener to the story in the frame—who would exchange the bountiful present for cash.

Melville and other inheritors of the Irving tradition in *Putnam's* and other 1850s magazines de-emphasize the frame narration but keep the genial narrator.[30] The genre is dependent on *non*astonished eyes. The narrators encounter people and events and are for a moment mildly amazed, discomforted, but their easeful confidence soon allows them to recover their balance. The stories are *about* the calm and balance of the imaginative point of view as a response to the encounter with a new set of conditions. One highly successful follower of Irving working in the early 1850s was Donald Grant Mitchell, and his books enjoyed the same enormous vogue as Curtis's. Mitchell's narrative persona was "Ik Marvell," and he dedicated his *Dream Life* (the title tells a good deal) to Washington Irving. The book, like so many mild narratives, argues for *feeling*: "Feeling has a higher truth in it, than circumstance."[31] Melville's narrator in "Bartleby" seems like the same kind of genial Irvingesque narrator as those in Curtis or Mitchell. He works in "the cool tranquillity of a snug retreat" doing a "snug business among rich men's bonds and mortgages and title-deeds" (14). He is a nonenergetic member of a profession with plenty of chances to observe human nature.

James A. Maitland's 1853 *The Lawyer's Story* is directly connected to Melville's "Bartleby." The first chapter of the novel was published as an advertisement in both the *New York Tribune* and *Times* for February 18, 1853, just at the time when Melville might have been thinking about "Bartleby." The novel begins with the lawyer's story of his remarkable clerk: "In the summer of 1843, having an extraordinary quantity of deeds to copy, I engaged, temporarily, an extra copying clerk, who interested me considerably, in consequence of his modest, quiet, gentlemanly demeanor, and his intense application to his duties."[32] The newspaper publication of the first part of Maitland's novel might have suggested directly to Melville a narrative structure and a theme he could use for "Bartleby." Like "Bartleby" *The Lawyer's Story* is a successful New York lawyer's first-person narration of his interest in and involvement with an unusual, "extra" scrivener. We never learn the name of either Maitland's lawyer or Melville's lawyer: the impression is that we would recognize it were it given. After he is engaged, Maitland's scrivener, named Adolphus Fitzherbert, copies with incessant industry. He uses Bartleby's famous verb (although not in its negative form) later in the first chapter when he begins the answer to a question with "I would prefer." He also has a characteristic that strongly suggests Bartleby: "the young man's countenance was shaded with constitutional or habitual melancholy—I judged the latter." (8) "Habitual" melancholy is more understandable than "constitutional" melancholy because it implies a knowable cause, a beginning and a history. But about his past life Adolphus is "reserved," and the lawyer does not at first press him. Bartleby's melancholy is, we know, more than "habitual" (if the terms are applicable at all), but Bartleby too declines "telling who he was, or whence he came, or whether he had any relatives in the world" (28).

When, after a few weeks, Maitland's lawyer no longer needs his extra scrivener's services, he lets him go. Adolphus, unlike Bartleby, leaves, but through a series of complicated coincidences the lawyer meets him again, and this time the lawyer actively investigates the mystery of Fitzherbert's melancholy and his origins. He shares with Melville's lawyer the charitable and confident nature the New York paradigm insists on and believes in the temporariness and ultimate explicability of human misery.

In the second chapter, which appeared only in the *Sunday Dispatch* and in the H. Long and Brother book, Adolphus's hopelessness and the lawyer's optimism clash dramatically. Adolphus announces that "hope for the future is dead within me," to which the lawyer responds, "I . . . urge you to view the matter differently. You are a young man: brilliant prospects may be before you; happiness may yet await you. . . . If not, recollect that others have suffered in a like degree, and if they have temporarily given way to despondency, it has not lasted forever" (27–29). The nonresisting, sentimental reader knows with the lawyer and the author that Adolphus's paralysis is a consequence of his separation from his family. This crisis is a standard one in the popular novel of the period, and *The Lawyer's Story* implicitly promises that a resolution will come in time and subsequent narrative event. Adolphus's hopelessness is the middle of a story, but its beginning and end will be known. And in fact the energetic lawyer discovers (after four hundred pages) that Adolphus is the lost heir to the Fitzherbert family fortune. Bartleby's motionlessness, however initially similar to Adolphus's, is without shape and end. Bartleby eludes analysis or resolution.[33]

Putnam's itself carried a very popular lost-heir story in its second issue (February 1853). Charles H. Hanson's "Is There a Bourbon Among Us?" attempted to prove that the lost dauphin had been reared in America by Native Americans and was living as a missionary by the name of Eleazar Williams.[34] All lost-heir stories insist that the tragedy is psychological: the "lost" person is separated from wealth and family and suffers in his solitude. The eventual reintegration with family (and money) is the chief sentimental event in nineteenth-century culture. The moment of meeting, or the moment of realization of who one's parents are, tells us of the importance of family as a bulwark against the confusions of the age. The lost-heir story also imagines that the legal complexities of the crisis require *professional* assistance. The unacknowledged heir, like so many others, needs a lawyer to sort through the complex paperwork so that his separation can end.

At the center of the lawyer story is an assumption about the nature of contemporary urban society. The lawyer—once necessary only for the aristocracy and then for the very wealthy—is more and more essential to middle-class life. The motion and change, the increasing disruptions, of urban domestic life overwhelm individuals and families. There is too much to interpret; there are tricks and traps set by experts in the new culture. The lawyer becomes an agent who represents the middle-class member in urban exchange. An article on "Doctors" in *Putnam's* in July 1853 and one on "Lawyers" in November 1856 explain these professionals as experts at "human nature" and in analysis and interpretation. They stand in for us in the intimacy of encounter with others. The doctor "is familiar with all the ills that flesh is heir to . . . he is admitted into sanctums where no other feet . . . enter. . . . Human nature, stripped of its conventionalities, lies exposed before him." "No profession," compared to the lawyer's, "affords better opportunities for the study of human nature; indeed, an acute insight of motives is a prerequisite of success."[35]

In June 1856, *Putnam's Monthly* published a story about a New York lawyer and a mysterious scrivener. Like Melville's 1853 story, "The Counterfeit Coin" is set in New York and is narrated by a genial, unaggressive lawyer: "Late one Saturday afternoon, in a certain December, I sat by a good sea-coal fire, in my office, trying to muster courage enough for an encounter with the cold winds and driving storm outside."[36] The narrator is counting the slim contents of his purse (his fees are small, he tells us), and the only coin he finds is a new half-eagle. Just at that moment there is a knock at the door. Because of the weather, the lawyer is surprised that anyone has come and is particularly taken aback to see a poorly clad young woman who has trudged through the storm from her "distant garret" to deliver some papers. She is a freelance law-copyist and she has completed her first job for the lawyer. The lawyer now has a small problem. He knows that the "trifling sum" he owes the law-copyist would be vital to her for food and fuel that very night, but the only money he has is his new half-eagle. She has no change. The lawyer continues to speculate to himself over her hard life and finally, charitably reckless of his own needs, gives her the half-eagle and asks her to come in on Monday to do more work for it.[37]

Monday comes and the young scrivener returns anxiously. The coin has been refused at her pawnbroker's: it is counterfeit! The lawyer has it tested and it is indeed a counterfeit, but he also knows it is not the same one he had given the woman on Saturday because it does not have a mark he had absently made on it with his penknife. The hapless woman is arrested, and the lawyer believes in her guilt. But soon a complicated series of events shows that the pawnbroker had expertly *switched* the true coin for a counterfeit and sent the scrivener away with it. The lawyer spends time arranging to prove this legally, and the truth comes out at the scrivener's trial. The pawnbroker is arrested, and the innocent woman is set free. The lawyer is chastened by the events, particularly by his initial failure to interpret them correctly. He ends by saying, "there is sadness on my heart, as I think of that scene in court, and I am garrulous no longer."

This *Putnam's* New York story of encounter is explicitly, like "Bartleby," a story of interpretation. The story presents a lawyer/narrator telling a story about a scrivener at which, as Bartleby's lawyer says, "good-natured gentlemen might smile, and sentimental souls might weep" (13). The lawyer encounters a woman whose poverty is not genteel like his own thinness of purse. At first the lawyer is full of sympathy, but then he thinks he has made a mistake, that the woman has tried to trick him and that she is therefore not what he thought she was. And then he is turned around again. In the lawyer's mind it comes out all right at the end and even proves to him how charitable and kind he himself is. One of his wealthy clients chides him for spending so much time on the indigent copyist's case: "Why, man, you would turn the whole fraternity [of lawyers] into a gang of knight-errants, roaming up and down Wall street seeking to set this crooked world straight again." The lawyer self-importantly responds, "And so they ought to be."

The lawyer is unnerved by his encounter with the law copyist first because of his sudden and intimate awareness of her terrible poverty and then by his complicity in her victimization. The language he uses to describe his discomfort is that of the supernatural. Her knock so startles him that he imagines a supernatural rapping; he thinks a ghost or worse has arrived. "Had spiritual rappings been invented then, I might have thought that Satan, his patience exhausted by this new development of wickedness, was about to foreclose the mortgage he is popularly supposed to hold on every member of our profession" (576). As it is, he just opens the door.

The copyist is strange to the point of being, to the lawyer, not quite human. She stands at the fireplace "as motionless as if she had been a carved pillar, placed there to support the mantel, against which her shoulder rested." She does not take pleasure in the flame; needful of its heat as she is, it does not cheer her. She is only barely resisting self-extinction. She "seemed to be bracing herself against an attraction that would draw her completely into the flame." The lawyer fancies that "if left to itself, her slender form would be drawn closer and closer, till, finally, it mingled with the flickering blaze, and, with it, passed into viewless air" (577).

The imaginative and literary conventions operating in "The Counterfeit Coin" are familiar in the Gothic tradition. We need only think of Poe's rapping, rapping at a chamber door to be reminded that knocking is a sign of another world that lies behind the manifest one and from which we may receive signs. The lawyer imagines the scrivener as having come into this world only briefly and being about to depart. The lawyer's "fancy," as he calls it, is only temporary. The scrivener—Alice Sumner is her name—does not come from another world; she is all too much from this one.

Like most of the mysterious characters New York lawyers encounter, but unlike Melville's Bartleby, the scrivener in "The Counterfeit

Coin" has a story the lawyer finally uncovers. She is not a lost heir but an ordinary woman in reduced circumstances. The story "need not be repeated here; it lacks, alas! the charm of novelty." It is "years of still deepening poverty—and yesterday . . . this poor child and her sick mother passed the long cold day without food or fire." The function of the story remains to reestablish a faith in explicability despite the difficulties of modern urban life. The ideological function is to show despite the complexities of interpretation, despite the lawyer's misreading of the scrivener, no fundamental change is necessary. Middle-class diligence and responsibility and charity will clear away the interpretive intricacies: the lawyer will see his way to the "truth" and use all his professional skill to defend the scrivener in court.

Dickens is, as always, the model in many contemporary minds. *Bleak House*, perhaps the era's best known fiction about urban life and lawyers, was being published serially as Melville was working on "Bartleby," and several scholars think that Melville had *Bleak House* in mind when he was composing "Bartleby."[38] Dickens's novel was the monthly feature of *Putnam's* chief competitor, *Harper's*, from April 1852 through October 1853. Dickens writes of London and not New York, but his influence was so immense in New York that American writers were always struggling with him, rejecting him and copying him at one and the same time. *Bleak House* provoked much reaction in New York and at *Putnam's*—the magazine that would not have published Dickens because he was not an American.

Putnam's takes up Dickens with respectful antagonism in "Characters in Bleak House," published in the same issue that ran the first installment of "Bartleby." For the writer of the article (perhaps Curtis?), Dickens's works live and die by their characters. His popularity is unmatched because he imagines so many. "As a delineator of persons, and the creator of distinct types of humanity, he stands second only to Shakspeare [*sic*]; while in the fertility of invention, he is fully the equal of the great poet of humanity." But Dickens doesn't write good stories; *Bleak House* is not a good story. The characters are at fault: "It is this permanency and fixedness of character which makes it necessary for Dickens to introduce new personages continually to keep up the interest of the reader; and it is his power of production that makes him careless of the conduct and consistency of his story." The characters are shown to us over and over in the same way, wearing the same clothes, using the same phrases, and presenting the same appearance. *Bleak House* shows Dickens at his best and worst at the same time.[39]

In Melville's "Bartleby," Turkey and Nippers are Dickensian characters. They are fixed and permanent: they wear the same clothes and do the same things, day after day. They and their lawyer boss exist in a small world balanced on each side by the eccentricities of their fixed characters. It is as if Melville were tossing off an example of a Dickensian routine to show that it is not difficult. He renders the stiflingly close office world of the lawyer and his scriveners in quick strokes. The physical details of the office and the mannerisms of the copyists all assume a heightened importance, as in *Bleak House*. Turkey, Nippers, and Ginger-Nut are as instantly knowable as their names imply. Bartleby arrives and is initially not so different from the character Nemo in *Bleak House*. Nemo, "no one," is at the heart of Dickens's mystery. Both characters are mysterious, silent, alone. Both suggest a world that lies alongside, and remains hidden from, the manifest one.

In *Bleak House* the obstacles to interpretation by the characters inside the book are monumental. The law case itself, *Jarndyce v. Jarndyce*, is lost in obscurity. Urban fog and labyrinthine complexities surround all the events in the novel; nothing is easy to understand. The mystery Nemo suggests is only revealed slowly through the expert and unprincipled investigations of the evil lawyer Tulkinghorn. That lawyer and the reader watch Lady Dedlock carefully, spotting early her envy for the simple domestic life she sees out her boudoir window at the keeper's lodge[40] and later her briefly unguarded reaction at seeing Nemo's copyist handwriting. The tiny bits of evidence accumulate, and interpretation of the main parts of the "hidden world" becomes possible. Bucket the detective, an expert in urban complications, assists the main parties and the reader, and we learn that however more sophisticated *Bleak House* is than, for example, James Maitland's *The Lawyer's Story*, at its heart is the terror and tragedy of the destruction of a (potential) happy middle-class family. Nemo and Lady Dedlock could have been Esther's Mum and Dad.

In *Bleak House* the individual is an object of knowledge. Nemo must be studied and understood. In "Bartleby" the individual Bartleby is also an object of knowledge. But the "world" of "Bartleby" is so closed and limited, so bounded in the quotidian, that the other world that lies alongside the manifest one seems completely inaccessible if it exists at all. Nothing can be *known* about Bartleby and, as the lawyer himself says, nothing can be *assumed* about him. He resists knowledge and assumption. Melville does what Donald Fanger says Dostoevsky does: he incorporates all the urban confusions into one ungraspable human personality that is "the ultimate repository of mystery."[41] The reader could only be helped by the lawyer/narrator, but his expertise, unlike that of the lawyers in the New York stories, is insufficient. We must see the reason for ourselves.

"Bartleby" is a "mutilated stump" in Melville's striking image for what great art is like. In *Pierre* the narrator attacks novels that end with clarification: "the countless tribes of common novels laboriously spin vails [*sic*] of mystery, only to complacently clear them up at last." These lesser works of art live in their promises to the reader to give a father to the bastard, a name to the phantom. These are the books that the literary marketplace insists Pierre write but he, afire with his mad idealism, refuses to. Great works, on the other hand, the "profounder emanations of the human mind," never end and never explain. They "never unravel their own intricacies, and have no proper endings; but in imperfect, unanticipated, and disappointing sequels (as mutilated stumps), hurry to abrupt intermergings with the eternal tides of time and fate."[42] Great art is never explicit and explanatory because truth is not directly visible. The mutilated stump suggests both our interpretive constrictions (no leg) and what might be imagined beyond those constrictions (the sense of the leg whole). Melville seems to think that there exists somewhere beyond our knowledge a Truth: it is just that we can have no access to it. In creating "Bartleby, the Scrivener: A Story of Wall Street" Melville becomes the self-conscious historian of the New York paradigm by cutting it off from its ordinary assurances and then by exploring its relationship to contemporary theological conjecture.

"I know where I am."
Bartleby

7

Key: "Bartleby, the Scrivener"

New York Words "Bartleby" substitutes for *Pierre*'s perceived excesses a limited narrator and an "inside narrative" of New York that shows us the walls, the movement, the food, the common usages that define a particular New York office. Like *Pierre*, "Bartleby" never names New York as its locale, but "Bartleby"'s failure to identify the city has an effect almost opposite that of *Pierre*. In *Pierre* the city is recognizably New York, but the omission of actual place-names is apparently intended to make readers understand Pierre's city as a mythic urban place appropriate for the destruction of youth's idealistic enthusiasms. In "Bartleby," on the other hand, while the parts of New York are named, the whole of it ("New York") is not. We know New York because of its own words, and most readily by its place-names: Wall Street, Broadway, Trinity Church. In order to read the story successfully, readers must assume New York from the geographical and cultural allusions that occur as they read. Places outside New York—Jersey City, Hoboken, Manhattanville, Astoria, Sing–Sing—are named and made to seem remote, and since we know that they are not really very far away, we see how limited the story's locale is. The provincialism of the New York point of view is a long tradition: even Sing Sing (since 1901 more respectably called "Ossining") is after all only thirty miles "up the river."

The narratives in the New York convention to which "Bartleby" belongs also use this metonymic device to create the sense of the inside story. Knowing New York from its parts is a game we can all be in on, and this is as true now when our national magazine *The New Yorker* refers without explanation to SoHo as it was when the national *Putnam's* referred to the Five Points. In "Bartleby" the same device is used, but the effect is quite different. The New York place-names "mean" New York in the same metonymic way, but the extraordinary limitation of the lawyer/narrator's field of vision makes the city place-names themselves seem remote from the law office. In "Bartleby" it is not just Hoboken that is alien and far away but also the streets outside the door. During one of the lawyer's infrequent descriptions of time spent away from the office, he tells us that while walking at the corner of Broadway and Canal Street he was so absorbed in thinking about Bartleby that he thought for an instant that a street conversation he overheard about a political candidate was about Bartleby.[1]

Some of the New York words in "Bartleby" are local enough to require explanation for the twentieth-century reader. Non–New Yorkers might have difficulty recognizing The Tombs as the New York City Prison whose Egyptian Revival architecture gave it its nickname. (The suggestiveness of the word was so powerful that it survives today as the nickname for the current city prison on Centre Street even though the original Egyptian-style prison, and other non-Egyptian buildings that replaced it, are long gone.) In reading "Bartleby," we must know that the "Directory" refers to the contemporary book of New York addresses, that John Jacob Astor was the prototype of new wealth in New York. We probably need more scholarly intervention to know that the legal system of Chancery and its Masters of Chancery like the narrator were abolished by the new New York State Constitution in 1848, or that the murder of Adams by Colt was a notorious New York office murder, or that the forger Monroe Edwards was a well-known criminal personality in New York.[2] The scholarship educates us on the particulars—explaining, for example, that John C. Colt killed Samuel Adams in his office in 1842 and committed suicide in The Tombs before he was to be executed—and our increased knowledge of Melville's handling of New York detail shows us how insistently local the created world of "Bartleby" is.

The two copyists and the office boy have New York names. The lawyer tells us "these may seem names, the like of which are not usually found in the Directory. In truth they were nicknames" (15). "Ginger Nut," the office boy, is named, as the story explains, after the New York term for the "small, flat, round, and very spicy" (18) cakes that the scriveners frequently sent him out for. "Turkey," the story does not explain, is New York slang of the period for drunkenness. The *Dictionary of Americanisms* cites the New York comic weekly the *Lantern*: "Him shall no Oysters from the Stews of Sliddon, nor Pork and Beans, so fat . . . arouse, till he's got rid [of] that Turkey in his hat." Or, also from the *Dictionary of Americanisms*, from Durivage: "it's a turkey I've got on, hiccuped Tom Links, as he noticed a singular disposition on the part of the *pave* to rise up and impede his progress." The turkey is something one has on one's back when one is drunk—analogous, perhaps, to the more recent but now also dated usage "he's got a monkey on his back" for drug addiction. And, to make a guess, to tie a turkey on one's back is perhaps the New York ancestor of our "to tie one on," meaning to get drunk.[3]

The name for the lawyer's other clerk, "Nippers," is probably also New York slang of the period, although the evidence is not as clear as it is with "Turkey." One kind of nippers is defined in chapter ninety-four of *Moby-Dick* as a word applied by whalers to "a short firm strip of tendinous stuff cut from the tapering part of Leviathan's tail," but in English and American cant "nippers" was a word for a thief or a pickpocket, or for handcuffs, or (most appropriately for "Bartleby") for "one who goes in for sharp practices." The metaphor is "nipping, grasping or squeezing a man more than the bargain purports" (*A Dictionary of Slang, Jargon & Cant*). Melville's "Nippers" is close to that. I imagine a closer New York fit, that "Nippers" is New York slang for the shady pseudolawyer who works, like Melville's character, on the steps of The Tombs.

Another example of the extreme locality of the story's New York words is Nippers's description of Turkey's money going "chiefly for red ink" (17). This is a pun on the red ink one uses for corrections but also the "red ink" one drinks. *The Dictionary of the Underworld* and *The Dictionary of Slang and Unconventional English* include "red ink," the former giving it as American "low slang, not cant, for red wine." Another word, "luny," an adjectival form of "lunatic" that Ginger Nut uses to describe Bartleby (22), is not cited in any dictionary as appearing earlier than 1869, making its appearance in the 1853 "Bartleby" significantly early and perhaps therefore another example of local slang being deployed by Melville.

I think Melville is using New York words, along with other devices, to sharpen and particularize the New York scene in "Bartleby." He writes "Bartleby" in a style he knows the editors of *Putnam's* will appreciate, but he also discovers in that New York convention a way of demythologizing its very assurances. The convention in the hands of George Curtis and others presented the "new," the initially extraordinary urban "other," in ways that allowed it eventually to be normalized. The slangy newsboy went to school to learn proper English, the starving children were adopted, the wild street people were calmed by religion. All joined or were made to join the regnant point of view of the middle class. The mythology that everything is explicable and that charitable interest solves every problem draws the new into itself and absorbs its strangeness. The initially alien words and scene become metaphoric in the sense that when they are decoded they come to stand for items within the ideological system that explains them. The hot-corn girl is the potential middle-class daughter, the melancholy clerk is a lost son, and both will gain meaning from the narrator's speculative attention. All is explicable.

In Melville's hands, the New York convention is recognizable but the outcome and effects are very different. Melville's use of the New York words forces the New York particulars away from metaphor and myth and explanation. The scene is identified so intensively locally that it remains local, particular. It is suggestive, certainly, but it is never explanatory, and this effect is created in part because the New York words themselves are so particular. In "Bartleby," the New York lawyer depends on his "own astonished eyes," and we in turn can only depend on the lawyer and not on myth. And the readers must try, as Bartleby "indifferently" suggests, to see the reason for ourselves.

"There was something about Bartleby" Bartleby's lawyer sympathizes with what he assumes is Bartleby's hopelessness, but he finds no way to understand what the "problem" is. Bartleby's silence shows how dependent on reaction, interest, talk, and response interpretation is. The lawyer writes about Bartleby not to show a lawyerly knowledge of human nature or a successful interpretation but to tell us about the strangest scrivener he ever knew. Like Alice Sumner's lawyer, Bartleby's expresses the strangeness with the language of the supernatural. He is, however, less self-consciously aware of the kind of language he is using than is the lawyer in "The Counterfeit Coin."

The lawyer indicates how odd Bartleby is by portraying him metaphorically as a ghost or a dead person. Bartleby appears from behind a screen "like a very ghost, agreeably to the laws of magical invocation" (25). At one point Bartleby is not Bartleby, he is "the apparition of Bartleby" (26). Bartleby has a "cadaverously gentlemanly *nonchalance*" (27), and his triumph over the lawyer is also a "cadaverous triumph" (35). When the lawyer comes into his office on a Sunday after having first been kept out because Bartleby's key was in the lock, he discovers that Bartleby is no longer there. But the phrase for Bartleby's absence is suggestive of a ghost: "Bartleby was not to be seen" (27). The lawyer once imagines walking into his office and "pretending not to see Bartleby at all . . . walk straight against him as if he were air" (35). Later, Bartleby is again an "apparition" (38), and the lawyer says "what does conscience say I *should* do with this man, or rather ghost?" (38). Bartleby is always near nonhumanity, from the time he first appears to the time he dies.

Bartleby is also nonhuman because he doesn't move. Like Alice Sumner or Adolphus Fitzherbert he is "motionless," but there is an extra edge. He is motionless when he *arrives*—a difficult feat for ordinary mortals: "a motionless young man one morning, stood upon my office threshold, the door being open" (19). When the lawyer calls Bartleby to come to him, Bartleby "appeared standing," and after preferring not to do as the lawyer asks, he "gently disappeared" (21). He is "a perpetual sentry in the corner" (23), he throws himself into "standing revery" with "great stillness" and "unalterableness" (26). His is a "long-continued motionlessness" (29). When told he must be conducted to The Tombs prison he acquiesces in an "unmoving" (42) way.

Mortals move, and they eat: Bartleby lives without dining. At first he "gorge[s]" (19) on documents, but the lawyer never sees him go to dinner (23); he never sees or knows of him eating anything other than ginger nuts (23); he does not dine in The Tombs even though the lawyer has paid off "Mr. Cutlets" (44).[4] Bartleby does not move or eat or read or have any family or friends or conversation or interest in the world around him. As the lawyer says, there seems not to be "any thing ordinarily human about him" (21). Melville handles these details expertly, carefully showing us a narrator using language that he knows is suggestive of worlds other than the manifest one but at the same time holding back from making imaginative leaps in interpreting the scrivener.

The lawyer does let us see the hints he has that something more might be known, something very hard to define. The comically vague word "something" is one way he tries to name some of the fugitive suggestions. I put the word in italics:

> But there was *something* about Bartleby that not only strangely disarmed me, but in a wonderful manner touched and disconcerted me. (21)

> There was *something* about Bartleby that forbade the supposition that he would by any secular occupation violate the proprieties of the day [Sunday]. (27)

> He seemed profoundly sleeping. *Something* prompted me to touch him. I felt his hand, when a tingling shiver ran up my arm and down my spine to my feet. (45)

Or, in similarly helpless language:

> *Somehow*, the things I had seen disqualified me for the time from church-going. (29)

The lawyer cannot help knowing that Bartleby's extraordinariness is powerful and suggestive. He catches the hints, but he carefully keeps himself from too vivid speculation. At one moment he says that "Presentiments of strange discoveries hovered round me" (28), but these he calls "sad fancyings—chimeras, doubtless, of a sick and silly brain" (28). The lawyer always calls himself back from any speculation about the supernatural.

The language the lawyer uses starts to resonate with the reader in a way that it does not with the lawyer. Again, the italics are mine.

Bartleby was one of those *beings* of whom nothing is ascertainable, except from *the original sources*. (13)

[Bartleby] had declined telling who he was, or whence he came, or whether he had any relatives *in the world*. (28)

"What *earthly* right [the lawyer asks Bartleby] have you to stay here? Do you pay any rent? Do you pay my taxes?" (35)

Readers of "Bartleby" recognize supernatural implications that the lawyer does not and entertain the possibility that Bartleby is not of this world, but that does not mean that they will be any more successful than the lawyer in interpreting what Bartleby is or represents. The hints are very faint, and our faith in our interpretive superiority might simply lead us to follies greater than that of the lawyer's unexcited straightforwardness. We do well to remember how "silent" the text is. H. Bruce Franklin is still right when he writes that if we "read 'Bartleby' well, we must first realize that we can never know who or what Bartleby is, but that we are continually asked to guess who or what he might be."[5]

Many readers have solved the problem of the story's suggestiveness by thinking that Bartleby is a Christ figure. The story itself quotes from Job and from John 13:31–35 ("A new commandment give I unto you, that ye love one another"), and readers have identified several parallels between Christ's story and Bartleby's. The ritualistic formulation of the scene in which Bartleby is taken to The Tombs is, for example, like the description of Christ's trip to his crucifixion in Luke 23:27. The lawyer, like Peter, denies Bartleby three times: "the man you allude to is nothing to me"; "I know nothing about him"; and "in vain I persisted that Bartleby was nothing to me" (39–40). H. Bruce Franklin thinks the heart of the biblical allusiveness in "Bartleby" is Matthew 25:34–45 where Christ says "Verily I say unto you, Inasmuch as ye have done it unto one of the least of these my brethren, ye have done it unto me." Bartleby is Christ-figure because he is the least of these my brethren.[6]

The modern critical idea that Bartleby is Christ's representative is a way of thinking about the interpretive problem that nineteenth-century liberal Christians would have liked. It is consonant with their happy response to the most important theological issue of the age, the construction of a new Christology. As I note in Chapter 4, the Christology that was accepted decisively in the nineteenth century was the view that all doctrines of Christ must start from and be grounded in human historical existence. The effort was to construct Christology "from below" rather than "from above." The old question was, since Jesus is divine, how could he be man? The new question was, since Jesus was human, what does it mean to speak of his divinity?

The movement toward this new view of Christ begins with Friedrich Schleiermacher, who argued that theology had to start from, articulate, and interpret a subjective view of the religious object. As Claude Welch has it, "[a]ny significant speech about God had to be talk in which the self was concerned, talk about God as the object of devotion, or of utter dependence, or of passionate concern and fidelity." Schleiermacher's "creative breakthrough . . . was his fresh interpretation of religion in its own integrity, according to its fundamental intuition and its locus in feeling or in the immediacy of human existence, [and] . . . a new possibility for understanding religion was opened." Theology does not then have any objective knowledge "but only this relational knowing of God as present."[7]

Hegel also sought to point a way beyond both the Enlightenment and religious orthodoxy by showing that religion is a necessary part of human experience.

In Hegel's system religion is the highest stage in the unfolding of Spirit, in the final development of subjectivity called "Absolute Spirit." Christianity is Absolute Religion. A new and final stage, the religion of freedom. Christianity is the religion of revelation (*offenbare Reli-*

gion), that is, positive religion in the sense that it has come to men from outside, with all its historically contingent character, as everything that exists for consciousness must come in an external way. Yet truth must become internal, rational, and essential, so that consciousness of the truth becomes identical with self-consciousness.[8]

Anything that has no conceptual relationship is simply nothing. The concept and the object are united. Christianity is the new and final stage in the process of the unfolding of the spirit, the final development of subjectivity. The dynamic unity Hegel sought is realized in Christianity and its human and divine love.

In the nineteenth century, liberal theologians became heavily influenced by these ideas, and even when they did not accept them completely, they formed the terms of the religious discourse of the period. David Friedrich Strauss added immensely to the debate (and the furor) by his "criticism" of the New Testament. His enormous book *Das Leben Jesu* (1835) identified in great detail the mythical elements in the Gospels and tried to show how those elements became attached to the historical Jesus. For Strauss, the strategy was a deeply religious one. He thought that giving up the historical reality of the narratives made it possible to preserve the absolute truth they expressed. One needed to abandon the supposition that the *idea* of the unity of God and man would manifest itself in only one person: it would not "lavish all its fullness on one exemplar and . . . be niggardly towards all others."[9]

The idea can appear in the street. God is related to us. More than that, it sounds as if he exists only if we find him in *feeling*. It is certainly easy to see how an emergent bourgeoisie flourishing in the new market economy in the United States would welcome a religious discourse based on the relational availability of God. The ideas were conveyed to them by American theologians like Horace Bushnell and their own ministers—like New York's Reverend Edwin Chapin. God and Meaning can be found in the street, and all—even the newly prosperous— had easy access. No membership in an old elite was necessary.

However elegant the theological thrusts are here, it is easy to sympathize with the conservatives who saw all this as a very convenient sort of God to have around or the radicals who thought that maybe this wasn't religion at all. Ludwig Feuerbach, for example, thought the new theology simply undid the need for theology. If "the divine is the human and the human is the divine," then one should simply study people. Feuerbach's principal aim was to change "the friends of God into friends of man, believers into thinkers, worshipers into workers, candidates for the other world into students of this world."[10]

As earlier chapters of this book have explained, the appearance of tests for Christianity on the streets of the city—in encounters with the "other"—was a staple of New York stories. For the lawyer/narrator of "The Counterfeit Coin" or Elizabeth Oakes Smith in her *The Newsboy*, the appearance of the melancholy scrivener or the smart-talking newsboy tests the quality of middle-class Christianity. More, it tests how advanced the Christianity is. The new Christian, for whom Christology starts "from below," should realize in the act of encounter that the person encountered can be "Christ" or "Christ figure" in the sense that the Christian *idea* can repose in any person on the street as well as it could in the historical Jesus. Narratives of the encounter are often stories of the light of that realization breaking over the middle-class person. The realization is difficult because the scrivener or the newsboy seems initially so alien. The encounter is also, I have suggested, an ideological expression of the need to preserve faith in the ability of the middle-class individual to explicate the complex and "mysterious" urban experiences. A simple self-justification was not, I hasten to add, what Feuerbach had in mind when he said that Christians should become "students of the world." For him a student would see the determining human social relations.

If Bartleby is Christ or Christ figure, if there are sufficient hints of that that we readers can recognize, and if the lawyer does *not* recognize these hints, then we could argue that the lawyer is an inadequate Christian. He does not recognize in his feeling the supernatural meanings of the Christ in his office; he does not, at least, do enough: he is insufficiently Christian. He represents a modern ethical pragmatism that Melville had Plotinus Plinlimmon articulate in *Pierre*. Plinlimmon contrasts "chronometricals," based on God's time or code, and "horologicals," based on society's. Plinlimmon thinks a "virtuous expediency" is the "highest desirable or attainable earthly excellence": that "in things terrestrial (horological) a man must not be governed by ideas celestial (chronometrical)."[11] Bartleby's lawyer is a horological man.[12]

Much of this kind of speculation about "Bartleby" is very helpful, but none of it is quite right. Bartleby is not Christ or Christ figure, and the lawyer is not fully explained by "virtuous expediency." "Bartleby" is perhaps the story of a god, but it is not Christ or Christ figure. Bartleby is on the one hand not *full* enough to be Christ and on the other not *empty* enough to be a Christ figure. The lawyer's story is instead a kind of new New Testament with a visiting god different from that envisioned in Matthew, Mark, Luke, and John.

Certainly we think (faintly) of the New Testament Christ story as we read "Bartleby" and it is the parallels, not the identities, between that story and Bartleby's that suggest ways to understand Melville's story. But Bartleby is not Christ come again: he is not full enough for that. Bartleby's arrival *is* described by the lawyer, unselfconsciously, as an "advent" (15), but there is no Epiphany, Sermon on the Mount, Last Supper, Crucifixion, Resurrection. Or if those things are represented in the story, they are such faint shadows of their New Testament versions as to be wholly different, even wholly opposite. Whatever Bartleby is, he does not break bread with humanity. There is nothing ordinarily human about Bartleby, nothing knowable, the way there is about Christ, who did break bread with humanity and who was seen and known and recorded. Christ spoke in parables, he was difficult to understand, but he spoke.

Bartleby is not a Christ *figure* either because he is not empty enough to be a Christ figure of the nineteenth-century sentimental kind. The many Christ figures of nineteenth-century sentimental urban literature were empty in the sense that they were convenient repositories of the fantasies of their creators. The figures were isolated from their social contexts and could then seem to be the missing children of nineteenth-century domestic religion. Bartleby is too full to be this Christ figure in that there is in him enormous force, and any ideas that the lawyer (or we) use to explain him, to fill him up, seem hopelessly insufficient. Bartleby, like Jackson or the dying family in *Redburn*, cannot be brought into a sentimental, bourgeois "reality."

"My heart in my mouth"   When the lawyer thinks he is seeing Bartleby for the last time, he unintentionally defines himself perfectly as the charitable and sentimental modern man: "I re-entered [the office], with my hand in my pocket—and—and my heart in my mouth" (39). The heart is too readily in the mouth, with the easy speech of the sentimental man, and the hand too readily in the pocket, with the easy small change of charity, for any true understanding. But for all his horological faults, the lawyer does finally offer the most the nineteenth-century sentimental person can offer: "will you go home with me now—not to my office, but my dwelling . . . Come, let us start now, right away." Bartleby responds: "No: at present I would prefer not to make any change at all" (41).

What we are (dimly) to understand, I think, is that Bartleby is a new god who is appearing on earth. Even "on earth" is far too grand: appearing in a lawyer's office on Wall Street is more like it. He may be Christ come again but come in such a different way that we might as well think of him as a different god. He is so ununderstandable as to make the suggestion that he is a new god tentative, not demonstrable. His life in the office and The Tombs parallels Christ's life in some faint ways and because of those parallels we—unlike the lawyer—can imagine his existence. But he is barely here: we don't really understand. We can only imagine in a way that the lawyer cannot. His heart is in his mouth, and he is an image of the new superficial man, the "sugared" narrator of the *Putnam's* New York stories. He is untouched by woe, by any deep tragedy or high thoughts. He lives in the modern world where god is defined "from below."

If we readers have difficulty interpreting some of Christ's biblical parables, we have hugely more trouble with Bartleby precisely because he gives no sermons. There is no help, no explanatory apostles other than the lawyer, who doesn't understand what he is seeing even though he was there. The lawyer is the new god's Matthew, Mark, Luke, and John—he is his Saint Peter, his doubting Thomas, his Saint Paul. Bartleby's Sermon on the Mount simply turns it back on us all: "Do you not see the reason for yourself?" (32). Just at the moment Bartleby might be having his Last Supper, when he would break his divinity into bread and wine for humanity, Bartleby tells the lawyer, "I prefer not to dine to-day" (44). His other statements in The Tombs prison, "I know you . . . and I want nothing to say to you" and "I know where I am" (43), are completely unlike Christ's statements of forgiveness and suffering from the cross. When the lawyer touches him after death a

"tingling shiver ran up my arm and down my spine to my feet" (45),
but there is no proof for the not-even-doubting Thomas.

The Chola Widow   In his journal of 1857 of his visit to Patmos, where
Saint John preached, Melville is disappointed in the way the physical
place does not read of transcendence, does not speak of God the way
that John once did there.

> Patmos is pretty high, & peculiarly barren looking. No inhabitants.—
> Was here again afflicted with the great curse of modern travel—
> skepticism. Could no more realize that St: John had ever had revela-
> tions here, than when off Juan Fernandez, could beleive [sic] in
> Robinson Crusoe according to De Foe. When my eye rested on arid
> heigth [sic], spirit partook of the barreness [sic].—Heartily wish Nie-
> buhr & Strauss to the dogs.—The deuce take their penetration & acu-
> men. They have robbed us of the bloom. If they have undeceived any
> one—no thanks to them.[13]

The "Historical Note" of the Northwestern-Newberry edition of the
Journals calls this comment on Niebuhr (the German historian Barthold
Niebuhr) and Strauss "intellectual petulance," a "deprecation of Niebuhr and Strauss for destroying the romance of myth" (185). It is rather
more than that. Melville thinks Niebuhr and Strauss deserve no thanks
because they have disconnected the truth of Christianity from the historical reality of Jesus. They and the liberal theologians have "freed"
religious truth from the shackles of history and physical space, but they
have also, Melville thinks, taken from religious truth its "bloom" in
history. And if there is no historical bloom, then our spirits partake of
the barrenness of the stony cities and we are left to wonder which of
the many human ideas is "absolute truth" and which is absolute false-
hood. The new god is one that is not there, or is hardly there: he is a
god not knowable because he is in the street with the crowd.[14]

What is exciting about the New Testament's God is not only that
he appears on earth in human form but that he allows ordinary human
beings to recognize him. It happens again and again. John recognizes
him as he baptizes him, the Apostles recognize him as they decide to
follow him, and so does the woman at Samaria and all who witness his
miracles. Christ is God coming on an ass, but some of the humans

who saw him *knew*. The New Testament encounter is what gives the nineteenth-century charity visitor a model for understanding what she is doing. She is recognizing in the slum child the representation of "truth": she needs no aid other than her own feeling. Melville turns this around: if there is no historical manifestation, then there may indeed be a god in the street, but it is a god who engenders, in the rush of the crowd, no feeling at all.

The threat of heavenly silence is always in Melville's mind. In *Pierre* the narrator talks about the difference between the Bible and the world. From the Sermon on the Mount flows "an inexhaustible soul-melting stream of tenderness and loving-kindness; and [enthusiastic youths] leap exulting to their feet, to think that the founder of their holy religion gave utterance to sentences so infinitely sweet and soothing as these; sentences which embody all the love of the Past, and all the love which can be imagined in any conceivable Future" (207). But those youths, like Pierre, find that the practical world is full of lies, "soaking with lies." The youths try, and fail, to find the "Talismanic Secret" that will reconcile the world with their own souls. They find, and then reject, those who claim to have found the secret, like Plato and Spinoza and Goethe "and many more [who] belong to this guild of self-impostors, with a preposterous rabble of Muggletonian Scots and Yankees, whose vile brogue still the more bestreaks the stripedness of their Greek or German Neoplatonical originals" (208).

And then, less chaotically, the narrator speaks directly of God's silence: "That profound Silence, that only voice of our God, which I before spoke of; from that divine thing without a name, those impostor philosophers pretend somehow to have got an answer; which is absurd, as though they should say they had got water out of stone; for how can a man get a Voice out of Silence?" (208). Silence is the only voice of "that divine thing without a name." This god too is like the god of the liberal theologians, a god who speaks only to individuals—the impostor philosophers, each of whom proceeds to announce his view of the secret as if it were undisputed truth.

At the same time as Melville must have been working on "Bartleby"—in early 1853—he was probably working on the "Agatha" project that Hershel Parker thinks may have developed into a unpublished book called "The Isle of the Cross."[15] Melville had written to

Nathaniel Hawthorne on August 13, 1852, telling him that he had recently visited Nantucket and there made the acquaintance of a New Bedford lawyer (probably John H. Clifford) with whom he discussed the island women's "great patience, & endurance, & resignedness" in the face of the long absences of their seafaring husbands. The lawyer then told him a story that awakened "the most lively interest" in Melville as material to be worked up into fiction. Melville tells Hawthorne that he thinks the story of Agatha Robertson's patience and endurance after her desertion by her husband "seems naturally to gravitate" to Hawthorne's interests and suggest his friend make use of it, attaching a copy of an entry from Clifford's journal. Melville's recommendations on how to handle the story are elaborate enough to make it obvious to even the least thoughtful letter reader that Melville was unconsciously asking to be encouraged to write the story himself. Hawthorne finally does that and sends back the journal entry.

Clifford knew the story of Agatha's long suffering because of his investigation of events surrounding a contested will. James Robertson was shipwrecked off the coast of Pembroke, Massachusetts, where Agatha Hatch was then living. The sailor, "hospitably entertained and cared for" by the young woman, married her. Two years later Robertson left his pregnant wife to look for work, and for seventeen years Agatha never heard from him. He then returned, gave Agatha and her daughter money, and went off again. Agatha understood then that her husband was living in St. Louis with a second wife, but apparently she saw no point in exposing him. She and her daughter Rebecca did, however, lay claim to Robertson's property after he and his second wife died.

What interested lawyer Clifford so much was that the story was a "striking instance of long continued & uncomplaining submission to wrong and anguish on the part of a wife, which made her in my eyes a heroine." When Melville imagines the story itself, he makes the most suggestions to Hawthorne about the potential first scene: young Agatha walking along the beach and seeing the shadow of a sheep on a cliff above and behind her. There "in strange & beautiful contrast," Melville says, "we have the innocence of the land placidly eyeing the malignity of the sea." In his suggestions for the character of the deserting husband, Melville mentions Hawthorne's own story, "Wakefield," in which a London husband leaves on an impulse and lives in the next street for twenty years, although Melville thinks the "Wakefield" example and the Agatha one "rudely contrast." In a letter written after November 25, 1852, Melville says that with Hawthorne's permission he will make use of the "Isle of Shoals" they discussed as far as the "name" (title?) goes. Hawthorne had visited the Isles of Shoals with Franklin Pierce between September 3 and 16 of that year and probably discussed with Melville the islands' stories of women waiting for departed sailors. Celia Thaxter later collected the folklore of the rocky and barren islands off the coast of Portsmouth in *Among the Isles of Shoals* (1873), and she includes a tale of an island ghost, a woman the narrator sees when he rows to the island that is apparently Appledore. The ghost is fascinating to the narrator. Her only words are the sentence: "He *will* come again."[16]

One cannot help thinking that whatever the fate of "The Isle of the Cross," Melville's "Agatha" writing may have been part of what became "The Encantadas; or, Enchanted Isles," published in *Putnam's* in March, April, and May 1854.[17] The series is organized as a description of the Galapagos Islands in ten separate sketches, and it has a format one might easily imagine the Agatha project (with its discussions with Hawthorne about the Isles of Shoals) having evolved to— with the first sketch describing the isles at large and the rest individual islands. "Sketch Eighth" of "The Encantadas," "Norfolk Isle and the Chola Widow," is most easily imagined as part of "The Isle of the Cross" project in that the principal image for Norfolk Island is the "rude cross" (155) that the Chola Widow Hunilla has put up as memorial for her dead husband, Felipe.

The island cross in "Norfolk Isle and the Chola Widow" is not a sign of Christian faith triumphant over death: it is a "cross of withered sticks; the dry, peeled bark still fraying from it; its transverse limb tied up with rope, and forlornly adroop in the silent air" (160). The island cross is the sign of human endurance through the sometimes unspeakable suffering that Hunilla has endured. It is Christianity imagined as *just* the suffering on the cross, without the religion's radiating assurances of transcendence: Christ as man crucified. Melville's narrator worships the defeated but enduring Hunilla: "Humanity, thou strong thing, I worship thee, not in the laurelled victor, but in this vanquished one" (157). It seems to me quite possible that this story was in some way part of the "Agatha" project, particularly since we can probably name the "Agatha" project "The Isle of the Cross." It shares with lawyer Clifford the original interest in uncomplaining submission to wrong and anguish. This same submission makes Hunilla a heroine, although what she suffers is far more than Agatha. On an ordinary day on the innocent land she looked out to the malignant sea and was forced to watch the waves overturn her husband and brother's boat and drown them. She was then completely alone on Norfolk Island for we know not how long, and she suffered not only total isolation but also endured horrors that the narrator will not name for us—that we think have to do with whale crews that stopped at the island.

What the "Agatha" story suggests, and the "Norfolk Isle and the Chola Widow" enacts, is the theme that "uncomplaining submission" is the admirable human reaction to the horror of a world in which God is silent. "Bartleby," written at approximately the same time as this work, does not portray submission. The lawyer doesn't understand enough of the heavenly silence to submit, and Bartleby—whether god or not—does not submit. But heavenly silence is the theme of Melville's New York story just as much as it is of the Encantadas sketch. The prison turnkey asks the lawyer, "Are you looking for the silent man?" (44).

In the Old Testament the essential word is "obey." In the New Testament it is "love." In "Bartleby, the Scrivener," it is "prefer." The lawyer's office has gotten "the word":

> "With submission, sir," said [Turkey], "yesterday I was thinking about Bartleby here, and I think that if he would but prefer to take a quart of good ale every day . . ."
> "So you have got the word too," said I, slightly excited.
> "With submission, what word, sir," asked Turkey, respectfully crowding himself into the contracted space behind the screen, and by so doing, making me jostle the scrivener. "What word, sir?"
> "I would prefer to be left alone here," said Bartleby, as if offended at being mobbed in his privacy.
> "*That's* the word, Turkey," said I—"*that's* it."
> "Oh, *prefer*? oh yes—queer word. I never use it myself. But, sir, as I was saying, if he would but prefer—"

"Turkey," interrupted I, "you will please withdraw."
"Oh certainly, sir, if you prefer that I should." (31)

The comedy of the office's unknowing adoption of Bartleby's word is a comedy on the theme of a new *Logos*. Again, this is a faint parallel to New Testament thought, to the Christian assertion of the word of God made flesh. In Bartleby a word is made flesh, all right, but the word is only the word of an individual's isolated, and apparently momentary, inclination—his preference. There is no eternity, no transcendence in the word that this god brings. And in the lawyer there is no apostolic proclamation, no awareness that the word is the Word. We, not Turkey or the lawyer, catch the implications of the "word." We catch suggestions, not proof.

The word "prefer" is Melville's perfect choice. Bartleby is the god of preferences, the god of that office. He brings the word that is most appropriate to a people who live entirely horologically, entirely without imagination of the supernatural blooming in history. This way of thinking is also the beginning of an explanation of what is hardest to understand about the story, and that is why it stresses again and again that Bartleby *belongs* in the office. Bartleby does not come, he "appears." He never leaves the office, he in fact lives in the office. When asked to leave, he doesn't. When the lawyer moves his whole office, Bartleby stays. It is as if he were always there. Most suggestively, Bartleby mysteriously has the key to the office even though no one gave him one. The key enables the scrivener to lock the door from the inside on the Sunday the lawyer chooses to visit the office. Bartleby says he is deeply engaged and asks the lawyer to walk around the block. While he does so, the lawyer tries to imagine what Bartleby could be *doing* in the office on Sunday—not copying, nothing immoral, nothing "secular" (27).

The key Bartleby has is a faint parallel to the "key" to the house of David, the keys to the kingdom that Jesus gives Peter, the keys that justify the whole practice of the Christian faith after Christ's death.[18] Compared to the subtlety of the rest of the story, Melville's "key" is a heavy-handed touch (like the interpretive "knot" presented to Delano and the reader in "Benito Cereno"). Bartleby has the key to what we don't understand, and he is deeply engaged doing something analogous

to "His Father's business" in the office on that holy day. What is striking is that this means that the New York office itself is the holy place
of this new New Testament of silence. The key to the kingdom is the
ordinary key to a lock in an ordinary door. Bartleby isn't missing or
lost: he *belongs* in that place for the time he is alive. The office is his
place. Bartleby is our god after all, the god of the nineteenth-century
nontranscendental ordinary encounter. He is the god of nontranscen-
dence.

One interpretative temptation is to say that Bartleby does not exist
as the (new) Christ because the lawyer does not recognize him as such.
This fits the nineteenth-century liberal theologians' notion that the god-
head exists in the *feeling* of the Christian individual. If there is no
religious emotion, then the Christ does not appear.[19] Since the lawyer is
so horological a man, one interpretation might go, he cannot recognize
Bartleby as God and therefore God does not appear. But this is not
quite it either. The lawyer *is* the sentimental man with his heart in his
mouth. It is not enough to think that the lawyer doesn't see Bartleby as
a (new) Christ and therefore he doesn't exist. He does exist and the
lawyer doesn't see him. We readers do see him—very faintly—and only
if we are alert. He exists apart from our perception of him: even if there
is no "bloom," the god is there. We do not understand, but Bartleby
knows where he is.

PART FOUR

AWAKE IN OUR SLEEP?

If there ever was an era especially favorable to the exercise of my peculiar talents, it is this. The public seem generally prepared for this mighty truth. . . . Verily, the day of our national greatness is at hand. The people clamor with one voice for new altars, and the God which they worship, lo! is it not almighty Humbug!

Dr. Davy Hines
Life, Adventures and Opinions

8

Peter Funk:
Tales of Exchange

Tricky Business Cities have their own God. Hermes himself came to town when trade was no longer a matter of guarding cattle and sheep. He is the god first of the borders between territories where trade took place (his images were used as boundary markers), and then he is the god of the urban marketplace "border" between buyers and sellers.[1] New York narratives of the antebellum period took a Homeric pleasure in warning New Yorkers and visitors about the clever gods of commerce in New York. They told and retold stories of encounters between representative people and a "genius" who was a tutelary god or attendant spirit attached to New York the way Hermes was attached to Athens. This is a genius with a readiness of speech and adroitness of action that still characterize the stereotypical New Yorker in American culture. He, like Hermes, seemed to control the borders of exchange between strangers. In the antebellum language of New York, he is "Peter Funk" or "the Confidence Man."[2]

Sometimes the narratives tell of long-established citizens of New York being tricked by extraordinarily well-spoken swindlers. These stories are like Ned Buntline's account of Frank Hennock, who masquerades as a threadbare poet sentimentalizing the poor to fool Peter Precise (see Chapter 5 above). Just as often the narratives are warnings to the truly "green," the inexperienced newcomers to the city or the tourists. Guidebooks, novels, and journalism of the period all alert their readers to "mock auction houses," "patent medicine men," "pocket book dropping," and the like. Hennock found his way to Precise through the services of an "intelligence office" (an employment agency), and they too were often on the list of New York scams.[3]

George G. Foster tells a version of an often retold story, a "browning" of someone "green" from upstate: "Mr. Zerubbabel Green, eldest son and hope of Deacon Hezekiah Green, and Thankful Green, his wife, all of Stephentown, New York state, arrived in the city last evening by the Albany boat, on his first visit to town, for the express purpose of seeing the world and knocking about a little."

Green encounters a real New York gentleman, Mr. Browning, who offers him assistance with his baggage and takes him to a hotel. They go several places to drink, where Green is overwhelmed by paintings of naked women. At the theater Browning introduces Green to the Countess of Astoria. They all drink as Green stammers and blushes. The countess proposes that Green go home with her, but Browning whispers, "No you don't, Moll! . . . this is *my* job." He takes Green to the Five Points with the chief of police, but the trip is so dangerous that Green must deposit all his money with the chief before they go. Later in the Points they are short of money for drinks, and Green out of the goodness of his heart reveals his well-stuffed money belt. They go to "Dickens' Place" and see blacks and whites dancing naked together. They proceed to an oyster place, where they play a thimbles game. Browning puts up his gold watch, Green his substantial silver one, the rigger a hundred dollars. Browning and Green confer on where the ball is. It's not there. Green protests that it's cheating and a fight starts. Green wakes up in the gutter, bloody and stiff but not dead.

He recalls, at his leisure, his urban education, "the process of being put through a course of sprouts."[4]

None of this is very different from the oldest sort of cony-catching, the kind described by Robert Greene in his sixteenth-century pamphlets. "Cony" was the Elizabethan cant term London gamblers applied to rural suckers they would "catch" and lure into rigged card games. In "Barnard's Law" a conspiracy of gamblers is arranged, and the "Taker" picks up the country victim on the streets and attempts the ancient "unremembered old acquaintance" routine. They are both country folk: they must know each other. If he does nothing else, the Taker learns the victim's name and passes it covertly to the "Verser," who then can approach the victim more effectively as an unremembered old acquaintance. In celebration of their finding each other in the big city, the country boys go to an inn. The "Barnard" is the expert card player, and he is the extraordinary character, the genius of the game. He is extravagantly urban and extravagantly drunk, and when he proposes a card game, the country lads just know they can clean him out. The cony is then fleeced like the rural lamb he is, and the "Putter" starts a fight with the other catchers to scare the victim off.[5]

New York journalism and guidebooks and fiction of the antebellum period all told warning stories; all are highly entertaining lessons intended to make up for the lack of urban experience.[6] Walt Whitman narrates one of the oldest and most long-lasting of street cons in "Advice to Strangers," published in *Life Illustrated* in 1856.

The old tricks of 'watch-stuffing,' pocket-book-dropping, and 'patent-safe' swindling are just now a little out of use. However, it is only the other day that a friend of our own was accosted by a shabby-looking chap, who asked him to step up an alley for a moment.

'Come here a moment, will yer? I've found suthin.'

'What is it?' said the gentleman, following fearlessly but cautiously.

'We've just picked up this pocket-book'—he held out a well-filled wallet, which he received from a companion who had been waiting for him—'and it's full of money. We can't keep it, for 'taint ours, and we're poor men; now, p'rhaps you'd hand us over a little for finding it, and you find the owner and settle with him for what you pay us.'

Our friend looked the speaker steadily in the eye, with a half smile, saying nothing. In a moment, the confederate remarked,

'You've waked up the wrong passenger, Jim; come let's be off,' and they sneaked out of sight. It was perhaps an even chance that they would have attempted a robbery.

Don't be in haste to make city street acquaintances. Any affable stranger who makes friendly offers is very likely to attempt to swindle you as soon as he can get into your confidence. Mind your own business, as we said before, and let other people mind theirs.

This pocket book (men now call it a "wallet") swindle is as old as cities and is still with us.[7]

As he often does, Whitman catches a wonderful piece of local language: "You've waked up the wrong passenger." This is an expression in use in New York during the period, and it means (roughly) trying to trick someone who is wise, who is awake in his sleep. It may originate in stories about gambling on the Mississippi steamboats where one trick was to have a victim think he was to trick a sleeping passenger when in fact the sleeper was the sharper.[8] It is, at least, used frequently by Jonathan H. Green, the "reformed gambler" who wrote a series of books in the 1840s and 1850s warning Americans about the tricks and traps of gambling. The books were very successful in New York in part because his cause was taken up by "respectable" society there and in part because his accounts of gambling tricks are so entertaining. At least twice Green tells stories about times he feigned sleep on a steamboat so the suckers would think they could fleece him. The suckers wake up the wrong passenger.[9]

Green's gamblers are always what we now call confidence men. Gamblers are particularly dangerous because "they often come under the garb of friendship, and in the most artful way insinuate themselves into the confidence and good graces of those they intend to destroy, and then make a fearful plunge at their victim, when they once have him in their power."[10] They masquerade as "Hoosiers" or clergymen or respectable merchants, all to make them seem the innocents they are not. The steamboat gamblers often operate as a team, like the Elizabethan cony-catchers described by the sixteenth-century Greene. Jonathan Green writes that it is all a matter of how much the victim is worth, what class he is. He is first approached by the most finished of the confidence men, "number 1."

When in company, we are too apt to form hasty acquaintances. . . . If number 1 should happen to meet you, he will converse with you in such a manner as is calculated to deceive you as to his designs. He will have the audacity to approach you in any form that he may think he can reach you. If on a steamer, they have many ways to approach you. If they think you worthy of their attention . . . they will inquire what part you are from; and as there are very few of number 1 that have not been to any one portion of our country, they are generally ready to discourse with you. They will ask you how Judge A or B comes on, or how such a merchant is getting along—is he solvent or not, and all such questions, which will make you think that you are certainly talking to a man of some importance; and becoming prepossessed in his favor, you are apt to enter into an intimacy with him. After he has gained your confidence in him as a gentleman, he will then find out what your business is, where you are going, how long you expect to stay, and all that can be beneficial to him. . . . [H]e soon finds out your prevailing dispositions; and then, by some ingenious way, he will ascertain how much money you have. . . . and thus having possessed himself of all the information he wishes, if he should think that you are not high enough game for him, he will apprise number 2 of you. An individual of this class now approaches you, and being fully acquainted with your position from number 1, his course is a comparatively easy one.

And if you are not good enough for number two, he passes you to number three, and number three may send you on to number four. If number four doesn't think you're worth much, a pickpocket will be sent after you. Or a thug will simply hit you over the head and take what small pickings you have. Green's conclusion is direct: "you should never allow yourselves to repose confidence too soon in a person, because he may have the appearance of a gentleman merchant, or any other respectable avocation."[11]

Green establishes himself as *the* authority on gambling and develops a market for his books and for the services of the Association for the Suppression of Gambling (which Greeley helped him form). The association served New York merchants who were employing young men they didn't know, any of whom could be a gambler. Among other activities, the association started an agency to provide information on office clerks who were gambling. Merchants could subscribe to "The Intelligence Office, J. H. Green, Chief Agent" and have the opportunity to read a "private book" that listed the young men who frequented gambling hells.

But soon Green was writing warnings that gambling was a vast conspiracy that undermines not just young men but even commercial relationships. As historian of gambling Ann Fabian puts it, "For his New York mercantile clientele, Green described a world in which gamblers threatened the credit relations that had become the real network of social interdependence."[12] He finally imagined for his readers a full-blown conspiracy akin to those in the fiction of George Lippard; in his *The Secret Band of Brothers* (1846) Green demonstrated how conspiratorial gamblers have a nationwide organization to overthrow networks of personal and financial relationships. Green's fantasy of a gigantic conspiracy fed a middle-class audience increasingly concerned that the social and commercial relations between them were breaking down under the excessive force of entrepreneurial thirst for gain. The criminals were no longer just thugs who clubbed one down on the street. The new business principles seemed to some dangerously close to rigged gambling, and perhaps a "secret band" of evil-doers was fleecing honest men and women.[13]

More than a decade earlier, Asa Greene published a parable about business life in New York entitled *The Perils of Pearl Street* (1834). The novel was remembered in its time for its description of "Peter Funk." Peter Funk is an apparent New York invention, an imp of deception, a supernatural shape-shifter who appears wherever there is deceit in business. He is a being without heritage, a "little, bustling, active, smiling, bowing, scraping, quizzical fellow, in a powdered wig, London-brown coat, drab kerseymere breeches, and black silk stockings."

> This is the standing portrait of Peter Funk—if a being who changes his figure every day, every hour, and perhaps every minute, may be said to have any sort of fixed or regular form. The truth is, Peter Funk is a very Proteus; and those, who behold him in one shape to-day, may, if they will watch his transformations, behold him in a hundred different forms on the morrow. Indeed there is no calculating, from his present appearance, in what shape he will be likely to figure next. He changes at will, to suit the wishes of his employers. . . . [Peter] will figure in the shape of a box, bale, or package of goods; he will appear in twenty different places, at the same time, on the shelf of a jobber—

sometimes representing a specimen of English, French, or other goods—but being a mere shadow, and nothing else—a phantasma—a show without the substance.[14]

Peter Funk shifts his shape to suit the circumstance, but he always appears where there is business trickery. Like Proteus he can change his shape at will, and like Hermes he is the tricky god of a new commercial age. He is the conspiracy of deceitful businessmen concentrated into one mythic and demonic figure. He is the local genius. Greene's section on Funk became a well-known bit of humorous New York folklore and was reprinted as late as 1858, by the dramatist William E. Burton in his *The Cyclopedia of Wit and Humor*.[15]

Many other New York writers of the 1840s and 1850s tell stories of Peter Funk. On the one hand the stories are dire warnings to greenhorns not to be fooled in "mock auction" shops (which Peter frequents), and on the other they are funny urban stories, whether in journalism or fiction.[16] George G. Foster, Ned Buntline, and Cornelius Mathews all describe him, as does Whitman in the *New Orleans Daily Crescent* in 1848 and *Life Illustrated* in 1856. Mathews's version is a character named Peter Funk in a play performed first at Burton's on December 3, 1856. The play sets the good mercantile family, the Crockerys, against the filthy rich social parvenus, the Milledollars. Funk is the swindler who seeks to operate on the borders of the complicated action to make himself a millionaire. He boasts that he has "ground the fine edge off every man I met." His only business is fraud; he has no tears, no morality.[17]

Professors of Appropriation Fear of the new principles of business and human interaction was made more understandable and at the same time more remote from the public by ascribing the tricks to secret conspiracies or to particular notorious individuals, mythic figures of deceit, the "coming man" conceived as highly finished criminal. The wildly inventive and wholly unreformed *Life, Adventures and Opinions of David Theo. Hines, of South Carolina* is a striking example of a satire on one such great figure, James Gordon Bennett.[18] This remarkable criminal autobiography, published in New York in 1840, is nominally "Davy" Hines's life story as told in a series of letters he wrote from City Prison to James Gordon Bennett, editor of the *New York Herald*.

Hines's narrative recounts his rise from humble beginnings in rural South Carolina to the exalted financial and social station of the greatest and most respected forger and confidence man that the great cities of Charleston and New York had ever known. He describes with pride his picaresque adventures throughout the country in which he set the standard for tasteful and nonviolent "appropriation." In addition, Hines sets forth for Bennett, sometimes at great length, his "opinions" about the state of the nation and the role that the "gentlemen of the road" should play in the country's affairs. He predicts a millennium in which America will properly honor its confidence men and draws evidence for his prediction from himself and his own age. Already he is honored and respected:

> If there ever was an era especially favorable to the exercise of my peculiar talents, it is this. The public seem generally prepared for this mighty truth. . . . Verily, the day of our national greatness is at hand. The people clamor with one voice for new altars, and the God which they worship, lo! is it not almighty Humbug! (19)

There was a real David Hines, or "Dr. Hines," from South Carolina active during the era, and several contemporary newspaper accounts attest both to his confidence methods and to his notoriety. But the *Life* is really an elaborate satire on Americans and American society of the period. We are meant to see Hines's criminal success and his apparently unopposed "opinions" as a commentary on American ideals and behavior in 1840. Because Hines is writing to Bennett we are also meant to recognize an analogy between Hines's methods and goals and those of the successful newspaper editor.[19]

To argue that the *Life* is a satire is to assert also that the book is a "confidence book" about a confidence man, that its narrator Davy is a voice created by an author, the satirist, and not the voice of a real Davy Hines, autobiographer. The assertion is tricky because the *Life* admits to no paternity other than Hines's. But the satiric purpose seems evident to a reader who recognizes in the narrator Hines a complete lack of awareness that his means or ends might not be approved or admired by his audience. Hines assumes that his views are in harmony with those of Bennett and the majority of the society, and this too forms part of the satire on Bennett and his New York humbug society. On the other hand, as we have seen, Bennett's own boastings in the early *Herald* might seem to be a satire on Bennett too! It is clear who the genius is: "Shakespeare is the great genius of the drama, Scott of the novel, Milton and Byron of the poem—and I mean to be the genius of the newspaper press."[20]

The 1840 publication of the *Life* makes it a good supposition that it was another salvo in the "moral war" on Bennett. By associating Hines with Bennett (just as Henry Fielding associated Jonathan Wild with Sir Robert Walpole), the satirist makes us see the "great" newspaperman and the "great" criminal as nearly identical.[21] Hines's episodic *Life* is not structured on urban encounters, but the text alludes to a kind of urban encounter that Bennett made famous—the visit of the important editor to the unsavory scene, in this case Hines's jail cell. Both Hines and Bennett call for a new order, and Hines's *Life* argues that the true god of that era would be Almighty Humbug (Hines calls it explicitly "New York humbug"), and the god's avatars are Davy Hines and James Gordon Bennett. Hines shows how the Humbug-worshipping society might function once fully established. The teachers would be experts like Hines. He calls himself the "Professor of Appropriation" and a "Master of Arts," and he firmly believes that a scholar can make an excellent teacher as well.

> The next day I operated with signal success upon several parties. . . . I have no doubt that they learned a great deal from my freedom of speech and manner, and the brief, but well occupied hours of association, which we had together. They were all young men, and such should always be made to pay well for their experience. It is of little value to them unless they do; and knowing its importance, I strove, and with some success, I think, to impress its lessons upon them as solemnly as possible. The next day one of them went off into the country, and another shot himself through the head. The losses of the latter at faro were said to have prompted this very ridiculous act, which, had the poor youth been sufficiently prepared by useful lessons of adversity at an earlier period, would never have taken place. (112)

Lessons in the new morality are hardly survivable. Hines practices medicine too: "Finding a young fellow sick where I staid that night, I resumed my old profession and prescribed for him without charge, but also without success. The willful youth died a few hours after, in spite of all my medicine and skill" (168). In the humbug order, the patient dies because he is "willful," not because the physician knows only bedside manner. Davy Hines operates in America as though his millennium has already arrived. His success and fame—his position as a man of "greatness"—are due to his faithfulness in making himself in the image of his god Humbug. What small discomfort he still suffers (jail) results from truth's not being widely enough known. Bennett will help spread the news.

Hines professes the Age of Humbug, and P. T. Barnum happily accepts a role as the benign spirit of the age. Barnum began his career with a hoax that the penny newspapers made famous and then developed a whole entertainment business from it. Before Barnum, the most famous New York trick was the "moon hoax" perpetrated by Richard Adams Locke in the *New York Sun* (described in Chapter 1).

Asa Greene comments on the Locke hoax in his 1837 guidebook, *A Glance at New York*, and notes that hoaxes in general "are got up for the purpose of making money—of picking the pockets of the credulous." He observes that New York City seems to be the place where hoaxers operate most successfully: "A great city affords a very rich field for the hoaxers harvest. There are abundant materials to be wrought upon. Folly, credulity, and ignorance are rife. The hoaxability is catching. And, provided it be skillfully and prudently managed, will continue to prevail very much in proportion to the number and density of the population."[22] Greene cannot bring himself to condemn Locke's hoax—its ingenuity overcomes him—but he has no use for the "evil" hoax perpetrated by the man who made the hoax a business, P. T. Barnum. Greene tells us that "A great city may be considered as the mother—the 'nursing mother' of rogues," and in his view Barnum was a chief rogue.

Greene is thinking of Barnum's first hoax, in which he offered New York the person of Joice Heth, 160-year-old nurse of George Washington. Heth was exhibited with great success in Niblo's Garden in New York and then around the Northeast. The old lady died and was dissected to "ascertain" her true age. In attendance were numerous famous surgeons and clergymen—and Richard Adams Locke. Locke wrote an article for the *Sun* (February 25, 1836) entitled "Dissection of Joice Heth: Precious Humbug Exposed," and his piece made a sensation itself. The ensuing events show the complications of hoaxing and newspaper competition. New York lawyer and Barnum associate Levi Lyman went, after the great success of the *Sun* article, to James Gordon Bennett, the editor of the *Herald*, and told him that he and Barnum had been humbugging about the dissection, that Heth was alive and being exhibited in Connecticut, and the body the notables and Locke examined was that of an old black woman who had died in Harlem. Bennett swallowed this whole. He exposed the hoax dissection in the *Herald* on February 27 and was thus hoaxed himself about the "hoax" dissection of the hoax nurse. When that hoax was exposed, Lyman told him another . . . and so on. As Barnum well understood, all these complications and newspaper articles, far from injuring his reputation, furthered his great cause: the fame and notoriety of P. T. Barnum.[23]

P. T. Barnum personified the urban encounter: he made the encounter with New York sharpness and trickery, the skills of the new culture, an *entertainment*. People went to his events and his American Museum because they knew they were going to be tricked and were delighted that they were. It made the urban encounter safe in that instead of being robbed of hundreds by a Peter Funk, one could go to the American Museum for twenty-five cents. Barnum provided tamed urban encounter: it was like meeting wild animals in a zoo. Barnum did not sell the seamless illusion of a true confidence game. He sold controversy, and his most successful exhibits were those, like the Fejee Mermaid, that had been condemned in the newspapers but looked pretty real all the same. A skeptical person could go to the American Museum and have the fun of trying to catch Barnum at his game. Charles Godfrey Leland, who edited the *Illustrated News* with Barnum during the early 1850s, recalled in his *Memoirs* Barnum's technique: "When he had concocted some monstrous cock-and-bull curiosity . . . [Barnum] was wont to advertise that 'it is with great reluctance that he presented this unprecedented marvel to the world, as doubts had been expressed as to its genuineness—doubts inspired by the actually incredible amount of attention in it. All that we ask of an enlightened and honest public is, that it will pass a fair verdict and decide whether it be a humbug or not.'" The public paid and decided it was humbug, "and

Barnum abode by their decision and then sent it to another city to be again decided on."[24]

Neil Harris explains the public's interest in trying to catch the hoaxer as a "delight in learning," and that Barnum's tricks "trained Americans to absorb knowledge." He calls it an "aesthetic of the operational, a delight in observing process and examining for literal truth."[25] I would add that the ideological education that Barnum provides is an assertion that the new deceptive culture of the market society is at base benign and manageable. The Barnum urban encounter is *comic* and controlled, and Barnum symbolically collects the era into himself and makes it seem only good-naturedly terrible. It's hard to be angry about a man who has an elephant plowing his fields next to the New Haven Railroad in Bridgeport. We *know* it's for publicity but we also know he knows we know.[26]

Barnum's own *Life of P. T. Barnum* (1855) was another use of the media to gain notoriety. The book, probably ghosted by New York writer Rufus Griswold,[27] is the genial and unabashed confession of the "original genius" Barnum. He humbly acknowledges himself a master of tricks, and the book reads like a joke book.

> A propensity of keeping out of harm's way has always stuck by me. I have often thought that were I forced to go to war, the first arms that I should examine would be my legs. I should scarcely fulfill the plan of the Yankee soldier who fired a few stray shots at the enemy on his own hook, and then departed, singing,
> "He that fights and runs away,
> May live to fight another day."
> I am decidedly a man of peace, and the first three words of the first line would never correctly apply to me if it was possible for me to appropriate the three words which follow them.[28]

Serious contemporary observers of Barnum saw in him the decline of American culture. Curtis writes in *Harper's* "Easy Chair" that Barnum has many good points, but "What a pity that [his] shrewdness is too shrewd! . . . How sad the infatuation that persuades us to show every man who admires our pretty palace that it is not marble, only ingenious stucco!" Every person is insulted by the publication of the *Life*: "Is a-something, a something else, because it is called humbug? . . .

Does the public applaud this kind of thing?" This "shrewd gentleman thought that he was never shrewder than when he felt sure of the approving sympathy of the public, if he could only show that he made enough money."[29] A *Knickerbocker* article, "Town and Rural Humbugs," published in March 1855, reviewed both Barnum's *Life* and Thoreau's *Walden*, the most important books of the year. Both authors live by their wits, neither works hard, both are humbugs.

> Both are good-natured, genial, pleasant men. One sneers at and ridicules the pursuits of his contemporaries with the same cheerfulness and good-will that the other cajoles and fleeces them. The rural philosopher measured the length, breadth and depth of Walden Pond, with the same jovial contentedness that the metropolitan show-man measured the length, breadth, and depth of the public gullibility.

Respectable New York journalists and magazinists were concerned with precisely the brazenness of Barnum's celebration of his entrepreneurship. They approved of entrepreneurial capitalism, but they were concerned about its excesses, and Barnum seemed to glorify the deceit in the market society culture. More than that he was not only selling fake products but also the *idea* of selling fake products. The *New York Tribune* printed in 1854 "America a Humbug," an article translated from the *Atlantische Studien*, and with the publication the *Tribune* signals its serious concern about the superficiality of American life. The writer is distressed by the "repulsive contradictions" in American life. It is the republic of Rousseau but enslaves human beings; it runs the commerce of the world but has faith in ghosts. Most of all, America shows a "complete stagnation of everything that is not of a material or commercial character." The contemporary American is lost in contradiction.

> [He] has outgrown his old clothes, and has not yet found any new ones to fit him. . . . He likes to be everything, and he is so, but whatever he does smacks of the last thing in which he was engaged. In short, he is never consistent, he adapts himself to his situation, in order to take the best advantage of it—he is more a man of interest than of principle, and will seldom hesitate in his choice between honor and gain.

The expression the writer always hears in America is "It is all humbug." Humbug never fails of its end because people are so one-sided that even though they know the principle, they are tricked. The article concludes: "Here, everything is humbug, as sure as there is a God in Heaven, everything in America is humbug! All America is a humbug!"[30]

The Original Confidence Man   If the whole of the new culture was a series of confidence games, as the writer for the German magazine thought, then the democratic experiment would have been given over to the confidence men. The term "confidence man" is itself a piece of New York language: it did not exist until the summer of 1849, when it was applied to a particular swindler. Before that time there were of course swindlers who took people's confidence, even those who used the word "confidence" in their swindle. The "City Matters" column of the *New York Daily Globe* for May 29, 1847, gives an account of "The Knowing Ones 'Done.' " A very genteelly dressed young gentleman was introduced to "mine host," as being the son of the late and distinguished Nicholas Biddle. Young Biddle flashes money and then tells the host that he is going to invest some money tomorrow. He asks, " 'Dare you put confidence enough in me to give me what you have got? Remember, I do not want it, unless you have confidence in me.' " " 'Certainly . . . I do put confidence in you.' " " 'I like to be sure,' said [Biddle] then, 'and as confidence is the link that binds friendship between man and man I will put you to the test. Let me have your gold watch, while I go around the block.' " That's it, of course, and young Biddle never returns. The host is advised by the *Daily Globe* "to have his hotel painted GREEN."[31]

The same swindler—or at least one using the same con—was arrested in New York two years later, on July 7, 1849, on the complaint of Mr. Thomas McDonald, who claimed that he had been tricked out of an expensive gold watch. The arrest made a newspaper sensation because of the swindler's remarkable method. The *New York Herald* describes the arrest of William Thompson:

> *Arrest of the Confidence Man.*—For the last few months a man has been travelling about the city, known as the "Confidence Man;" that is, he would go up to a perfect stranger in the street, and being a man of genteel appearance, would easily command an interview. Upon this

interview he would say, after some little conversation, "have you confidence in me to trust me with your watch until to-morrow;" the
stranger, at this novel request, supposing him to be some old acquaintance, not at the moment recollected, allows him to take the watch,
thus placing "confidence" in the honesty of the stranger, who walks
off laughing, and the other, supposing it to be a joke, allows him so to
do.[32]

The swindler Thompson used an extremely concentrated version of the
age-old confidence game. Thompson compressed "Barnard's Law" into
a brief encounter on the street. The confidence man makes the victim
assume that he can have confidence in him and then asks that the
confiding man demonstrate the confidence. What is noteworthy about
Thompson is not just his adeptness at compressing the steps but also
that his game provides a strikingly clear illustration of just what a
confidence game is. As if in tribute to that, he was the first such swindler to whom the term "confidence man" was applied.

The *Herald* kept the new term and the subject before its public by
publishing " 'The Confidence Man' on a large Scale" on July 11. Written by Bennett's close associate George Houston, the long article retells
the story of the arrest but then goes on to generalize on the principle.
Houston observes that splendid *palazzos* meet the eye on all New York's
fashionable streets while the Confidence Man resides in The Tombs.
His genius was exercised on too small a scale! He should have gone to
Albany and obtained a charter for a new railroad company and issued
a prospectus and sold shares. Then he should have quietly got rid of
his own stock while running the company into debt and drawing a
munificent salary. So:

Let him rot in "the Tombs" . . . while the genuine "Confidence Man"
stands one of the Corinthian columns of society—heads the lists of
benevolent institutions—sits in the grandest pew of the grandest temple—spreads new snares for new victims. . . . Success, then, to the
real "Confidence Man." Long life to the real "Confidence Man!"—the
"Confidence Man" of Wall street—the "Confidence Man" of the palace uptown—the "Confidence Man" who battens and fattens on the
plunder coming from the poor man and the man of moderate means!
As for the "Confidence Man" of "the Tombs," he is a cheat, a humbug,
a delusion, a sham, a mockery! Let him rot![33]

Only four days after the arrest of the criminal who inspired the term, the *Herald* had found satiric possibilities in the idea of a "Confidence Man." The angry article exposes a confidence man in operation in New York who is far more dangerous than paltry Thompson. The Wall Street manipulator, using the same techniques as the small-time swindler, defrauds larger numbers of people on a larger scale. The satire condemns not just the financier but the society that admires and respects him. The *Herald*, true to its methods, uses the satire as an attack on the alliance it perceived between the old elites and the criminal class.

The Duyckincks' *Literary World* for August 18 copied for its readers the *Merchant's Ledger*'s defense of confidence in one's fellow man: "It is a good thing, and speaks well for human nature, that, at this late date, in spite of all the hardening of civilization, and all the warning of newspapers, men *can be swindled*. . . . The man who is *always* on his guard, *always* proof against appeal . . . is far gone, in our opinion, toward being himself a hardened villain." That a paper called the *Merchant's Ledger* finds a meaning in the arrest of the "Confidence Man" quite different from that found by the *Herald* is perhaps understandable. The article seems almost the business community's reply to the "warning of newspapers." In any case, the rebuttal indicates the complexity and contradiction possible in what was becoming the theme of the "Confidence Man" in New York.

William E. Burton's Chambers Street Theatre put on a farce called "The Confidence Man" for the first time on July 23. The play was created by John Brougham, the Dublin-born actor and playwright who worked with Burton. It was most likely a play with hardly a script, an interlude put together by the company. In any case, no manuscript or prompt copy seems to survive, although the play was reviewed in at least the *Herald*, the *Spirit of the Times*, and the *Albion*.

The *National Police Gazette*, always on the track of unique criminals, wrote extensively about the "Confidence Man" in its weekly issues from July through October. The *Gazette* mentions many aliases, but the swindler is usually called "The Confidence Man," or even just "Confidence." The August 18 issue finds the "Confidence Man is fulfilling a greater destiny than even he, in the vastness of all his self-complacency ever expected for himself." Formerly, other criminals thought him simply an adroit, but now, thanks to the press, "he claims to be considered as a great man in the eyes of the world." The man in jail in The Tombs was very aware of his own notoriety. A letter published in the *Gazette* for September 22 records a visit to his cell: "Natural impudence he possesses in a high degree. . . . When I visited the Tombs, I was preceded upstairs by two country looking individuals. When they arrived at the landing in the second tier, they were accosted by our hero, who sat in the keeper's chair, in this way, 'Gentlemen, have either of you a cigar? I am the *Confidence Man.*' " Proud as Thompson here was of his title and his place in social and linguistic history, at other times he seems to have claimed he was not the original Confidence Man.

The *Dollar Weekly Herald* for September 10, 1849, notes the arrest of "Dusty Bob," or the "Original 'Confidence' Man." George Spencer, alias George Sabins but better known as "Dusty Bob" was arrested on suspicion of burglary. "Thompson, 'the Confidence man,' now in the Tombs, maintains that 'Dusty Bob' is the original Confidence man, and that he (Thompson) was his pupil." Three years earlier, in 1846, there was a series of news accounts of arrests of "Dusty Bob" in the *New York Morning News*: "Dusty Bob Arrested" (April 17); "Dusty Bob Released" (May 15); "[Dusty Bob Arrested]" (August 3); "Dusty Bob Again Arrested" (September 11). There are no specific descriptions of Dusty Bob's cons in these *Morning News* accounts. Any newspaper reader who tried to follow the attempts to identify the Confidence Man would quickly become aware of how shifting his identities were.[34]

The *National Police Gazette* produced a dictionary of cant terms, *Vocabulum; or, The Rogue's Lexicon*, in 1859, and the term "confidence man" gets a definition far longer than that of any other term.

CONFIDENCE MAN. A fellow that by means of extraordinary powers of persuasion gains the confidence of his victims to the extent of drawing upon their treasury, almost to an unlimited extent. To every knave born into the world it has been said that there is a due proportion of fools. Of all the rogue tribe, the Confidence man, is, perhaps, the most liberally supplied with subjects: for every man has his soft spot, and nine times out of ten the soft spot is softened by an idiotic desire to overreach the man that is about to overreach us. This is just the spot on which the Confidence man works. He knows his subject is only a knave wrongside out, and accordingly he offers him a pretended gold watch at the price of a brass one; he calls at the front door with presents from no where, as none could be expected; he writes letters in the most generous spirit, announcing large legacies to persons who have no kin on the face of the earth who cares a copper for them. The Confidence man is perfectly aware that he has to deal with a man who expects a result without having worked for it, who gapes, and stands ready to grasp at magnificent returns. The consequence is, that the victim—the confiding man—is always *done*. The one plays a sure game; his sagacity has taught him that the great study of the mass of mankind is to get something and give nothing; but as this is bad doctrine, he wakes up out of his 'brown study,' and finds himself, in lieu of his fine expectations, in possession of a turnip for a watch, a cigarbox in place of a casket. The Confidence man always carries the trump card; and whoever wishes to be victimized can secure his object by making a flat of himself in a small way, while attempting to victimize somebody else.[35]

The capitalization of "Confidence man" in the *Vocabulum*'s definition indicates a continuing tendency in the 1850s and beyond to think of "the Confidence Man" in a *singular* sense. The casual impression grew that the "Original Confidence Man" of 1849 appeared and reappeared, ubiquitously and almost supernaturally. Whether or not all the incarnations of "the Confidence Man" were in fact appearances of Dusty Bob or Thompson is not as important as the recognition that, given the interest in them in 1849, any subsequent adventures of men who dealt in confidence and who had no stable identities were bound to make an observer think of the singular "Confidence Man," especially since the term was so new, so apt, and so particularly applied originally to an 1849 swindler. All of this made the "the Confidence Man" seem much more ingenious and important: besides being the first, he seemed to be all over, in many places at once. He must have seemed like Ben Jonson's Mosca, a man who could "be here, and there, and here, and yonder, all at once" or perhaps even like the whale Moby Dick, "not only ubiquitous, but immortal (for immortality is but ubiquity in time)."

"Yes, we golden boys, the moderns, have geniality everywhere—a bounty broad-cast like noonlight."

Herman Melville
The Confidence-Man

9

"We Golden Boys, the Moderns":
The Confidence-Man

Drummond Light Melville's *The Confidence-Man: His Masquerade* (1857) digresses three times from its description of the encounters on a Mississippi steamboat between a series of victims and the many shapes of the Confidence-Man. The digressions speculate about the novelist's craft and whether characters should be consistent. In the last digression, Melville (directly, it seems) asks where *original* characters come from. He answers himself: "For the most part, in town. . . . Every great town is a kind of man-show, where the novelist goes for his stock, just as the agriculturist goes to the cattle-show for his." But even in great towns the original character is rare, and a "due conception" of one would make him in fiction the equivalent in real history of "a new law-giver, a revolutionizing philosopher, or the founder of a new religion."

[The original character is] a revolving Drummond light, raying away from itself all round it—everything is lit by it, everything starts up to it (mark how it is with Hamlet), so that, in certain minds, there follows upon the adequate conception of such a character, an effect, in its way, akin to that which in Genesis attends upon the beginning of things.

Melville is not modest. He is saying that his Confidence-Man is such a character. But an original character does *not*, he tells us, just leap out of the author's imagination. "To produce such characters, an author, beside other things, must have seen much, and seen through much: to produce but one original character, he must have had much luck."[1] Melville's man-show was New York. The Confidence-Man comes from there just as the image of the Drummond light comes from the revolving limelight on the top of P. T. Barnum's American Museum.[2] Melville's *The Confidence-Man* is a compendium of the forms used in the New York discourse of urban encounter between the ordinary individual and the extraordinary stranger—even though the novel is set on a Mississippi steamboat. It is true of Melville and New York what Henry James said about Balzac and Paris: "whenever in his novels Paris is not directly presented she is even more vividly implied."[3]

The Confidence-Man's well-known interpretive difficulties exist in part because Melville crowds so many changes on the discourse into one book. There is no relief from the form, and the repetition of encounter after encounter forces readers to see the form the book uses *as* form. In many ways *The Confidence-Man* is nothing *but* the moment of encounter, and the interpretive gap I have previously described—the moment when the ordinary person encountering the extraordinary one loses the ability to understand—expands to all parts of the book. Each encounter is so brief, and the narrative authority so unhelpful, that the reader wanders within the interpretive gap. Or rather, the wise reader wanders in the gap. The unwise reader leaps to the other side, to *an* interpretation.

The book enlarges the conventional metaphor of the period that New York's Broadway is a "Mississippi" of different peoples just as the great river is a combination of many waters. The urban crowd is like the turbulent and wide river south of St. Louis which, in Melville's words, unites "the streams of the most distant and opposite zones, pours them along, helter-skelter, in one cosmopolitan and confident tide" (9). For the New York novelist Cornelius Mathews, Broadway was an "ever flowing wave," a "perfect Mississippi" of different human types.[4] Melville also used the metaphor in "Bartleby" to contrast the populous crowd with the solitary scrivener: "I remembered the bright silks and sparkling faces I had seen that day, in gala trim, swan-like sailing down the Mississippi of Broadway."[5]

The Confidence-Man is not only about New York. The novel is a national panorama that makes satiric suggestions about the shallowness of the *whole* American cosmopolitan tide.[6] The steamboat *Fidèle* and its heterogeneous mass of peoples and languages is a carnival of elements where meanings wander loose. We are at a national marketplace of dialogues, trying to distinguish genuine from false goods. The cleric may be a misanthrope, the modest merchant a swindler, the charitable lady a fool. The simple tricks and traps of New York tradition, the Peter Funk business spirit of New York, dilates to define the whole country and to embrace theological and aesthetic issues unimagined by early workers in the discourse. *The Confidence-Man* is built on New York incident, New York metaphor, New York personages, and New York encounter, but it is New York discourse nationalized.

The Confidence-Man structures itself nearly entirely on encounters between one person and another, but the beginning of the book shows us a crowd very much like one on Broadway and describes the crowd's encounters with two extraordinary street people. The first interpretive test in *The Confidence-Man* is the man in cream colors who writes sentences about charity from 1 Corinthians on a slate for all to read. The man's "cheek was fair, his chin downy, his hair flaxen, his hat a white fur one, with a long fleecy nap." We take him for a deaf-mute because of his slate and because he doesn't react when warned of a bump by a man carrying a trunk. The man in cream colors is "in the extremest sense of the word, a stranger," with an aspect the crowd takes "to be somehow inappropriate to the time and place" (3–5).

Characters in, and readers of, *The Confidence-Man* know immediately that the "stranger" is an interpretive crux. He must be thought about to be understood. Various as is the panorama of characters in even the opening scene of the novel, we know that the man in cream colors is a "stranger" to the rest. Like so many extraordinary characters before him—Adolphus Fitzherbert, Bartleby—the true "stranger" assaults our assumption that everything we see and read can be fitted quickly into preexisting interpretive patterns. The failure to understand the man in cream colors immediately—is he a man of confidence preaching charity and love or a confidence man softening up the crowd?—begins a *process* in which characters in, and readers of, the book try to recognize and interpret what he and his many ambiguous followers in the novel represent, "mean." We expect at first, at the hopeful start of things, that although we do not understand the man in cream colors now, we will understand him later, from the book that comes after him. We suspend our frustration and conceive our task as the local one of interpretation: we will ultimately "figure it out." We assume this because of the narrative assurances of the sentimental tradition, or of narrative tradition altogether. Urban encounter narratives, as we have seen, usually show us how the stranger will be adopted into bourgeois understanding.

The second chapter of *The Confidence-Man*—"Showing that many men have many minds"—begins the struggle toward interpretation in earnest with the characters of the book themselves suggesting one understanding after another about the man in cream colors: " 'Odd Fish!' ... 'Casper Hauser.' ... 'Humbug!' ... 'Kind of daylight Endymion.' ... 'Escaped convict, worn out with dodging.' ... 'Jacob dreaming at Luz' " (7). The crowd's reactions to the man in cream colors are Melville's rapid introduction to the comedy of interpretation in the rest of the book. He tosses the interpretive list off so quickly that we see it as example, as introduction. Each test of interpretation that follows in the rest of the book is an immediate, local encounter between one character and another, and between book and reader, for which one knows only what is immediately *there* in the text. The book is full of interpretive possibility, yet no authority in the text assists us and no interpretive system seems permanently operative. We struggle to understand simply what is going on—who is the confidence man or men, what are the terms of the financial and spiritual exchanges recounted. We know that it is foolish to trust the men preaching confidence so eloquently, and yet we also know that it is impossible and perhaps immoral to have confidence in nothing.

If the man in cream colors is in the extremest sense of the word a stranger, then the second character to set himself up against the crowd, Black Guinea, is the most familiar of street people, the talkative beggar. The difference between Black Guinea and the mute is, the reader recognizes, the difference between words and silence, between black and white. Black Guinea makes everyone smile in recognition: he is the "negro cripple, in tow-cloth attire and an old coal-sifter of a tamborine in his hand," begging for money. He is no stranger: one can chat with him, tease him, call him "old boy," compare him to a dog. He tells his interlocutors that chiefly he "libs in der city," where he sleeps out "on der pabements o'nights" (11). African American beggars were familiar sights in New York, and some were well known. Lydia Maria Child describes one who was always on Broadway, as does Elizabeth Oakes Smith, writing ten years later.[7] These familiar characters were staples of the sentimental description of street life, but other New York writers warned about the dangers of "swindling beggars," whose disabilities were fiction created to encourage charity. Melville mixes the two conventional representations and makes it hard to tell whether Black Guinea is real or false. The crowd's reaction goes both ways too: the people are charitable—they give Black Guinea money—but they play a horrible game of charity, tossing coins that the beggar catches in his mouth, like the grotesque mechanical bank where the coin is shot into a wide, red-lipped black mouth that clanks open and closed.

When Black Guinea is challenged as a possible fraud, he appeals to the crowd to find the men who can speak for him. The challenge is to the reader too: we must find and identify the men of confidence—or the confidence men: "Oh, find 'em, find 'em . . . and let 'em come quick, and show you all, ge'mmen, dat dis poor ole darkie is werry well wordy of all you kind ge'mmen's kind confidence" (13). One bystander, thinking about the complexities of urban identities, asks the right question: "how are we to find all these people in this great crowd?" (13). The reader is still asking that question at the end of the book.

The man in cream colors and Black Guinea are together the Drummond light of *The Confidence-Man*. They announce the book the way Barnum's rotating light advertised his American Museum, illuminating briefly and brightly its forms and ideas. The reader, like the crowd, is either softened up or forewarned, or both together. The beginning of the book also dramatizes and predicts the future solitude of the reader in the act of reading. Each reader will, like Bartleby's lawyer, have to see the reason for himself.

New Yorkers   All the encounters in the chapters that follow have the shape of the isolated meetings of the New York discourse paradigm. The victim, if that is who it is, has to decide to act (give or withhold confidence, or money) based on what is happening at the instant. *The Confidence-Man* is exact where Melville's earlier novels were loose, and the pleasures for the reader come in sharing the interpretive isolation of the characters, in considering the suggestions in each sentence. Each paragraph is, to use Black Guinea's tricky language, "wordy" of close attention. As the reviewer of *The Confidence-Man* for the distinguished *Westminster Review* wrote of Melville, "Few Americans write so powerfully as Mr. Melville, or in better English." Or as H. Bruce Franklin says, "I say to anybody who thinks he finds a wasted or misplaced word, 'Read the book again.' " Thought no longer seems, in Fitz-James O'Brien's phrase about *Pierre*, to "stagger through each page like one poisoned."[8] It is the reader who staggers.

O'Brien might want to think that the difference was the discipline of the highly crafted short pieces Melville had written for *Harper's* and *Putnam's*. *The Confidence-Man* itself, with its self-contained chapters, was most likely written to appear first serially in *Putnam's Monthly* and later as a published book. Melville proposed to Joshua A. Dix a project that must have been *The Confidence-Man* sometime before the end of June 1855. We know that because George W. Curtis, acting as manuscript adviser to *Putnam's*, wrote to Dix on June 29: "I should decline any novel from Melville that is not extremely good." Curtis's condescending advice might be taken as a sign of Curtis's denseness and the consequent frustrations of Melville's career, but since Dix and Edwards did take the book—and Curtis probably read it—they all must have thought it *was* extremely good.[9]

Putnam's writers frequently wrote a series or a serialized novel for the magazine and then published it separately. Melville himself had published both *Israel Potter* and *The Piazza Tales* from the pages of the magazine, and we can see that many of *The Confidence-Man*'s chapters could have been published alone, some as small encounter sketches, some as whole stories. Despite the novel's deserved reputation for complexity, then, Melville was probably directing his work toward popular distribution in *Putnam's* with collected publication to follow. However, a serialization in *Putnam's* must not have been agreed on because no parts of the novel were published in the magazine before the whole book came out.[10]

The individual chapters of *The Confidence-Man* abound in the kind of New York character and allusion that would have suited *Putnam's*: there are Bowery b'hoys, pauper boys, stock brokers, sick people, charity visitors, veterans of The Tombs prison, and, most of all, confidence men. The herb doctor, for example, meets two New Yorkers. He is giving *out* charity when a man with "the appearance of a day-laborer, with a white bandage across his face, concealing the side of the nose, and who, for coolness' sake, had been sitting in his red-flannel shirt-sleeves, his coat thrown across one shoulder, the darned cuffs drooping behind" arose and "with a pace that seemed the lingering memento of the lock-step of convicts, went up for a duly-qualified claimant" of the charity (91). The laborer wears the red flannel associated with the New York workingman of the period, so often recorded by New York writers like Mathews and George G. Foster or embodied in Walt Whitman's costume. This day laborer, however, is specifically *not* the happy-go-lucky Mose, the Bowery b'hoy of journalistic fantasy. That imagined b'hoy might need a bandage for his nose after a raucous "muss," but he would be too proud for charity. Melville's workingman is an anti-Mose whose bandages speak of real injury, real sorrow, and real jails.[11]

In the next chapter the herb doctor meets another bandaged veteran. He approaches a man with paralyzed legs ("stiff as icicles" in Melville's stunning simile) and asks him, in his genial way, "Mexico? Molino del Rey? Resaca de la Palma?" The bitter response is "Resaca de la *Tombs!*" The man is in other words a veteran of the same New York City Prison in which Pierre and Bartleby died. Thomas Fry is a "soldier of fortune" who has survived a sequence of terrible events only suggested by the bandaged man in red flannel of the previous chapter. Fry is a born New Yorker, a cooper, and he was imprisoned in a wet cell in The Tombs because he witnessed a murder. Unlike the murderer he does not have friends for bail. By the time the trial finally comes his legs have been damaged. The murderer is released, again because he has friends, and Fry goes off to the Corporation Hospital on

Blackwell's Island. There he just gets worse, and finally he is sent hob-
bling off with five silver dollars and his crutches. No one believes his
story, so he tells a different one. His street patter is "Sir, a shilling for
Happy Tom, who fought at Buena Vista. Lady, something for General
Scott's soldier, crippled in both pins at glorious Contreras" (97). Fry is,
then, a New York swindling beggar, with a believable fake story that
stands for the unbelievable real one. His fake is real.

The Confidence-Man frequently alludes to New York's street boys.
The Philosophical Intelligence officer and the cynical Missourian, Pitch,
debate the subject of boys. Pitch needs help but he distrusts the whole
category of boys, and the agent tries to convince him to try one. Pitch
took twenty-nine boys previously, and finally even a thirtieth boy, one
sent out by "the Commissioners of Emigration, all the way from New
York, culled out carefully, in fine, at my particular request, from a
standing army of eight hundred boys, the flowers of all nations, so they
wrote me, temporarily in barracks on an East River island" (117–18).
The boy, in other words, has been sent out from a New York prison by
an organization like Charles Loring Brace's Children's Aid Society to
work in exchange for "adoption" into a farm family. Pitch's thirtieth
boy is "Chesterfieldian," polite and intelligent and filial. But he is the
worst, destroying and stealing Pitch's things and denying the thefts
point-blank. Despite his previous experience with thirty boys and the
sentimental illusions of New York charities, despite his determination
not to take another boy, and despite his determination to be like his
name and stick to what he says, Pitch is convinced to have confidence
in the Philosophical Intelligence Office agent and in boys and try one
more.

A pauper boy like those described in sentimental New York novels
appears in chapter 29. Frank Goodman, the cosmopolitan, and Charlie
Noble are engaged in their long dialogue, and Frank has just said that
he thinks that a man capable of a good loud laugh cannot be a heartless
scamp. Right on cue, Noble laughs and points to the "figure of a pale
pauper-boy on the deck below, whose pitiableness was touched, as it
were, with ludicrousness by a pair of monstrous boots, apparently some
mason's discarded ones, cracked with drouth, half eaten by lime, and
curled up about the toe like a bassoon." "Look," says Noble, "ha, ha,
ha!" As Noble continues to laugh at poverty, Frank goes on to say that

those who "heard that laugh . . . would as naturally argue from it a sound heart as sound lungs" (163). Frank Goodman, shape-shifting confidence man though he might be, exposes the cruelty of Noble's good humor, his utter lack of sympathy.

The herb doctor's encounters, Pitch's encounter with the agent for boys, and the exchange between Goodman and Noble about the pauper boy all take New York materials and rework them so that they stand out as starkly untranscendable as the family Redburn watches die in Liverpool. The charitable and uncharitable languages of the confidence men Goodman and Noble, for example, cannot make the pauper boy into a sentimental (and therefore transcendable) icon because Melville's description is so exact, so graphic, and because the optimistic language seems all too obviously facile and the misanthropic language too obviously cruel.

The Confidence-Man also reworks stories of minor street cons familiar in New York. As we have seen, hundreds of newspaper articles, guidebooks, and pamphlets about New York warned about New York patent medicine men like Melville's herb doctor, intelligence office operators like the philosophical one, or people selling counterfeit detectors like the boy in Melville's last chapter.[12] Mathews even warns in a novel against people like Melville's man with the weed. Mathews's character Small always wears a weed in public: "it was more respectable, and made the public sympathize with him as a bereaved young gentleman."[13]

The most important New York street confidence game Melville had in mind was that of the New York swindler who was the Confidence Man. The Confidence Man of 1847 and 1849 appeared again in 1855, in Albany, when Melville was living on his farm, Arrowhead, in Pittsfield, Massachusetts. The reappearance of the first Confidence Man in Albany in April and May 1855 could easily have been the stimulus for Melville's conception of the novel he proposed to Dix before June of that year. An *Albany Evening Journal* news item of April 28, 1855 was headed, "The Original Confidence Man in Town:—A Short Chapter on Misplaced Confidence." The article describes the activities of "Samuel Willis" in an Albany jewelry store.

> He called into a jewelry store on Broadway and said to the proprietor: "How do you do, Mr. Myers?" Receiving no reply, he added "Don't

you know me?" to which Mr. M. replied that he did not. "My name is Samuel Willis. You are mistaken, for I have met you three or four times." He then said he had something of a private nature to communicate to Mr. Myers, and that he wished to see him alone. The two then walked to the end of the counter, when Willis said to Myers, "I guess you are a Mason,"—to which Myers replied that he was—when Willis asked him if he would not give a brother a shilling if he needed it. By some shrewd management, Myers was induced to give him six or seven dollars.[14]

The *Springfield Daily Republican* reprinted this piece on May 5, and Melville reasonably could easily have seen either newspaper.

The *Albany Evening Journal* also published on the same day a separate article, not reprinted by the Springfield paper, entitled "Brief History of the Confidence Man." This piece specifically connects the "Willis" arrested in Albany to the Thompson arrested in New York in 1849. The writer explains that he has searched the files of the *National Police Gazette* and discovered the facts. On May 5, the Albany paper had a note reporting on the visit of William Stokeley, one of the "Independent Police of Wall-st.," to the Albany jail. Stopping in front of Willis's cell he points in and exclaims, "Here is No. 1, the Original Confidence Man. I arrested him the first time in New-York." The *New York Times* and the *Tribune* reprinted the *Evening Journal* note about Stokeley's identification, thus showing that the "Original Confidence Man" was still notorious enough in New York that his whereabouts would be of interest.

In chapter 4 of *The Confidence-Man*, "Renewal of Old Acquaintance," the first man on Black Guinea's list of men who could recommend him, the man with the weed, approaches a merchant and asserts an old acquaintance unremembered by the victim, and finally uses exactly the same trick and, in part, the same words that "Willis" does.

> "If I remember, you are a mason, Mr. Roberts?"
> "Yes, yes."
> Averting himself a moment, as to recover from a return of agitation, the stranger grasped the other's hand; "and would you not loan a brother a shilling if he needed it?" (21)

The gold watch borrowing of the 1847 and 1849 stories does not appear in the 1855 accounts, but Melville probably also knew of the earlier New York newspaper accounts. In *The Confidence-Man* Frank Goodman proposes to Pitch that they should go dancing. "I shall fling them off a Scotch jig, while . . . you hold my loose change; and following that, I propose that you, my dear fellow, stack your gun, and throw your bearskins in a sailor's hornpipe—I holding your watch" (135). And of course, like the original New York Confidence Man, Melville's apparent swindlers often use the word "confidence" in asking for it. The agent for the Seminoles, for example, asks "a charitable lady" for just that: "Could you put confidence in *me* for instance?" (44). Or, in the funniest version, Goodman beats Charlie Noble to the key question by inverting the formula and putting confidence in Noble!

> "How shall I express what I mean, unless I add that by your whole character you impel me to throw myself upon your nobleness; in one word, put confidence in you, a generous confidence?"
>
> "I see, I see," with heightened interest, "something of moment you wish to confide. Now, what is it, Frank? Love affair?"
>
> "No, not that."
>
> "What, then, my *dear* Frank? Speak—depend upon me to the last. Out with it."
>
> "Out it shall come, then," said the cosmopolitan. "I am in want, urgent want, of money." (178)

As I will demonstrate, Melville's use of the New York Confidence Man source is important in many ways. At the least we can know that Melville picked a highly topical and popular theme for his difficult novel. In its review the *Newark Daily Advertiser* thought it all too popular. It condemned Melville's novel and acidly remarked that "a certain class of persons, those who read police reports, will relish this record of trickery and deceit." Another reviewer, in the *Boston Evening Transcript*, thought Melville was not only after popularity but that he had achieved it: "One of the indigenous characters who has figured long in our journals, courts, and cities, is 'the Confidence Man:' his doings form one of the staples of villainy, and an element in the romance of roguery. . . . It is not to be wondered at, therefore, that the subject caught the fancy of Herman Melville. . . . The plan and treatment are . . . Melvillish; and the story more popularly eliminated [*sic*] than is usual with the author."[15]

The Founder of a New Religion   I think Melville discovered in New York's Confidence Man, and in New York discourse as a whole, a way to see in the quotidian a whole new principle. He finds in urban encounter narratives a dim embodiment of his most serious theological and aesthetic concerns. In chapter 44, as I have noted, Melville describes the original character as having an effect akin to Genesis, but he goes on to say that in such a character there is "something prevailingly *local*, or of the age" (239, my italics). Melville thinks that the original character "cannot be born in the author's imagination—it being as true in literature as in zoology, that all life is from the egg" (239). In the local Confidence Man of New York Melville says he has found "the founder of a new religion" (239).

In shaping his novel Melville is aware of the linguistic peculiarities in the penny paper invention of the term "Confidence Man." He is aware that the term originates in singular form only—as *the* "Confidence Man" and not as a category of "confidence men." In the newspaper crime reports this meant, as I have said, that swindles of various sorts and swindlers in many different places all seemed to be manifestations of the one Confidence Man. Melville thinks this ubiquity itself is a hint of how a kind of supernatural effect resides in the local. The Confidence-Man is like Peter Funk who is here and there, everywhere, or like Dickens's Bucket who appears everywhere "all at wunst," but in *The Confidence-Man* the immortality is a modern one, defined not by dual citizenship in this world and the next but by pervasive and continuing presence in this.

Many readers try to deal with the ubiquity of the Confidence-Man by fixing him into meaning. One repeated method is to recognize in the book a series of satiric portraits of well-known literary or political figures among Melville's contemporaries. The portraits are masked: the courageous interpreter unmasks. Fitz-James O'Brien suggests this line of thinking in 1857, although he has the sense to reject it immediately. He quotes the description of the mute in chapter 1 and comments: "But for the fact that this singular being is presented to us as being quite *dumb*, one might suppose that Mr. Melville meant to give us the portrait of a distinguished metropolitan editor, and, in this way, to suggest some clue to his purpose in the story."[16] O'Brien has in mind Horace Greeley because the mute's fairness of coloring and clothing remind him of

Greeley's flaxen hair and white coat.[17] Whether O'Brien was aware that either sheeplike man might be a wolf in costume he doesn't say.

Twentieth-century readers have unmasked more historical figures than O'Brien, living in that history, might have imagined. Despite all the book's warnings against leaping across the gap to *an* interpretation, readers quite naturally persist in doing so. They are the "confident" readers in William Ramsey's anatomy of the book's interpreters, and they set out to clarify *The Confidence-Man*'s confusions.[18] They identify, for example, the character Mark Winsome in chapters 36 and 37 as a portrait of Ralph Waldo Emerson. Other identifications are of Winsome's disciple Egbert as Henry David Thoreau, the cold-hearted Goneril of chapter 12 as the actress Fanny Kemble Butler, and the poetry peddler of chapter 36 as Edgar Allan Poe. Still more see Pitch as James Fenimore Cooper, John Ringman as William Cullen Bryant, Egbert as George William Curtis (and therefore not Thoreau), Frank Goodman, the cosmopolitan, as Bayard Taylor or George William Curtis.[19] Helen Trimpi has written the definitive analysis of this kind, identifying nearly all of the characters in Melville's novel with his contemporaries and thus understanding the book as highly specific social satire. Perhaps all such "confident" identifications fail to convince because at crucial moments something must be forced to make the fit. Trimpi identifies the wooden-legged cynic with the gimlet eye as the cross-eyed James Gordon Bennett of the *New York Herald*, but Bennett didn't have a wooden leg. Or as Fitz-James O'Brien says, the man in cream colors might be Horace Greeley but he's mute.[20]

Less confident readers—Ramsey's "imperiled" ones—find that there are hints of goings-on more theological than social. They suspect the Devil is aboard the steamboat and see in Melville's vision an imperiled human state where the Devil operates freely without being recognized. The argument for the Devil is relatively easy to follow. We see that the characters refer to each other, and this leads quickly to thinking that there is a conspiracy of swindlers aboard the *Fidèle*. This seems a fair assumption in the light of Jonathan H. Green's warnings in *An Exposure of the Arts and Miseries of Gambling* about teams of confidence men aboard steamboats who passed a victim from one kind of sharper to another depending on which con better suited him, and passed on useful information about the victim at the same time. But the games the members of the team play in *The Confidence-Man* seem so unprofitable compared to the effort expended that the interpreter moves to the possibility that the characters are in fact all the guises of one man, a single extremely gifted criminal. This fits the otherwise unnecessary detail that the separate characters never appear at the same time, but since such rapid and complete shape-shifting hardly seems humanly possible, the interpreting mind goes quickly on to that supernatural shape-shifter, the Devil himself.

Taunting hints of the Devil pervade the novel. Snakes, for example, slither everywhere. Pitch realizes that he has yet again ordered a boy and thinks he has just been with the supernatural Snake: "the insinuator's undulating flunkyisms dovetail into those of the flunky beast that windeth his way on his belly" (130). In talking with Winsome, Goodman says that he has confidence in the latent benignity of the rattlesnake, but Winsome, all transcendental, wants to be one! Winsome says, "When charmed by the beauty of that viper, did it never occur to you to change personalities with him? to feel what it was to be a snake? to glide . . . your whole beautiful body one iridescent scabbard of death? In short, did the wish never occur to you to feel yourself exempt from knowledge, and conscience, and revel for a while in the care-free, joyous life of a perfectly instinctive, unscrupulous, and irresponsible creature?" (190). Winsome of course has been charmed by the snake Goodman, but Goodman seems to reject the transcendental folly of imaginative reveling in irresponsibility. He says he needs to be "genial," and if he were a snake people would be afraid. But he perhaps is that genial original snake, and the transcendentalist who examines the ideas of snakes in his brain does not see the snake before him. Goodman is later described as having the power of "persuasive fascination" over the barber: "the power of holding another creature by the button of the eye" (234).[21]

The snake evidence is highly suggestive, but we can never be sure whether we can build a consistent interpretation on a character's suspicion, a transcendentalist's folly, or even the novelist's metaphor. I conclude that it is a mistake to recognize the Confidence-Man only as the Devil just as I think it is a mistake to recognize Christ in Bartleby. The Confidence-Man is not the Devil in the sense that he is stealing souls by opposing the God of the Old or New Testament: he is far too incon-

sistent, too modern, for only that interpretation. Consistency is the first
requisite of recognition, and *The Confidence-Man* is most of all not a
book of consistencies. Everything that might seem familiar and predict-
able is defamiliarized.[22] Characters change within chapters, from chapter to chapter, and if we can say that there is *a* Confidence-Man who is
shifting his shape again and again, then the leading character is the very
type of inconsistency. But we can observe inconsistency even without
assuming the supernatural. The man with the weed is different in
chapter 5 from what he was in chapter 4: he, "throwing off in private
the cold garb of decorum, and so giving warmly loose to his genuine
heart, seemed almost transformed into another being" (25). The man
in gray of chapter 7 is full of enthusiasms—he will "quicken" charitable
missions with "the Wall street spirit" (40)—while in chapter 8 he goes
"laggingly into the ladies' saloon, as in spiritless quest of somebody,"
seating himself "with an air of melancholy exhaustion and depression"
(43). The Collegian is first a melancholy reader of Tacitus and then a
stock market enthusiast hot in his hatred of bears. Pitch, the Missourian
who says he sticks to what he says, does not stick and orders a boy.
Charlie Noble, after all his smoothness in his long dialogue with the
Cosmopolitan, is stunned when Goodman asks him for money first. He
undergoes "a metamorphosis more surprising than any in Ovid" and
curses the Cosmopolitan (179).

In chapter 14—"Worth the consideration of those to whom it may
prove worth considering" (!)—Melville comments on the inconsistency
of the merchant Roberts in the chapter before. The narrator asks
whether the author should be blamed for an inconsistent character
since, after all, "in real life, a consistent character is a *rara avis*" (69). He
knows that novelists ordinarily present humans not in obscurity but in
transparency. There are some novelists who create characters who seem
at first inconsistent but later turn out, through the author's cleverness,
to be consistent after all. Melville's prejudices are clear, however (intentionally) murky his prose: "Upon the whole, it might rather be thought,
that he, who, in view of its inconsistencies, says of human nature the
same that, in view of its contrasts, is said of divine nature, that it is past
finding out, thereby evinces a better appreciation of it than he who, by
always representing it in a clear light, leaves it to be inferred that he
clearly knows all about it" (70).

Popular novelists are adept at "throwing open," Melville says bitterly, "the last complications" of character. These are the "psychological" novelists who think they have found all the consistencies of human character. As we have seen, the leading novelist of this kind in the 1840s and 1850s was Charles Dickens, and reviewers always commented on and praised his inventiveness in making characters. The article on "Characters in *Bleak House*" in the November 1853 issue of *Putnam's Monthly* (the same issue as the first installment of "Bartleby") is a contrary example. The writer thinks that Dickens is prodigal in his characters and that this is astonishing since "there is nothing so rare in literature as the creation of a new character," but the writer goes on to complain that Dickens is a simple daguerreotypist because the first sight of a Dickensian character exhausts our interest in him. A later *Putnam's* article, "The Genius of Charles Dickens" (March 1855), probably written by Curtis, disagrees, arguing that the characters are extraordinary and "where we recognize here and there the *second* appearance of some familiar person, he comes under such new relations, and with such different combinations, as to have all the effects of complete novelty."[23] Melville, writing his book for *Putnam's*, uses *The Confidence-Man* to join this *Putnam's* debate on the nature of fictional character. The novel says:

> As for original characters in fiction, a grateful reader will, on meeting with one, keep the anniversary of that day. True, we sometimes hear of an author who, at one creation, produces some two or three score such characters; it may be possible. But they can hardly be original in the sense that Hamlet is, or Don Quixote, or Milton's Satan. That is to say, they are not, in a thorough sense, original at all. They are novel, or singular, or striking, or captivating, or all four at once. (238)

Like other parts of *The Confidence-Man*, Melville's digressions on character could easily have been intended for separate publication in *Putnam's*. Melville clarifies the logic of the first *Putnam's* article, distinguishing more carefully between "new" characters of the kind Dickens creates and "original" ones that are altogether different. *The Confidence-Man*, like "Bartleby" before it, strikes out at Dickens's authority both in his literary comments and in the novel's portrayal of the original character it finds in New York.

The novelist who goes in for inconsistency is doomed to a small readership, however much his book participates in a recognizable New York discourse. Good sales are particularly unlikely if he does not finally clear away the inconsistencies by a clever plotting that uncovers a final consistency (Esther Summerson is Lady Dedlock's daughter!). As I have noted, Melville thinks great works never explain themselves and do not end in anything other than "mutilated stumps," but the contemporary reviewers of *The Confidence-Man* were frustrated by its inconclusiveness. The *Philadelphia North American* said about it that "you read on and on" only to be "choked off at the end of the book like the audience of a Turkish story teller, without getting to the end of the story." O'Brien in *Putnam's* was mystified, saying Melville "evidently had some occult object in his mind, which he has not yet accomplished, when he began to paint the 'Masquerades' of this remarkable personage."[24]

No authority within the text helps the reader recognize the Confidence-Man for what he consistently is, if anything. *The Confidence-Man* hints at the Devil, but this only helps the wise reader understand how he is not that conventional Devil. The principle the book teaches—the principle of the Confidence-Man—is inconsistency. With the Confidence-Man there is only surface, inconsistency, in addition to something "prevailingly local." With the old Devil or devils there was always some true standard against which they could (eventually) be measured and found wanting. Like Bartleby, the Confidence-Man is a devil or god in the street of everyday human life. All meaning in their stories lies on the surface; if there are hidden truths or explanations of the new system, we have no access to them. The Confidence-Man is a postmodern devil or god who comes to Melville from New York discourse, from his contemplation of narratives that force observers into unmediated individual interpretive encounters—with starving children, with silent copyists, or with talented tricksters. The narratives were themselves ideological creations intended to normalize and justify the superficiality of encounter in modern life, to adopt the "other" into the middle-class understanding. Melville takes those narratives and discovers in them the conflation of humanity and a new divinity.[25]

Melville most often thinks "truth" exists, and not only that, he thinks that truth gives us signs that it exists. We live perpetually with the knowledge that there is another world, a world of certainty and perfect explanation, and it is our torment that we have little access to that world—despite the incessant masquerade of hints it provides us. Sometimes it is art that provides the look into, and the connection with, the world of correct understanding and interpretation. Seven years before the publication of *The Confidence-Man*, in 1850, Melville wrote that he admired Hawthorne because Hawthorne understands that truth is "forced to fly like a scared white doe in the woodlands; and only by cunning glimpses will she reveal herself, as in Shakespeare and other masters of the great Art of Telling the Truth,—even though it be covertly, and by snatches."[26]

By the time of the writing of *The Confidence-Man* Melville is less willing to create the "cunning glimpses" and more concerned with the wanderings of the person trying to catch sight of the doe, if one exists. The attempt to see the doe, to interpret, has become the principle of his art: the reader becomes the person faced with a world studded with interpretations. We know that we, like many of the characters in *The Confidence-Man*, reveal ourselves by the strategies, the politics, we use in the struggle to read the book. The Confidence-Man reveals *our* assumptions, not his own: he is the revolving Drummond light, "everything is lit by it, everything starts up to it" (239). The reason we (readers in 1857 or the 1990s) cannot look back through the brightness of the limelight to its source to understand *it* is that we have no hold on the framing context in which we should understand things. If we are wise, we will know this and hold back from the paradoxical blindness that comes of looking into the light, but we cannot always help ourselves. We try to interpret, and because we do so we reveal ourselves as being as full of wisdom and folly, charity and greed, community or isolation as the characters in *The Confidence-Man*.

Geniality *The Confidence-Man* opens the interpretive process up. In the urban encounters between middle-class lawyers or journalists and extraordinary characters there was for an instant the failure of interpretation before the old interpretive systems took hold again in a new way. In *The Confidence-Man*, particularly in its first half, the victims often react extremely: they are conned with no sense of their victimization or they viciously reject being deceived. Both kinds of victims are consistent, and their geniality or misanthropy reveals them in a flash either as foolish or heartless. Other, more attractive, victims, like Pitch, react both ways in different encounters and contain both geniality and misanthropy. The early parts of the book establish a dialectic between geniality and misanthropy as ways of managing the confusions of individual encounter, and the reader looks forward to some resolution as the book goes on. How can a victim behave sensibly? How can the reader read?

John Bryant thinks that the chief character in the second half of the book, Frank Goodman, is Melville's complex development of the cultural type of the cosmopolitan. For Bryant, Goodman is the book's culminating "two-sided genial misanthrope" who can sustain both a "good-natured love and a healthy hatred of man." Everything leads up to Goodman.

> [He] knows human iniquity but is fully committed to human society. Pitch, Moredock, Hall, Polonius, even Noble himself anticipate this figure, for each exhibits an experimental combination of geniality and misanthropy, but these fractional men only whet our taste for something whole, someone like Goodman, whose instinctual benevolence and misanthropy fuse in one cosmopolitan tide. In grounding his geniality upon a misanthropic awareness, Melville's new "monster" brings others in their ill-fated extremism toward his fused sensibility.[27]

Goodman is a character who teases characters and readers out of false geniality as well as false misanthropy: he is the saving character of the world of *The Confidence-Man*. Goodman provides salvation on a completely social level, in a world where all meaning lives in social exchange, where we survive by our social wits: "Goodman's indeterminacy [is] the very model of survival for our own immersion in doubt" (250).

I agree with much of Bryant's argument because I concur in his understanding that the pleasures and meanings of the book exist in its representations of social interactions, but I think that Bryant accepts much more easily than Melville does the modern and flattened new world the Confidence-Man presents. Melville sees in "geniality" the word of the new world just as "prefer" was the word for Bartleby. Geniality was once a private virtue, "mostly confined to the fireside and table," but now it lives in public. The modern creatures of the coming world, the "coming century" as the book says, will distribute this geniality throughout religious and political public culture. Goodman says it himself, "Yes, we golden boys, the moderns, have geniality everywhere—a bounty broadcast like noonlight."

Soon, Goodman tells us, the entire world will be genialized.

> In a word, as the progress of Christianization mellows those in manner whom it cannot mend in mind, much the same will it prove with the progress of genialization. And so, thanks to geniality, the misanthrope, reclaimed from his boorish address, will take on refinement and softness—to so genial a degree, indeed, that it may possibly fall out that the misanthrope of the coming century will be almost as popular as, I am sincerely sorry to say, some philanthropists of the present time would seem not to be. (175–77)

This passage imagines an interpretive order that is *replacing* Christianity. The Confidence-Man is the founder of that new religion, its lawgiver and teacher. What will arrive is either a mellow Christianity that is concerned only with manner and not mind or, more terrifying, Geniality itself. The world will be only surfaces—genial politicians, genial entertainers, genial theologians, genial novelists, genial readers. I think that Melville wants us to recognize the demonism of this genial new order. I think, in other words, that there *is* something that the wise reader can recognize, and that is the existence of the principle of the Confidence-Man.

New York's Boy   In the last chapter of the novel, a "solar lamp" is burning in the gentlemen's cabin. On its shade is "the image of a horned altar, from which flames rose, alternat[ing] with the figure of a robed man, his head encircled by a halo" (240). These images are of the Old Testament (the horned altar) and the New Testament (the robed man).[28] At the end of the chapter the cosmopolitan, who has been conversing with an old man, says that he will "extinguish" the lamp, and the "waning light expired, and with it the waning flames of the horned altar, and the waning halo round the robed man's brow" (251). The lights of the Old *and* the New Testament are out; a new order and its unknowable devil or god have arrived.

There is hope only in the voice that speaks from the berth. It provides resistance to all of the cosmopolitan's talk in the last chapter: it surprises the cosmopolitan. The cosmopolitan is quoting Ecclesiasticus on the subject of "good news" to the old man, and a voice speaks from the berth: "Too good to be true." The cosmopolitan later quotes a section about the enemy who speaks sweetly: "Observe and take good heed. When thou hearest these things, awake in thy sleep." At this the voice speaks again:

> "Who's that describing the confidence-man?" here came from the berth again.
> "Awake in his sleep, sure enough, ain't he?" said the cosmopolitan, again looking off in surprise. (242)

In this case the cosmopolitan has awakened "the wrong passenger"; someone recognizes the con, someone calls him by his name. This use of the term "confidence-man" is the *only* one in the entire book other than in the title, and the scene is unlike any other in *The Confidence-Man*. The person in the berth recognizes the game that is going on. He is in the position of the wise reader. He notices Goodman and recognizes him as principle. Although the man in the berth is nameless, and could be another avatar of the Confidence-Man, he still affords us some hope that the truth can be spoken, even in the dark. We readers also hope that we as individuals may be able to confront the shallowness of our superficial modern experience and speak some brief and incomplete truths. We may not continue to be victims of geniality: we may be awake in our sleep.

Toward the end a ragged boy joins the cosmopolitan, a boy whose "pointed and fluttering" rags look like "the painted flames in the robes of a victim in *auto-da-fe*" (244). He is selling traveler's conveniences—travelers' patent locks, money belts, counterfeit detectors—and he has a patter that overwhelms the old man into buying. The boy is a friendly competitor to the cosmopolitan, trying to live the principle that the cosmopolitan is rather grandly illustrating. The boy tips the cosmopolitan "a wink expressive of a degree of indefinite knowingness, not uninteresting to consider in one of his years" (244–46). They seem related to each other the way that Hermes is related to his brother Apollo—

antagonists, then friends after a trading of gifts.[29] The boy certainly seems the child-god of commerce, the Hermes of the new order. But like his brother god the cosmopolitan this Hermes is a god of the street. His rags are those of a "red-flannel shirt," and he has "no allotted sleeping-place." He is New York's boy.

NOTES

Prologue: The Man in Cream-Colors

1. Frank Kermode, *The Genesis of Secrecy: On the Interpretation of Narrative* (Cambridge: Harvard University Press, 1979), p. 101.

2. Edward K. Spann, *The New Metropolis: New York City, 1840–1857* (New York: Columbia University Press, 1981), p. 15. See also Robert G. Albion, *The Rise of New York Port* (1939; reprint, New York: Scribner's, 1970), pp. 16–37, 405.

3. See Thomas C. Cochran and William Miller, *The Age of Enterprise: A Social History of Industrial America* (New York: Harper & Row, 1961), pp. 43–48, 81–86. They quote Sydney Smith, editor of the *Edinburgh Review* and apparently an investor in Pennsylvania bonds, as saying that he never met a citizen of Pennsylvania at a London dinner "without feeling a disposition to seize and divide him—to allot his beaver to one sufferer and his coat to another—to appropriate his pocket handkerchief to the orphan, and to comfort the widow with his silver watch, Broadway rings, and the London Guide which he always carries in his pockets. . . . He has no more right to eat with honest men than a leper has to eat with clean" (p. 48). Smith was thinking of the $35 million in Pennsylvania bonds that many in England bought to their regret.

4. Sean Wilentz, *Chants Democratic: New York City and the Rise of the*

American Working Class, 1788–1850 (New York: Oxford University Press, 1984), p. 107.

5. A good account of the population growth during the 1845–60 period is in Ira Rosenwaike, *Population History of New York City* (Syracuse, N.Y.: Syracuse University Press, 1972). See particularly chapter 3, "The 'Foreign City,'" pp. 33–54, from which I draw my statistics.

6. Carroll Smith Rosenberg, *Religion and the Rise of the American City* (Ithaca: Cornell University Press, 1971), p. 168.

7. See, for example, Christine Stansell, *City of Women: Sex and Class in New York, 1789–1860* (Urbana: University of Illinois Press, 1987). Although Stansell uses the writings of journalists and charity "home visitors" to New York slums as evidence in her account of the material conditions of women in New York, she stresses their unreliability as evidence: "Journalists and writers, in translating the experiences of the home visitors into narratives, popularized the geography of vice as a metaphor through which genteel New Yorkers could see themselves as both brave explorers of a dangerous city and elect guardians of civilized culture" (p. 75).

8. Roland Barthes, "Myth Today," in *Mythologies*, ed. and trans. Annette Lavers (New York: Farrar, Straus and Giroux, 1972), p. 112.

9. F. O. Matthiessen, *American Renaissance: Art and Expression in the Age of Emerson and Whitman* (1941; reprint, New York: Oxford University Press, 1964), p. vii. Myra Jehlen's "Introduction: Beyond Transcendence" in Sacvan Bercovitch and Myra Jehlen, eds., *Ideology and Classic American Literature* (Cambridge: Cambridge University Press, 1986), pp. 1–18, is persuasive in showing Matthiessen's insistence on the nonideological character of the United States' master texts.

10. See John Stafford's study of literary criticism of the period, *The Literary Criticism of "Young America": A Study in the Relationship of Politics and Literature* (1952; reprint, New York: Russell & Russell, 1967). There is also John Paul Pritchard, *Literary Wise Men of Gotham: Criticism in New York, 1815–1860* (Baton Rouge: Louisiana State University Press, 1963); Thomas Bender, *New York Intellect: A History of Intellectual Life in New York City* (Baltimore: Johns Hopkins University Press, 1987); and Nina Baym's more general *Novels, Readers, and Reviewers: Responses to Fiction in Antebellum America* (Ithaca: Cornell University Press, 1984).

11. Perry Miller, *The Raven and the Whale: The War of Words and Wits in the Era of Poe and Melville* (New York: Harcourt, Brace and World, 1956), pp. 94–97. The speech was printed in the *New York Tribune* for February 21, 1842.

12. Lawrence Buell, *New England Literary Culture: From Revolution through Renaissance* (Cambridge: Cambridge University Press, 1986), pp. 416–17n.

13. David S. Reynolds, *Beneath the American Renaissance: The Subversive*

Imagination in the Age of Emerson and Melville (New York: Alfred A. Knopf, 1988), pp. 443–44, 563.

14. John Bryant, *Melville and Repose: The Rhetoric of Humor in the American Renaissance* (New York: Oxford University Press, 1993), pp. ix, 265–67.

15. I take the dramatic metaphor from Terry Eagleton, *Criticism and Ideology: A Study in Marxist Literary Theory* (1975; reprint, London: Verso, 1978), pp. 64–101.

16. From "The Problem of Ideology in American Literary History," *Critical Inquiry* 12 (Summer 1986): 636.

17. Carolyn Porter, *Seeing and Being: The Plight of the Participant Observer in Emerson, James, Adams, and Faulkner* (Middletown, Conn.: Wesleyan University Press, 1981), p. 30.

18. See Hershel Parker, "The 'New Scholarship': Textual Evidence and Its Implications for Criticism, Literary Theory, and Aesthetics," *Studies in American Fiction* 9 (Autumn 1981): 181–97, as well as his *Flawed Texts and Verbal Icons: Literary Authority in American Fiction* (Evanston: Northwestern University Press, 1984).

19. Herman Melville, *Correspondence*, ed. Lynn Horth (Evanston and Chicago: Northwestern University Press and the Newberry Library, 1993), p. 186. See Sanford E. Marovitz, "Melville's Problematic *'Being,'* " *ESQ* 28 (1982): 11–23.

20. Hawthorne shared Melville's effusion about *The House of Seven Gables* with his wife, Sophia, and she sent the letter to her sister Elizabeth Palmer Peabody. Sophia asked Elizabeth not to show it but to study it as a piece of sincerity by "a boy in opinion." Melville's speculations "would be considered perhaps impious, if one did not take in the whole scope of the case." Nothing pleases her better than to hear "this growing man dash his tumultuous waves of thought up against Mr. Hawthorne's great, genial, comprehending silences." Most interesting in Sophia's letter is how aware she is of the *silence* of Hawthorne's comprehension. She writes in another letter to Elizabeth that Melville had said to her that Hawthorne's "great but hospitable silence drew him out—that it was astonishing how *sociable* his silence was." Jay Leyda, *The Melville Log: A Documentary Life of Herman Melville* (1951; reprint, New York: Gordian, 1969), "Supplement," pp. 925–26.

21. Herman Melville, *The Piazza Tales and Other Prose Pieces, 1839–1860*, ed. Harrison Hayford, Alma A. MacDougall, and G. Thomas Tanselle (Evanston and Chicago: Northwestern University Press and the Newberry Library, 1987), p. 246.

22. Eagleton, *Criticism and Ideology*, p. 179.

Chapter 1   The Penny Press: Anecdotes of New York

1. Walter Benjamin, *Illuminations*, trans. Harry Zohn, ed. Hannah Arendt (New York: Shocken, 1969), pp. 88–89.

2. Richard Terdiman, *Discourse/Counter-Discourse: The Theory and Practice of Symbolic Resistance in Nineteenth-Century France* (Ithaca: Cornell University Press, 1985), p. 120.

3. Benjamin, *Illuminations*, p. 90.

4. Frank Luther Mott, *American Journalism: A History of Newspapers in the United States through 250 Years* (1941; reprint, New York: Macmillan, 1962), pp. 181–92.

5. Frank M. O'Brien, *The Story of the* Sun (1928; reprint, New York: Greenwood Press, 1968), pp. 1–24; James L. Crouthamel, *Bennett's* New York Herald *and the Rise of the Popular Press* (Syracuse, N.Y.: Syracuse University Press, 1989), p. 20.

6. *New York Sun*, July 4, 1834, as reprinted by Mott, *American Journalism*, p. 223.

7. Mott, *American Journalism*, pp. 223–24, makes this point about the *Sun*'s reporting.

8. Mott, *American Journalism*, pp. 224–27. Constance Rourke thinks the scale of Locke's joke "western": "the tone that of calm, scientific exposition of wonders such as often belonged to western comic legend. Explorations of the moon by telescope . . . were explained in the imperturbable manner of the tall tale, verging aggressively toward the appearance of truth and sheering away again." *American Humor: A Study of the National Character* (1931; reprint, New York: Doubleday, 1953), p. 56. I think the scale of the joke and its imperturbable manner is just as New York as it is western.

9. Michael Schudson, *Discovering the News: A Social History of American Newspapers* (New York: Basic Books, 1978), pp. 60, 58.

10. Charles Dickens, *Martin Chuzzlewit* (London: Oxford University Press, 1951), pp. 255–56.

11. *Columbia (South Carolina) Spy*, May 21, 1844, as reprinted in *Doings of Gotham, as Described in a Series of Letters to the Editor of the Columbia Spy*, ed. Jacob E. Spannuth (Pottsville, Pa.: Jacob E. Spannuth, 1929).

12. Philip Hone, *The Diary of Philip Hone, 1828–1851*, ed. Allan Nevins (New York: Dodd, Mead, 1927), 1:484.

13. Dan Schiller, *Objectivity and the News: The Public and the Rise of Commercial Journalism* (Philadelphia: University of Pennsylvania Press, 1981), p. 15.

14. Crouthamel, *Bennett's* New York Herald, assesses Schiller and Schudson's evidence on the question of the *Herald*'s audience and concludes that we can't know for sure. What we can say is that "Bennett's paper had a large circulation and that its contents had a wide and diverse appeal" (p. 161). Nina Baym argues that the story papers (weekend papers with serialized novels) also had overlapping audiences, both middle and working class. Michael Denning sees these novels as class *forming* and thinks they were read by working-class readers. His argument complements Dan Schiller's about the penny press

audience. See Baym's *Novels, Readers, and Reviewers: Responses to Fiction in Antebellum America* (Ithaca: Cornell University Press, 1984), pp. 44–62, and Michael Denning's *Mechanic Accents: Dime Novels and Working-Class Culture in America* (London: Verso, 1987), pp. 27–46.

15. Merton M. Sealts, Jr., *Melville's Reading* (Columbia: University of South Carolina Press, 1988), pp. 88, 127.

16. See Crouthamel, *Bennett's* New York Herald, pp. 28–31. See also Patricia Cline Cohen, "Unregulated Youth: Masculinity and Murder in the 1830s City," *Radical History Review* 52 (1992): 33–52. Cohen notes that Bennett reprinted his April 11 article on April 12 and said that the demand for it had been so high that day-old copies were selling for a shilling, well above the newsboy price of one penny. She also discovers that Jewett was well known in the press before her murder and that she had a relationship with William Attree, a police-court reporter for the *Transcript*.

17. Mott, *American Journalism*, p. 303.

18. Ralph Waldo Emerson, *The Journals and Miscellaneous Notebooks*, ed. Merton M. Sealts, Jr. (Cambridge: Harvard University Press, Belknap Press, 1965), 5:462.

19. Henry D. Thoreau, "Slavery in Massachusetts" (delivered at the antislavery celebration at Framingham July 4, 1854), *Reform Papers*, ed. Wendell Glick (Princeton: Princeton University Press, 1973), p. 100.

20. William Charvat, *The Profession of Authorship in America, 1800–1870: The Papers of William Charvat*, ed. Matthew J. Bruccoli (Columbus: Ohio State University Press, 1968), pp. 64–65.

21. Ralph Waldo Emerson, "The American Scholar," *The Collected Works* (Cambridge: Harvard University Press, Belknap Press, 1971), 1:67–68.

22. *Log Cabin* for April 3, 1841, as quoted in James Parton, *The Life of Horace Greeley* (New York: Mason Brothers, 1855), p. 190.

23. Constance Rourke in her *Trumpets of Jubilee* has a perceptive analysis of Greeley's public image (1927; reprint, New York: Harcourt, Brace and World, 1963), p. 199.

24. Jonathan Raban, *Soft City* (New York: E. P. Dutton, 1974), p. 37.

25. Horace Greeley, *Hints toward Reforms, in Lectures, Addresses, and Other Writings* (New York: Harper & Brothers, 1850), p. 86.

26. Parton, *Life of Horace Greeley*, pp. 391–411. See also Charvat, *Profession of Authorship*, pp. 168–89, for the attacks on Ripley for working as a "hireling" for the *Tribune*.

27. Margaret Fuller, *Papers on Literature and Art* (New York: AMS Press, 1972), pp. 139–40. Edgar Allan Poe makes something of the same point: "we now demand the light artillery of the intellect; we need the curt, the condensed, the pointed, the readily diffused—in place of the verbose, the detailed, the voluminous, the inaccessible." *The Complete Works of Edgar Allan Poe*, ed. James A. Harrison (New York: Thomas Y. Crowell, 1902), 16:117–18.

28. Horace Greeley, *Recollections of a Busy Life* (New York: J. B. Ford, 1868), p. 179.

29. Bell Gale Chevigny, *The Woman and the Myth: Margaret Fuller's Life and Writing* (Old Westbury, N.Y.: The Feminist Press, 1976), p. 289.

30. Among later *Tribune* comments on Melville are those by Greeley on *Omoo* on June 26, 1847; those presumably by George Ripley on *Mardi* (May 10, 1849), and on *White-Jacket* (April 9, 1850); as well as reviews of *Moby-Dick* (November 22, 1851) and *The Piazza Tales* (June 23, 1856). For Fuller reviewing Melville see Jay Leyda, *The Melville Log: A Documentary Life of Herman Melville* (1951; reprint, New York: Gordian, 1969), p. 207, and for Melville's purchase of *Hints* see Sealts, *Melville's Reading*, p. 180.

31. One early reader who does is Fitz-James O'Brien, "Melville and Curtis," *Putnam's Monthly* 9 (April 1857): 384–93.

32. The most amusing account of Cooper's lawsuits is Greeley's own in his *Recollections*, pp. 261–65.

33. See *The Correspondence of Henry David Thoreau*, ed. Walter Harding and Carl Bode (New York: New York University Press, 1958), p. 232.

34. Erik S. Lunde, *Horace Greeley* (Boston: Twayne, 1981), p. 26.

35. Stuart Blumin, "Introduction," *New York by Gas-Light and Other Urban Sketches by George G. Foster*, ed. Stuart Blumin (Berkeley: University of California Press, 1990), p. 34.

36. Herbert Anthony Kellar, ed., *Solon Robinson: Pioneer and Agriculturist: Selected Writings* (1936; reprint, New York: DaCapo Press, 1968), 1:38.

37. Jeter Allen Isely, *Horace Greeley and the Republican Party, 1855–1861: A Study of the* New York Tribune (1947; reprint, New York: Octagon Books, 1965), p. 5.

Chapter 2   Windows on the World: Guides to New York

1. First published in *The New Yorker* for March 29, 1976, Steinberg's drawing has been reproduced and imitated again and again since. It is one of the most influential and popular images of New York City yet produced.

2. John A. Kouwenhoven, *The Columbia Historical Portrait of New York: An Essay in Graphic History* (1953; reprint, New York: Harper & Row, 1972), pp. 242–44.

3. The event was held on September 27, 1855. Dozens of well-known writers attended; others unable to come (including Melville) sent letters. Whitman was not invited. See Ezra Greenspan, *Walt Whitman and the American Reader* (New York: Cambridge University Press, 1990), pp. 3–4.

4. See Richard D. Altick, *The Shows of London* (Cambridge: Harvard University Press, Belknap Press, 1978), pp. 134–47.

5. See also John W. Reps's history of the lithographed urban view, *Views and Viewmakers of Urban America* (Columbia: University of Missouri Press,

1984). For the years 1848–59, Reps records fifty-two lithographed views of New York.

6. James L. Machor, *Pastoral Cities: Urban Ideals and the Symbolic Landscape of America* (Madison: University of Wisconsin Press, 1987), p. 88.

7. A significant later example is *Picturesque America; or, The Land We Live In* (1874; reprint, New York: Lyle Stuart, 1974), edited by William Cullen Bryant. The two volumes of this immense gift book contain hundreds of engravings of the most picturesque sights in the United States. Most of them are representations of well-known natural scenes, but Harry Fenn's engravings of New York scenes show the picturesque conventions at work. Most of the scenes are framed with foliage; the urban is made to appear balanced and calm. Even Fenn's two views from the top of Trinity steeple are framed by softened-looking parts of the tower, although in one the energy and crowding of Broadway is clearly visible far below.

8. "New-York Daguerreotyped" in *Putnam's Monthly* 2 (February 1853): 121–36. The panorama is given special prominence in the issue because it folds out. It demonstrates the magazine's special dedication to promoting New York and embodying its literary culture. See Kouwenhoven, *Columbia Historical Portrait of New York*, pp. 188–241, and Reps, *Views and Viewmakers of Urban America*, passim, for reproductions of other panoramas.

9. Edward K. Spann, *The New Metropolis: New York City, 1840–1857* (New York: Columbia University Press, 1981), p. 105.

10. "Editorial Appendix," Herman Melville, *The Piazza Tales, and Other Prose Pieces, 1839–1860*, ed. Harrison Hayford, Alma A. MacDougall, and G. Thomas Tanselle (Evanston and Chicago: Northwestern University Press and the Newberry Library, 1987), p. 702.

11. Herman Melville, *Redburn, His First Voyage* (Evanston and Chicago: Northwestern University Press and the Newberry Library, 1969), p. 149.

12. Edgar Allan Poe also imagines New York in the distant future in his short piece "Mellonta Tauta," published in *Godey's Lady's Book* in April 1848. The New York of 2848 is nonexistent, but the travelers aboard the balloon airship *Skylark* look out over their panoramic world and observe that the experts in "Amriccan [*sic*] antiquities" have been amazed at the number of churches on the small island. *The Short Fiction of Edgar Allan Poe*, ed. Stuart and Susan Levine (Indianapolis: Bobbs-Merrill, 1976), pp. 588–96.

13. Other similar guidebooks of the late 1840s period are Edward Ruggles, *A Picture of New-York in 1848* (New York: C. S. Francis, 1848) and the anonymously published *The Picturesque Tourist* (New York: n.p., 1849).

14. Ezekiel Porter Belden, *New York—As It Is; Being the Counterpart of the Metropolis of America* (New York: J. P. Prall, 1849), pp. 45–49, 125.

15. Asa Greene, *A Glance at New York* (New York: Author, 1837), pp. 79, 83.

16. Asa Greene, *The Perils of Pearl Street; Including a Taste of the Dangers of Wall Street, by a Late Merchant* (New York: Betts and Anstice, 1834).

17. Cornelius Mathews, *A Pen-and-Ink Panorama of New York City* (New York: John S. Taylor, 1853), p. 15.

18. Terry Eagleton, *Walter Benjamin; or, Towards a Revolutionary Criticism* (London: Verso, 1981), pp. 25–26.

19. Dana Brand, *The Spectator and the City in Nineteenth-Century American Literature* (New York: Cambridge University Press, 1991), pp. 1–10. Brand argues for a long history of the flaneur in England and shows that "the flaneur, understood by Benjamin and others as an exclusively and quintessentially Continental phenomenon, was in fact a significant presence in the culture of the United States in the three decades before the Civil War" (p. 9).

20. Priscilla Parkhurst Ferguson, "Reading Revolutionary Paris," in *Literature and Social Practice*, ed. Philippe Desan, Priscilla Parkhurst Ferguson, and Wendy Griswold (Chicago: University of Chicago Press, 1989), p. 48.

21. Judith Wechsler, *A Human Comedy: Physiognomy and Caricature in Nineteenth-Century Paris* (Chicago: University of Chicago Press, 1982), p. 20.

22. Ferguson, "Reading Revolutionary Paris," pp. 61–62.

23. Brand, *Spectator and the City*, p. 19.

24. There are, for example: Charles Knight, ed., *London* in six volumes (1841–43); the "London Penetralia" series in *Our Own Times*, April–July 1846; Albert Smith, ed., *Gavarni in London: Sketches of Life and Character* (1849); G. M. Smith, *Curiosities of London Life; or, Phases Physiological and Social of the Great Metropolis* (1853) and his *Little World of London; or, Pictures in Little of London Life* (1867); J. E. Ritchie, *The Night Side of London* (1857), and his *Here and There in London* (1859) and *About London* (1860). For a more complete list, see H. J. Dyos, "The Slums of Victorian London," *Victorian Studies* 11 (September 1967): 5–40.

25. Humphry House, *The Dickens World* (London: Oxford University Press, 1961), p. 135.

26. Dyos, "Slums of Victorian London," says, "Mayhew's work was essentially a form of higher journalism, not of social analysis." Mayhew's "findings . . . provided little more than a panorama of the poverty—and of the itinerant employment—to be seen on the streets. It is possible to say that they suffered from his under-disciplined curiosity and his spontaneous desire to make the poor known to the rich" (pp. 12–13).

27. Stuart Blumin, "Introduction," *New York by Gas-Light and other Urban Sketches by George G. Foster*, ed. Stuart Blumin (Berkeley: University of California Press, 1990), p. 38.

28. J. C. Derby, *Fifty Years among Authors, Books and Publishers* (New York: G. W. Carleton, 1884), pp. 130–31.

29. G[eorge] G. Foster, *New York Naked* (New York: Robert M. DeWitt, [1854]), p. 17.

30. Janis P. Stout, *Sodoms in Eden: The City in American Fiction before 1860* (Westport, Conn.: Greenwood Press, 1976), p. 37.

31. Fanny Fern, "Some Things in New York," in *Folly As It Flies* (New York: G. W. Carleton, 1868), p. 190.

32. Lydia Maria Child, *Letters from New York* (New York: C. S. Francis, 1844), p. 14.

33. Edwin Hubbell Chapin, *Humanity and the City* (1854; reprint, New York: Arno Press, 1974), p. 33.

34. See Richard Sennett's *The Conscience of the Eye: The Design and Social Life of Cities* (New York: Alfred A. Knopf, 1990) for thoughtful remarks on New York walking by a 1990s flaneur.

35. Up to about 1835 American publishing was predominantly local: most cities and towns in the Atlantic states produced their own books, and almost all publishers were primarily retail booksellers. See William Charvat, *The Profession of Authorship in America 1800–1870: The Papers of William Charvat*, ed. Matthew J. Bruccoli (Columbus: Ohio State University Press, 1968), p. 169. The biggest changes occurred in the 1840s. Before 1842, United States publishers issued about a hundred books a year and had revenues of about $2.5 million. In 1855, they published 1,092 books and had revenues of $16 million. Twelve million of these dollars were earned by houses in Boston, Philadelphia, and New York, and of this half was New York's share. John Tebbel, *A History of Book Publishing in the United States* (New York: R. R. Bowker, 1972), 1:262. See also Ezra Greenspan, *Walt Whitman and the American Reader* (New York: Cambridge University Press, 1990), pp. 13–38.

36. Perry Miller, *The Raven and the Whale: The War of Words and Wits in the Era of Poe and Melville* (New York: Harcourt, Brace and World, 1956), p. 15.

37. Brand, *Spectator and the City*, p. 73.

38. John Quincy Adams said he would not write for the *Democratic Review* for the reason that literature was "aristocratic; that democracy of numbers and literature were self-contradictory." Quoted in John Stafford, *The Literary Criticism of "Young America": A Study in the Relationship of Politics and Literature* (1952; reprint, New York: Russell & Russell, 1967), p. 5.

39. As quoted in Thomas Bender, *New York Intellect: A History of Intellectual Life in New York City* (Baltimore: Johns Hopkins University Press, 1987), p. 161.

40. Herman Melville, *White-Jacket; or, The World in a Man-of-War*, ed. Harrison Hayford, Hershel Parker, and G. Thomas Tanselle (Evanston and Chicago: Northwestern University Press and the Newberry Library, 1970), pp. 74, 144. Subsequent citations will appear in my text.

41. *White-Jacket*'s New York imagery is so precise that the New York side of the simile outruns the warship side. After an imagined cannonading, the ship's "bulwarks might look like the walls of the houses in West Broadway in New York, after being broken into and burned out by the Negro Mob" (69). The ship is so neat that you see "all the decks clear and unobstructed as the sidewalks of Wall Street of a Sunday morning" (87). Shoveling snow on board

is "like Broadway in winter, the morning after a storm, when rival shop-boys are at work cleaning the sidewalk" (117).

42. Miller, *Raven and the Whale*, p. 145.

43. On bourgeois voyeurism see Richard Sennett, *The Fall of Public Man: On the Social Psychology of Capitalism* (New York: Random House, 1976), passim, and Brand, *Spectator and the City*, pp. 1–10, passim.

44. Cornelius Mathews, *Big Abel and the Little Manhattan* (New York: Wiley & Putnam, 1845), p. 79.

45. Mathews, *Pen-and-Ink Panorama of New York City*, pp. 32–33.

Chapter 3 Walt Whitman: Over the Roofs of the World

1. Richard Maurice Bucke, *Walt Whitman* (Philadelphia: David McKay, 1883), pp. 19–20. I follow Paul Zweig, *Walt Whitman: The Making of the Poet* (New York: Basic Books, 1984), pp. 112–13, in quoting the passage as an example of Whitman's self-making myth.

2. A superb summary of Whitman's newspaper work is in Ezra Greenspan, *Walt Whitman and the American Reader* (New York: Cambridge University Press, 1990), pp. 39–62.

3. Emerson's letter is reproduced in facsimile in Horace Traubel, *With Walt Whitman in Camden* (New York: Rowman and Littlefield, 1961), vol. 4, following page 152.

4. Thomas L. Brasher, *Whitman as Editor of the* Brooklyn Daily Eagle (Detroit: Wayne State University Press, 1970), p. 141.

5. *Brooklyn Daily Times* (September 9, 1857), as reprinted in *The Uncollected Poetry and Prose of Walt Whitman*, ed. Emory Holloway (Gloucester, Mass.: P. Smith, 1972), 2:10–12.

6. As quoted in Betsy Erkkila, *Whitman the Political Poet* (New York: Oxford University Press, 1989), p. 27.

7. Walt Whitman, *The Gathering of the Forces: Editorials, Essays, Literary and Dramatic Reviews and Other Material Written by Walt Whitman as Editor of the* Brooklyn Daily Eagle *in 1846 and 1847*, ed. Cleveland Rodgers and John Black (New York: G. P. Putnam's Sons, 1920), 2:246–47.

8. Traubel, *With Walt Whitman*, 4:2.

9. See Erkkila, *Whitman the Political Poet*, passim.

10. Whitman, *Uncollected Poetry and Prose*, 1:262.

11. Walt Whitman, *The Early Poems and the Fiction*, ed. Thomas L. Brasher (New York: New York University Press, 1963), p. 152.

12. David S. Reynolds thinks that *Franklin Evans* shows that Whitman knew that in America moral fanaticism (on temperance) could be exploited as an avenue to the tabooed. Whitman "*knew the reformers better than they knew themselves*" and could see that their extremism could subvert the morality they ostensibly prized. *Beneath the American Renaissance: The Subversive Imagination*

in the Age of Emerson and Melville (New York: Alfred A. Knopf, 1988), p. 105. Betsy Erkkila, following Sean Wilentz, comments that temperance had important political content as well. The "issue . . . was basic to the cause of artisan republicanism in New York City, particularly among the Working-men's movement and the trade unions of the 1830s." *Whitman the Political Poet*, p. 32.

13. As quoted in Erkkila, *Whitman the Political Poet*, p. 35.

14. The "Sun-Down Papers" are reprinted in *Uncollected Poetry and Prose*, 1:35–51. "Sketches of the Sidewalks and Levees" is in 1:199–218. "Brooklyniana" is in 2:222–321. "City Photographs" is reprinted in *Walt Whitman and the Civil War: A Collection of Original Articles and Manuscripts*, ed. Charles I. Glicksberg (Philadelphia: University of Pennsylvania Press, 1933), pp. 16–62. "New York Dissected" is collected in *New York Dissected*, ed. Emory Holloway and Ralph Adimari (New York: Rufus Rockwell Wilson, 1936).

15. George G. Foster, *New York in Slices, by an Experienced Carver; Being the Original Slices Published in the New York Tribune* (New York: William H. Graham, 1849), pp. 43–49.

16. George G. Foster, *New York by Gas-Light and Other Urban Sketches by George G. Foster*, ed. Stuart Blumin (Berkeley: University of California Press, 1990), p. 173.

17. Sean Wilentz, *Chants Democratic: New York City and the Rise of the American Working Class, 1788–1850* (New York: Oxford University Press, 1984), pp. 300–301.

18. On Walsh see Wilentz, *Chants Democratic*, pp. 326–35.

19. Greenspan, *Walt Whitman*, p. 70.

20. Walt Whitman, *Daybooks and Notebooks*, ed. William White (New York: New York University Press, 1978), 3:668–83.

21. *Putnam's Monthly* 6 (September 1855): 321. Also, from the same review, a reaction to the word "kosmos": "Precisely what a kosmos is, we trust Mr. Whitman will take an early occasion to inform the impatient public" (p. 323).

22. *New York Tribune* (July 23, 1855).

23. Whitman, *Uncollected Poetry and Prose*, 1:44, 45.

24. Gay Wilson Allen, *The Solitary Singer* (New York: Grove Press, 1955), pp. 11, 53.

25. This account is from William Sloane Kennedy, *Reminiscences of Walt Whitman* (1896; reprint, New York: Haskell House, 1973), pp. 73–74. Cornelius Mathews describes newsboys who sell obscene material in his novel *Money-penny; or, The Heart of the World: A Romance of the Present Day* (New York: Dewitt & Davenport, 1849), p. 47. Herman Melville writes about sailor reading: "Their favorite authors were such as you may find in the book-stalls around Fulton Market; they were slightly physiological in their nature."

White-Jacket; or, The World in a Man-of-War (Evanston and Chicago: Northwestern University Press and the Newberry Library, 1970), p. 169.

26. On this point see James Dougherty, *Walt Whitman and the Citizen's Eye* (Baton Rouge: Louisiana State University Press, 1993), p. 32, and M. Wynn Thomas, *The Lunar Light of Whitman's Poetry* (Cambridge: Harvard University Press, 1987), pp. 155–61.

27. Brasher collects Whitman's descriptions of Broadway in *Whitman as Editor of the* Brooklyn Daily Eagle, pp. 38–41.

28. Cornelius Mathews, *A Pen-and-Ink Panorama of New York City* (New York: John S. Taylor, 1853), pp. 32–33.

29. Whitman, "Christmas at 'Grace,' " in *New York Dissected*, p. 47.

30. As reprinted in Whitman, *New York Dissected*, pp. 123–24.

31. Whitman, *New York Dissected*, p. 130.

32. Whitman, *Specimen Days* (1882), as collected in *The Portable Walt Whitman*, ed. Mark Van Doren (1945; reprint, New York: Viking Press, 1973), p. 401–2.

33. Whitman, "A Backward Glance O'er Travel'd Roads" in *The Portable Walt Whitman*, p. 298.

34. Herman Melville, "Hawthorne and His Mosses," *The Piazza Tales and Other Prose Pieces, 1839–1860*, ed. Harrison Hayford, Alma A. MacDougall, and G. Thomas Tanselle (Evanston and Chicago: Northwestern University Press and the Newberry Library, 1987), p. 246.

35. ["Preface"] to the 1855 *Leaves of Grass*, xi. My quotations from the 1855 edition of *Leaves of Grass* are from a facsimile edition edited by Richard Bridgman (San Francisco: Chandler Publishing, 1968). Subsequent page numbers of the preface will be in my text. The 1855 edition differs dramatically from Whitman's subsequent editions. I quote from it to show the local New York language that Whitman later edited out.

36. Walt Whitman, "A Backward Glance O'er Travel'd Roads" (1888), in *The Portable Walt Whitman*, p. 299.

37. Reynolds, *Beneath the American Renaissance*, pp. 512–15.

38. Roy Harvey Pearce, *The Continuity of American Poetry* (Princeton: Princeton University Press, 1961), p. 41.

39. Gay Wilson Allen, *Waldo Emerson* (New York: Viking, 1981), p. 582.

40. *Putnam's Monthly* 6 (September 1855), p. 321.

41. I quote "Peeps from under a Parasol," which appeared in the New York *Ledger* for April 19, 1856, from *Ruth Hall and Other Writings*, ed. Joyce W. Warren (New Brunswick, N.J.: Rutgers University Press, 1986), pp. 272–73. The letter is reprinted from William White, "Fanny Fern to Walt Whitman: An Unpublished Letter," *American Book Collector* 11 (May 1961): 9.

42. Parton, *Ruth Hall and Other Writings*, pp. 274–77.

43. Walt Whitman, *Democratic Vistas*, in *The Portable Walt Whitman*, pp. 326–27.

Chapter 4 "Hot Corn!": Encounters with Street Children

1. *New York Aurora* (April 16, 1842), as reprinted in *Walt Whitman of the New York Aurora*, ed. Joseph Jay Rubin and Charles H. Brown (State College, Pa.: Bald Eagle Press, 1950), pp. 50–52.

2. Alexander Welsh, *City of Dickens* (New York: Clarendon Press, 1971), p. 124.

3. Lydia Maria Child, *Letters from New York* (New York: C. S. Francis, 1844), pp. 14, 95–96.

4. Solon Robinson, *Hot Corn: Life Scenes in New York Illustrated* (New York: Dewitt and Davenport, 1854), p. 45.

5. [Sara Parton], *Fern Leaves from Fanny's Portfolio* (Auburn, N.Y.: Derby & Miller, 1853), p. 105.

6. Edwin Hubbell Chapin, *Humanity in the City* (1854; reprint, New York: Arno Press, 1974), p. 16. Subsequent citations will be in my text.

7. Claude Welch, *Protestant Thought in the Nineteenth Century* (New Haven: Yale University Press, 1972), pp. 59–60, 68, 78. See below, my Chapter 7.

8. Elizabeth Oakes Smith, *The Newsboy* (New York: J. C. Derby, 1854), p. 5. Subsequent citations will be in my text.

9. Charles Loring Brace, *The Dangerous Classes of New York, and Twenty Years' Work among Them* (New York: Wynkoop & Hallenbeck, 1872), pp. 40–41.

10. See Brace, *Dangerous Classes*, pp. 80–81, 110–13, 119–22, 195–211, 228–30, and passim. Subsequent citations will be in my text.

11. Samuel Halliday, *The Lost and Found; or, Life among the Poor* (New York: Blakeman and Mason, 1859), pp. 118–25. The book does not identify the engraver of the frontispiece.

12. The accounts from the *Evening Post* for December 16, 1846, and from the *Tribune* for March 31, 1847 are from Edward K. Spann, *The New Metropolis: New York City, 1840–1857* (New York: Columbia University Press, 1981), p. 67.

13. Thomas L. Brasher, *Whitman as Editor of the* Brooklyn Daily Eagle (Detroit: Wayne State University Press, 1970), p. 167.

14. Mrs. P. Roosevelt to S. R. Johnson, July 13, 1832, Roosevelt Papers, General Theological Seminary, New York City. As quoted in Carroll Smith Rosenberg, *Religion and the Rise of the American City: The New York City Mission Movement, 1812–1870* (Ithaca: Cornell University Press, 1971), pp. 36–37n.

15. I take my account of the progress of the 1849 epidemic from Charles E. Rosenberg, *The Cholera Years: The United States in 1832, 1849, and 1866* (Chicago: University of Chicago Press, 1962), pp. 101–20. Rosenberg's sources for the visit to 20 Orange Street include the first-person *Report of Seth Geer, M.D., Resident Physician of the City of New York* (New York, 1849). Other

Rosenberg sources are the *New York Evening Post* and the *New York Tribune* for May 17, 1849. These are all first-person encounter narratives.

16. Welsh, *City of Dickens*, p. 13.

17. Charles Dickens, *Bleak House*, ed. George Ford and Sylvère Monod (New York: W. W. Norton, 1977), p. 383. Subsequent citations are in my text.

18. "Characters in Bleak House," *Putnam's Monthly* 2 (November 1853): 561. The review is unsigned.

19. As quoted by Hershel Parker in his "Historical Note" to Herman Melville, *Redburn: His First Voyage*, ed. Harrison Hayford, Hershel Parker, and G. Thomas Tanselle (Evanston and Chicago: Northwestern University Press and the Newberry Library, 1969), p. 322.

20. Melville, *Redburn*, p. 3. Subsequent citations will be in my text.

21. Wai-chee Dimock writes, "where the *Bildungsroman* registers time as accretion, *Redburn* registers it as deficit. . . . Redburn is 'inconsistent' as a character because he fails to achieve a cumulative identity over time, but that failure is altogether consistent with the book's timeless environment": *Empire for Liberty: Melville and the Poetics of Individualism* (Princeton: Princeton University Press, 1989), p. 85.

22. Compare Whitman's "The City Dead House" (1867). It graphically states what the body of a prostitute looks like but still looks for transcendence. "Her corpse they deposit unclaim'd, it lies on the damp brick pavement, / The divine woman, her body, I see the body, I look on it alone." See William Chapman Sharpe, *Unreal Cities: Urban Figuration in Wordsworth, Baudelaire, Whitman, Eliot, and Williams* (Baltimore: Johns Hopkins University Press, 1990), p. 81.

Chapter 5   Five Points: Sketches of Hell

1. Carroll Smith Rosenberg, *Religion and the Rise of the American City* (Ithaca: Cornell University Press, 1971), p. 35. Rosenberg cites: *Minutes of the Common Council*, 1784–1831, 7:168–69, 8:257–58; *New York Mirror*, January 1, 1831, and May 18, 1833; the *New York Evening Post* for March 19, 1829, and June 22–25, 1835.

2. Charles Loring Brace says, for example, "The *mass* of poverty and wretchedness is, of course, far greater in [London] . . . but certain small districts can be found in our metropolis with the unhappy fame of containing more human beings packed to the square yard, and stained with more acts of blood and riot, within a given period, than is true of any other equal space of earth in the civilized world." *The Dangerous Classes of New York, and Twenty Years' Work among them* (New York: Wynkoop & Hallenbeck, 1872), p. 25.

3. General descriptions of the Five Points abound in the nineteenth and twentieth centuries. Useful among the twentieth-century accounts are those in Carroll Smith Rosenberg, *Religion and the Rise of the American City*; Charles

E. Rosenberg, *The Cholera Years: The United States in 1832, 1849, and 1866* (Chicago: University of Chicago Press, 1962); Robert H. Bremner, *From the Depths: The Discovery of Poverty in the United States* (New York: New York University Press, 1956); and even (less authoritatively) Herbert Asbury, *The Gangs of New York: An Informal History of the Underworld* (New York: Alfred A. Knopf, 1928). On African Americans in the Points, see Roi Ottley and William Weatherby, *The Negro in New York: An Informal Social History* (New York: New York Public Library, 1967).

    4. *New York Sun*, May 29, 1834.

    5. Edgar Johnson, *Charles Dickens: His Tragedy and Triumph* (New York: Simon and Schuster, 1952), 1:113.

    6. For Dickens in New York see Perry Miller, *The Raven and the Whale: The War of Words and Wits in the Era of Poe and Melville* (New York: Harcourt, Brace and World, 1956), pp. 95–99; for Cornelius Mathews at the City Hotel dinner see also Allen F. Stein, *Cornelius Mathews* (New York: Twayne, 1974), pp. 23–36. A general history of Dickens's several visits to the United States is William Glyde Wilkins, *Charles Dickens in America* (1911; reprint, New York: Haskell House, 1970).

    7. M. A. De Wolfe Howe, *Memories of a Hostess: A Chronicle of Eminent Friendships Drawn Chiefly from the Diaries of Mrs. James T. Fields* (Boston: Atlantic Monthly Press, 1922), p. 136.

    8. Charles Dickens, *American Notes* (London: Oxford University Press, 1957), p. 90.

    9. See Alexander Welsh, *The City of Dickens* (Oxford: Clarendon Press, 1971), pp. 9–15.

    10. See Ottley and Weatherby, *Negro in New York*, pp. 76–80.

    11. Evert Duyckinck's diary describes his strolling with Cornelius Mathews "through some of the more noisy electioneering quarters of the Five Points. . . . The lower part of Mulberry Street and the Points—'Dickens' place' presented a very squalid London-like admixture of fog and mud . . . In the green moss-roofed huts in the triangle sat an Irish family as unselfconsciously as if in their native bogs." As quoted by Eugene Exman, *The Brothers Harper* (New York: Harper & Row, 1965), p. 188.

    12. George C. Foster, *New York by Gas-Light and Other Urban Sketches by George G. Foster*, ed. Stuart Blumin (Berkeley: University of California Press, 1990), p. 146. See also pp. 130, 140–49.

    13. Solon Robinson, *Hot Corn: Life Scenes in New York Illustrated* (New York: DeWitt and Davenport, 1854), p. 208; Ladies of the Mission, *The Old Brewery and the New Mission House at the Five Points* (New York: Stringer & Townsend, 1854), pp. 21, 66.

    14. Joel H. Ross, *What I Saw in New York; or, A Bird's Eye View of City Life* (Auburn, N.Y.: Derby & Miller, 1852), pp. 88–104; Samuel Iraneus Prime,

Life in New York (New York: Robert Carter, 1847); and Edwin Hubbell Chapin, *Humanity in the City* (1854; reprint, New York: Arno Press, 1974), pp. 187–220.

15. Dr. John Griscom, *The Sanitary Condition of the Laboring Population of New York* (New York: Harper & Brothers, 1845); Ladies of the Five Points Mission, *Old Brewery and the New Mission House*; Publishing Committee, American Female Guardian Society, *Wrecks and Rescues* (New York: American Female Guardian Society, 1859); Charles Loring Brace, *The Dangerous Classes of New York, and Twenty Years' Work among them* (New York: Wynkoop and Hallenbeck, 1872), pp. 90–93, 195–96, passim.

16. George G. Foster, *New York Naked* (New York: Robert M. DeWitt, [1854]), p. 25.

17. Robinson, *Hot Corn*, pp. 70–71. See especially "Life at the Five Points," pp. 190–224.

18. Foster, *New York by Gas-Light*, p. 125–26.

19. American Female Guardian Society, *Wrecks and Rescues*, p. 41. As is so often true in accounts of New York, the Society's book has the intent of nonfiction but reads like fiction in its stories of people like "The Broadway Belle" or "The Actress" or "A Family in Prison."

20. Johnson, *Charles Dickens*, 1:442.

21. Griscom, *Sanitary Condition*, pp. 66–86.

22. Richard C. Maxwell, Jr., "G. M. Reynolds, Dickens, and the Mysteries of London," *Nineteenth Century Fiction* 32 (September 1977): 188–213.

23. See Heyward Ehrlich, "The 'Mysteries' of Philadelphia: Lippard's *Quaker City* and 'Urban' Gothic," *ESQ* 18 (1972): 50–65, and Janis P. Stout, *Sodoms in Eden: The City in American Fiction before 1860* (Westport, Conn.: Greenwood Press, 1976), pp. 44–66.

24. Peter Brooks, *The Melodramatic Imagination: Balzac, Henry James, Melodrama, and the Mode of Excess* (New Haven: Yale University Press, 1976), p. 152.

25. Michael Denning, *Mechanic Accents: Dime Novels and Working-Class Culture in America* (London: Verso, 1987), p. 86.

26. Jay Monaghan, *The Great Rascal: The Life and Adventures of Ned Buntline* (New York: Bonanza Books, 1951), pp. 168–81; Richard Moody, *The Astor Riot* (Bloomington: Indiana University Press, 1958); and Lawrence W. Levine, *Highbrow/Lowbrow: The Emergence of Cultural Hierarchy in America* (Cambridge: Harvard University Press, 1988), pp. 63–69. For Levine the riot is a "struggle for power and cultural authority within theatrical space" (p. 68) and is the sign of the loss of a public space that different classes could share. The literary journals followed the events and Buntline's trial. The Duyckincks' *Literary World*, for example, commented on September 29, 1849: "The trial of the Astor Place Rioters drags its slow length along. . . . Now and then in the

evidence we get a peep into the Mysteries of New York, to which once popular work of Ned Buntline that author is made to contribute a reluctant chapter" (279). *Literary World* also reported Buntline's conviction in its October 6 issue.

27. Foster, *New York by Gas-Light*, p. 143.

28. George G. Foster, *Celio; or, New York Above Ground and Under Ground* (New York: DeWitt & Davenport, 1850), p. 92.

29. David S. Reynolds, *Beneath the American Renaissance: The Subversive Imagination in the Age of Emerson and Melville* (New York: Knopf, 1988), p. 206; Denning, *Mechanic Accents*, pp. 105–6.

30. Denning, *Mechanic Accents*, pp. 103–5.

31. Walter Edward Hugins is helpful on these distinctions. See his *Jacksonian Democracy and the Working Class: A Study of the New York Working-man's Movement 1829–1837* (Stanford, Calif.: Stanford University Press, 1960), passim.

32. Steven Marcus, *Dickens: From Pickwick to Dombey* (New York: Basic Books, 1965), pp. 27–28. Marcus's quotation (on p. 61) of Melbourne's remark about *Oliver Twist* is from David Cecil's biography.

33. Reynolds, *Beneath the American Renaissance*, pp. 205–6, 460.

34. [Edward Zane Carroll Judson], *The Mysteries and Miseries of New York: A Story of Real Life, by Ned Buntline* (New York: Berford & Co., 1848), pp. 20–80.

35. Charles Dickens, *Bleak House*, ed. George Ford and Sylvère Monod (New York: W. W. Norton, 1977), p. 559.

36. Herman Melville, *Pierre; or, The Ambiguities*, ed. Harrison Hayford, Hershel Parker, and G. Thomas Tanselle (Evanston and Chicago: Northwestern University Press and the Newberry Library, 1971), pp. 231, 359.

37. Dickens, *American Notes*, p. 90. In calling the spoken language he hears "Cant" or "the Flash," Dickens asserts that it is a special criminal argot used to exclude the lawabiding from understanding.

Chapter 6   *Putnam's* and New York Stories

1. Herman Melville, "Bartleby, the Scrivener," in *The Piazza Tales, and Other Prose Pieces, 1839–1860*, ed. Harrison Hayford, Alma A. MacDougall, and G. Thomas Tanselle (Evanston and Chicago: Northwestern University Press and the Newberry Library, 1987), p. 32. Subsequent citations will be in my text.

2. One of the most interesting summaries of the earlier criticism is Milton R. Stern's "Towards 'Bartleby the Scrivener,' " in Duane J. MacMillan, ed., *The Stoic Strain in American Literature* (Toronto: University of Toronto Press, 1979). See also my "Melville's Tales" in John Bryant, ed., *A Companion to Melville Studies* (New York: Greenwood Press, 1986), pp. 241–78, and Dan

McCall, *The Silence of Bartleby* (Ithaca: Cornell University Press, 1989), particularly pp. 1–32.

3. For an account of the critical reaction to *Pierre*, see Leon Howard and Hershel Parker's "Historical Note," in Herman Melville, *Pierre; or, The Ambiguities*, ed. Harrison Hayford, Hershel Parker, and G. Thomas Tanselle (Evanston and Chicago: Northwestern University Press and the Newberry Library, 1971), pp. 365–421.

4. Fitz-James O'Brien, "Our Young Authors—Melville," *Putnam's Monthly* 1 (February 1853): 164. O'Brien wrote about Melville again in "Our Authors and Authorship: Melville and Curtis," *Putnam's* 9 (April 1857): 384–93. O'Brien makes the same criticisms even though he has read the short pieces and *The Confidence-Man*. In my view O'Brien is more wrong in 1857 than in 1853 because he has misread the new work.

5. See Edward Cary, *George William Curtis* (Boston and New York: Houghton Mifflin and the Riverside Press, 1894), and, particularly, Gordon Milne, *George William Curtis and the Genteel Tradition* (Bloomington: Indiana University Press, 1956). At first, Curtis shared the "Easy Chair" with Donald G. Mitchell ("Ik Marvel"), but in April 1854 Curtis took over completely and wrote the column for forty years. For the new *Harper's Weekly*, founded in 1857, he wrote "The Lounger," but in December 1863 he became the *Weekly's* political editor. By "the end of 1863 [Curtis's political column] was being read by 120,000 people" every week (Milne, *Curtis*, p. 118).

6. Warner Berthoff, *The Example of Melville* (Princeton: Princeton University Press, 1962), p. 138.

7. *Putnam's Monthly* 1 (January 1853): 1.

8. See Frank Luther Mott, *A History of American Magazines, 1850–1865* (1938; reprint, Cambridge: Harvard University Press, 1966), pp. 383–405. In its first issue (June 1850), *Harper's* announced that it would "transfer as rapidly as they may be issued all the continuous tales of Dickens, Bulwer, Croly, Lever, Warren, and other distinguished contributors to British Periodicals."

9. Perry Miller thinks that *The Trippings of Tom Pepper* is quite different from *The Adventures of Harry Franco* because of the intervening influence of Charles Dickens. The "reality" of poverty has made the later collection more "serious." See Perry Miller, *The Raven and the Whale: The War of Words and Wits in the Era of Poe and Melville* (New York: Harcourt, Brace and World, 1956), pp. 178–80.

10. Thomas Bender, *New York Intellect: A History of Intellectual Life in New York City* (Baltimore: Johns Hopkins University Press, 1987), p. 165.

11. George William Curtis, *Nile Notes of a Howadji* (New York: Harper & Bros., 1851), p. 201. *Howadji* is an Arabic word that signifies merchant or peddler, but by Curtis's time it meant any "up the Nile" tourist.

12. The narrator and his friends hike in the Catskills, and the artist

"Swansdowne" sees Kensett paintings in the landscape: "With his delicately sensitive artistic eye, Swansdowne glanced among the trees, and from time to time, announced 'a Kensett,' as a broad bit of mossed rock, or a shapely stretch of trees with the mountain outline beyond, recalled the poetic accuracy and characteristic subjects of that artist." This is in-group writing, in which readers who know the joke—that Kensett traveled with Curtis and is himself "Swansdowne"—enjoy its inclusion. George William Curtis, *Lotus-Eating: A Summer Book*, illustrated by John F. Kensett (1852; reprint, New York: Dix, Edwards & Co., 1856), p. 55.

13. Curtis, *Lotus-Eating*, p. 132. Subsequent citations will be in my text.

14. Van Wyck Brooks, *The Times of Melville and Whitman* (1947; reprint, New York: E. P. Dutton, 1953), p. 20.

15. I take the editorial history of *Putnam's* from Arnold G. Tew's 1969 Case Western Reserve University dissertation, "*Putnam's Monthly*: Its Men and their Literary and Social Policies." Tew's work clarifies and corrects details in Mott, *History of American Magazines*, and in Milne, *Curtis*. Sources other than Tew often describe Curtis as an "editorial adviser" to Dix and Edwards rather than as the "secret" editor. This may come to the same thing. Dana's participation is to my knowledge described only in Tew.

16. See the *Tribune*'s welcoming of the new magazine in its issue for February 3, 1853, or the description of "Horace Greeley" in *Putnam's* for July 1855.

17. "The Great Exhibition and Its Visitors," *Putnam's Monthly* 2 (December 1853): 577–93. The article features descriptions of the out-of-town visitors the exhibition has drawn and complains about the New Yorkers who are not going. It concludes with familiar New York boosterism: "[The exhibition's] avenues are crowded more and more, and whoever can speak and write in our land begins to feel its inspiration. . . . The Crystal Palace is at last the fashion, and its projectors, builders, encouragers, abettors, and contributors, have quietly ascended to the position due to their liberality, discernment, skill, faith and courage. May their light never be less!" (p. 593).

18. "The World of New York," *Putnam's Monthly* 8 (July 1856): 108.

19. *The Potiphar Papers* (New York: G. P. Putnam, 1853), p. 32. See the praise of the magazine generally, and "Our Best Society" in particular, in the *New York Tribune* for February 3 and 5, 1853.

20. Curtis had met Thackeray in London in 1850 and then again during the English novelist's first American lecture tour in the winter of 1852–53. In 1855 they saw much more of each other and became good friends, enjoying convival good times on the town. One early notice of Curtis's engagement to Anna Shaw is in a November 14, 1855, letter from Thackeray to his sisters: "A niece of Russell Sturgis, quite a young girl, is going to marry the cleverest and most gentlemanlike man in New York" (Milne, *Curtis*, pp. 80–84). See also Curtis's "Thackeray in America," *Putnam's Monthly* 1 (June 1853): 638–

42. Longfellow's account of Thackeray's London dinner remark was reported to Curtis by Samuel Ward. See Jay Leyda, *The Melville Log* (1951; reprint, New York: Gordian Press, 1969), p. 507.

21. George Templeton Strong, *Diary* (New York: Macmillan, 1952), 2:114.

22. Curtis traveled in Egypt with Quincy Shaw, his future wife's uncle, and calls him the "Pacha of the Nile" in *Nile Notes of a Howadji*, passim. Perhaps Kurz Pacha is a portrait of Quincy.

23. Leon H. Vincent, *American Literary Masters* (Boston and New York: Houghton Mifflin and the Riverside Press, 1906), p. 430.

24. George William Curtis, *Prue and I* (New York: Harper & Brothers, 1856), p. 19. Subsequent citations will be in my text.

25. Melville sticks in Curtis's mind; as late as 1865 he is remembering *Moby-Dick*. He states his good opinion of the eleven-year-old book in his *Harper's* "Easy Chair" column for September 1862, and three years later in the same column suggests, in describing a dazzling snow scene, that "Herman Melville could have found a fresh hint for his wonderful chapter upon whiteness in 'The Whale' " (March 1865). Barton Levi St. Armand noticed that the 1892 deluxe reprint of *Prue and I* by *Harper's* has an illustration of "Bartleby the scrivener" done by Albert Edward Sterner (p. 115). See St. Armand's "Curtis's 'Bartleby': An Unrecorded Melville Reference," *Papers of the Bibliographical Society of America* 71 (1977): 219–20.

26. Mott, *American Magazines*, p. 423. The Godwin quotation is from *Putnam's* 5 (January 1855): 97.

27. Charles Eliot Norton, ed., *Orations and Addresses of George William Curtis* (New York: Harper & Brothers, 1894), p. 2. The text of Curtis's speech is reprinted in this same volume, pp. 1–35.

28. George Monteiro, "More on Herman Melville in the 1890s," *Melville Society Extracts* 30 (May 1977), p. 14. I am not aware that Donald Grant Mitchell ever published in *Putnam's*. His mild prose appeared in *Harper's*. See Wayne R. Kime, *Donald G. Mitchell* (Boston: Twayne, 1985), who lists no *Putnam's* contributions.

29. As quoted in Thomas Inge, ed., *Bartleby the Inscrutable: A Collection of Commentary on Herman Melville's Tale "Bartleby the Scrivener"* (Hamden, Conn.: Archon Books, 1979), p. 37.

30. R. Bruce Bickley thinks Irving's stories are the model for Melville's short narratives, and he points out that Melville was given two volumes of Irving in June 1853. *The Method of Melville's Short Fiction* (Durham: Duke University Press, 1975), pp. 26–44.

31. *Dream Life: A Fable of the Seasons* (New York: Charles Scribner, 1851), p. 25. Subsequent citations appear in the chapter text. *Dream Life's* introduction states the book's purpose: "I would catch up here and there the shreds of feelings, which the brambles and roughness of the world have left tangling in my heart, and weave them out into those soft, and perfect tissues, which—if

the world had been only a little less rough,—might now perhaps enclose my heart altogether" (p. 16).

32. I quote from the book publication of the novel: James D. Maitland, *The Lawyer's Story; or, The Orphan's Wrongs* (New York: H. Long & Brother, 1853), p. 7. Subsequent citations appear in the chapter text.

33. See my " 'Bartleby' and *The Lawyer's Story*," *American Literature* 47 (1975): 432–36.

34. See also "The Problem of the Lost Prince," *Putnam's Magazine* 3 (February 1854): 202–12.

35. "Doctors" in *Putnam's* 2 (July 1853): 66–71, and "Lawyers" in *Putnam's* 8 (November 1856): 449–58. Richard Sennett writes about the new authority figures in the nineteenth century: "There were also attempts to enshrine individualism itself, so that the expert—the engineer, doctor, or scientist with modern technological skills—working alone according only to the dictates of his expertise, yet controlling others, became a figure of authority. Tocqueville calls 'the independent ones' the only people of his time securely able to command respect from others and make them afraid. . . . The autonomous expert would doctor, engineer, or plan cities for other people—yet the conditions of entry into these professions became more and more restricted, so that the need for services always outstripped the supply. The market shaped the appearance of these figures of strength, even as they gave the appearance of rising above it." *Authority* (New York: Alfred A. Knopf, 1980), p. 45.

36. "The Counterfeit Coin," *Putnam's Monthly* 7 (June 1856): 576–83. I have not found an author.

37. Patricia Barber analyzes "Bartleby, the Scrivener" by asking how different our interpretation would be if Bartleby were a woman. We would see a story about a man "who comes to love a person he cannot save." In "The Counterfeit Coin" the Bartleby-like character *is* a woman. The lawyer reacts strongly and sentimentally to his imagination of the law copyist's life, and her gender increases his terror of her poverty. The relationship does not have the love that Barber sees in the one between Bartleby and his lawyer, and the woman copyist's lawyer thinks he *has* saved her. See Barber's "What if Bartleby Were a Woman" in *The Authority of Experience*, ed. Arlyn Diamond and Lee R. Edwards (Amherst: University of Massachusetts Press, 1977), pp. 212–23.

38. Brian Foley, "Dickens Revised: 'Bartleby' and *Bleak House*," *Essays in Literature* 12 (Fall 1985): 241–50; David Jaffe, *"Bartleby, the Scrivener" and "Bleak House": Melville's Debt to Dickens* (Arlington, Va.: Mardi Press, 1981); Charlotte Walker Mendez, "Scriveners Forlorn: Dickens's Nemo and Melville's Bartleby," *Dickens Society Notes* 11 (1980): 33–38.

39. "Characters in Bleak House," *Putnam's Monthly* 2 (November 1853): 558–62. George W. Curtis was responsible for a later *Putnam's* piece on Dickens, "The Genius of Charles Dickens," which appeared in June 1855. Nina

Baym discusses the first *Putnam's* piece and other contemporary reviews of "character" in fiction in her *Novels, Readers, and Reviewers: Responses to Fiction in Antebellum America* (Ithaca: Cornell University Press, 1984), pp. 82–97.

40. The domestic imagery of the scene is perfectly done. "My Lady Dedlock . . . looking out in the early twilight from her boudoir at a keeper's lodge, and seeing the light of a fire upon the latticed panes, and smoke rising from the chimney, and a child, chased by a woman, running out into the rain to meet the shining figure of a wrapped-up man coming through the gate, has been put quite out of temper. My Lady Dedlock says she has been 'bored to death.' " *Bleak House*, ed. George Ford and Sylvère Monod (New York: W. W. Norton, 1977), p. 11.

41. Donald Fanger, *Dostoevsky and Romantic Realism: A Study of Dostoevsky in Relation to Balzac, Dickens, and Gogol* (Cambridge: Harvard University Press, 1967), p. 264.

42. Melville, *Pierre,* p. 141.

Chapter 7   Key: "Bartleby, the Scrivener"

1. Herman Melville, "Bartleby, the Scrivener," in *The Piazza Tales, and Other Prose Pieces, 1839–1860,* ed. Harrison Hayford, Alma A. MacDougall, and G. Thomas Tanselle (Evanston and Chicago: Northwestern University Press and the Newberry Library, 1987), p. 34. Subsequent citations will appear in the chapter text.

2. The most interesting article on "Bartleby" and Chancery is still Herbert M. Smith, "Melville's Master in Chancery and his Recalcitrant Clerk," *American Quarterly* 17 (1965): 734–41. T. H. Giddings details the famous murder in "Melville, the Colt-Adams Murder, and 'Bartleby,' " *Studies in American Fiction* 2 (1974): 123–32.

3. See my " 'Turkey on his Back': 'Bartleby' and New York Words," *Melville Society Extracts* 90 (September 1992): 16–19.

4. In Herman Melville's *White-Jacket* one of the ship's corporals is "Leggs," who had been "a turnkey attached to 'The Tombs' in New York" *White-Jacket; or, The World in a Man-of-War,* ed. Harrison Hayford, Hershel Parker, and G. Thomas Tanselle (Evanston and Chicago: Northwestern University Press and the Newberry Library, 1970), p. 306.

5. H. Bruce Franklin, *The Wake of the Gods: Melville's Mythology* (Stanford, Calif.: Stanford University Press, 1963), p. 126. Dan McCall's *Silence of Bartleby* (Ithaca: Cornell University Press, 1989), which also quotes the Franklin passage, is an interesting summary of how resistant "Bartleby" is to its many interpretive assaults. McCall's premise is: "the more we see of what went into the story, the less we understand the story itself" (p. 9).

6. Christ and Christ-figure interpretations of "Bartleby" include: Franklin, *Wake of the Gods*, pp. 126–36; William Bysshe Stein, "Bartleby: The Chris-

tian Conscience" in Howard P. Vincent, ed., *A Symposium: Bartleby the Scrivener* (Kent, Ohio: Kent State University Press, 1966), pp. 104–12; H. Bruce Franklin, *The Victim as Criminal and Artist* (New York: Oxford University Press, 1978); John Seelye, *Melville: The Ironic Diagram* (Evanston: Northwestern University Press, 1970), pp. 96–99; John Gardner, " 'Bartleby': Art and Social Commitment," *Philological Quarterly* 43 (January 1964): 87–98; Donald M. Fiene, "Bartleby the Christ," *American Transcendental Quarterly* 7 (1970): 18–23; and Walter E. Anderson, "Form and Meaning in 'Bartleby the Scrivener,' " *Studies in Short Fiction* 18 (1981): 383–93.

7. Claude Welch, *Protestant Thought in the Nineteenth Century* (New Haven: Yale University Press, 1972), 1:59–60, 68, 78. This part of my discussion is heavily dependent on Welch's fine book.

8. Welch, *Protestant Thought*, p. 99.

9. Strauss, as quoted in Welch, *Protestant Thought*, p. 150.

10. As quoted in Welch, *Protestant Thought*, p. 177, from Feuerbach's Heidelberg lectures, *Vorlesungen über das Wesen der Religion* (1845) translated by Ralph Manheim as *Lectures on the Essence of Religion* (New York: Harper & Row, 1967).

11. Herman Melville, *Pierre; or, The Ambiguities,* ed. Harrison Hayford, Hershel Parker, and G. Thomas Tanselle (Evanston and Chicago: Northwestern University Press and the Newberry Library, 1971), p. 214. Subsequent citations will appear in the chapter text.

12. Two scholars examine the relationship between Plinlimmon and the lawyer: Hershel Parker in "The 'Sequel' in 'Bartleby,' " in M. Thomas Inge, ed., *Bartleby the Inscrutable: A Collection of Commentary on Herman Melville's Tale* (Hamden, Conn.: Archon Books, 1979), pp. 159–65; and Lea Bertani Vozar Newman in *A Reader's Guide to the Short Stories of Herman Melville* (Boston: G. K. Hall, 1986), pp. 36–37.

13. Herman Melville, *Journals*, ed. Howard C. Horsford and Lynn Horth (Evanston and Chicago: Northwestern University Press and the Newberry Library, 1989), p. 97. Subsequent citations will be in my text.

14. Melville in his journal is always disappointed at the ordinariness of place. Visiting Cyprus he writes, "From these waters rose Venus from the foam. Found it as hard to realize such a thing as to realize on Mt. Olivet that from there Christ rose." (*Journals*, p. 95). And in a miscellaneous entry about Jerusalem, he writes "J.C. should have appeared in Taheiti [*sic*]" (p. 154).

15. See Hershel Parker, "Melville's *The Isle of the Cross*: A Survey and a Chronology," *American Literature* 62 (March 1990): 1–16. For the "Agatha story" see Melville's letters to Hawthorne in Herman Melville, *Correspondence*, ed. Lynn Horth (Evanston and Chicago: Northwestern University Press and the Newberry Library, 1993), pp. 153–63.

16. Celia Thaxter, *Among the Isles of Shoals* (Boston: James R. Osgood, 1873), pp. 177–84. The first words of the book mention Melville's "Encanta-

das" as the series of sketches that made the world acquainted with the volcanic crags and desolate beaches of the Galapagos Islands, which, Thaxter thinks, are no more barren than New Hampshire's own Isles of Shoals. See also Lyman V. Rutledge, *The Isles of Shoals in Lore and Legend* (Barre, Mass.: Barre Publishers, 1965).

17. See Merton M. Sealts, Jr., "Historical Note," *The Piazza Tales*, p. 483, and also Robert Sattelmeyer and James Barbour, "The Sources and Genesis of Melville's 'The Norfolk Isle and the Chola Widow,'" *American Literature* 50 (November 1978): 398–417. A direct response to Hershel Parker's "Melville's *Isle of the Cross*" is Basem Ra'ad, "'The Encantadas' and 'The Isle of the Cross': Melvillean Dubieties, 1853–54," *American Literature* 63 (June 1991): 316–23.

18. From Isaiah: "And the key of the house of David will I lay upon his shoulder; so he shall open, and none shall shut; and he shall shut, and none shall open" (22:22). From Matthew: "And I will give unto thee the keys of the kingdom of heaven: and whatsoever thou shalt bind on earth shall be bound in heaven: and whatsoever thou shalt loose on earth shall be loosed in heaven" (16:19). And from Revelation: "I *am* he that liveth, and was dead; and, behold, I am alive for evermore, Amen; and have the keys of hell and of death" (1:18), and "And to the angel of the church in Philadelphia write; These things saith he that is holy, he that is true, he that hath the key of David, he that openeth, and no man shutteth, and no man openeth" (3:7).

19. "Yet it is of course also true that for Hegel God has his self-consciousness in man's consciousness of him, that Spirit thus comes to self-consciousness. God, one may say, is true though not real apart from his manifestation in the world" (Welch, *Protestant Thought*, p. 102).

Chapter 8 Peter Funk: Tales of Exchange

1. See Norman O. Brown, *Hermes the Thief* (1947; reprint, Great Barrington, Mass.: Lindisfarne Press, 1990), passim.

2. The *Oxford English Dictionary* defines "genius" as the word for the tutelary god or attendant spirit allotted in pagan belief to every person at birth. A genius is also a spirit similarly connected to a place, an institution. Another meaning is a demon or spiritual being in general, like the one in the bottle. Yet another is natural ability or capacity, and a late one (not in Johnson's *Dictionary*) is the familiar "native intellectual power."

3. George G. Foster tells us about them in the *Tribune*: "The ostensible business of many intelligence offices is mostly sham or imposition. The keepers generally do nothing for either employer or employed until they have been feed [*sic*]; and when the silver is fingered their interest in the matter, either way, ceases. Nine-tenths of the indescribable trouble, the disaster, the agony, of house-keeping in New York, which constitute such constant themes of elo-

quent lamentation whenever two or three housekeepers meet, arise from the loose, dishonest Intelligence Office system. No careful housewife will ever apply a second time at an Intelligence Office for a servant." *New York in Slices, By an Experienced Carver; Being the Original Slices Published in the New York Tribune* (New York: William H. Graham, 1849), pp. 37–40.

4. George G. Foster, *New York by Gas-Light and Other Urban Sketches by George G. Foster,* ed. Stuart Blumin (Berkeley: University of California Press, 1990), p. 178.

5. Robert Greene's many pamphlets are collected in Gamini Salgado's *Cony-Catchers and Bawdy Baskets: An Anthology of Elizabethan Low Life* (Harmondsworth: Penguin, 1972). See also Frank Wadleigh Chandler, *The Literature of Roguery* (Boston: Houghton Mifflin Co., 1907), 1:93–111.

6. John Hovey Robinson's *The Life and Adventures of William Harvard Stinchfield* (n.p., 1851) has an account of the young man's fleecing in New York. See also the series of pamphlets *The Rogues and Rogueries of New York* (New York: Haney & Co., 1865). Also: *Humbug: A Look at Some Popular Impositions* (New York: S. F. French, 1859) and Joel H. Ross, *What I Saw in New York; or, A Bird's Eye View of City Life* (Auburn, N.Y.: Derby & Miller, 1852).

7. Walt Whitman, "Advice to Strangers," *Life Illustrated* (August 23, 1856), as reprinted in *New York Dissected,* ed. Emory Holloway and Ralph Adimari (New York: Rufus Rockwell Wilson, 1936), p. 141. A twentieth-century version of the same game is described in Mel Ziegler's "The Harlem Hustle," *New York Magazine* (June 3, 1968).

8. See for example T. W. Lane's "The Thimble Game," an 1850 story collected in William E. Burton's *The Cyclopedia of Wit and Humor* (New York: Appleton, 1858), 1:305–8. Peter Wilkins from backwater Georgia is going to Augusta to sell the crops. His father has warned him about "them gimblit fellers," but the cotton buyer introduces him to the game of thimbles and he is taken for $451: "Alas for poor Peter! He had awakened the wrong passenger."

9. The earliest use of the expression I have found is in a *New Orleans Daily Picayune* account of the arrest of someone mistaken to be the notorious "Negro stealer" Dr. Hines (June 10, 1840). Jonathan Green's "waking up the wrong passenger" story is in his *Gambling Unmasked!* (Philadelphia: G. B. Zieber & Co., 1847), pp. 189–93, and in *An Exposure of the Arts and Miseries of Gambling* (Philadelphia: G. B. Zieber & Co., 1847), pp. 68–69. Newspaper clippings from the controversy in the New York newspapers about Green and his books are conveniently copied in Green's own *Twelve Days in the Tombs* (New York: T. W. Strong, 1851), pp. 76–99. *Tribune* articles are September 16, 1844, September 23 and 26, 1848, and April 27, 1850. See also *Knickerbocker* 33 (January 1849): 63–64.

10. Green, *Gambling Unmasked,* pp. 279–80.

11. Green, *Arts and Miseries of Gambling,* pp. 106–9.

12. Ann Fabian, *Card Sharps, Dream Books, and Bucket Shops: Gambling in Nineteenth-Century America* (Ithaca: Cornell University Press, 1990), p. 75.

13. Jonathan H. Green, *The Secret Band of Brothers; or, The American Outlaws* (Philadelphia: G. B. Zieber & Co., 1847). Edgar Allan Poe's "Gambling" in the *Broadway Journal* 1 (March 1, 1845), 133–34, praises Green highly and makes the connection between gambling and respectable capitalist business. "There are other gamblers than those who shuffle cards and rattle dice. Nine tenths of our leading politicians are gamblers. . . . Wall street operators are nearly all gamblers. . . . Merchants are generally strongly imbued with gambling propensities." He goes on to describe the gambling "hells" of New York. Melville may have those same hells in mind when he describes Redburn's visit to a London gambling hell in *Redburn*.

14. Asa Greene, *The Perils of Pearl Street: Including a Taste of the Dangers of Wall Street, by a Late Merchant* (New York: Betts and Anstice, 1834), pp. 50–55.

15. Among Peter's many appearances are: "Peter Funk," *Brother Jonathan* (October 10, 1840); "Peter Funkiana," *New York Morning News* (April 14, 1846); "Intelligence Office Funk," *New York Morning News* (June 27, 1846); [Walt Whitman], "Sketches of the Sidewalks and Levees . . . Peter Funk," *New Orleans Daily Crescent* (March 13, 1848), as reprinted in *Uncollected Poetry and Prose*, ed. Emory Holloway (Gloucester, Mass.: P. Smith, 1972), 1:199–202; Harrison Gray Buchanan, *Asmodeus; or, Legends of New York* (New York: Munson & Co., 1848), pp. 75–78; [Edward Z. C. Judson], *Mysteries and Miseries of New York: A Story of Real Life by Ned Buntline* (New York: Berford & Co., 1848), 5:74; "The Peter Funk's Watch," *Dollar Weekly Herald* (October 8, 1849): 3; G[eorge] G. Foster, *New York in Slices*, pp. 30–33; "Swindlers and Adventurers in the City of New York," *Illustrated News* (January 1, 1853): 6–7; J. Holbrook, *Ten Years Among the Mail Bags; or, Notes from the Diary of a Special Agent of the Post-Office Department* (Philadelphia: H. Cowperthwait & Co., 1855), p. 343; [Walt Whitman], "Advice to Strangers," *Life Illustrated* (August 23, 1856), as reprinted in *New York Dissected*; the anonymously written *Tricks and Traps of New York City* (Boston: C. H. Brainard, 1857), pp. 10–22; Burton, *Cyclopedia of Wit and Humor*, 1:98–100 [Asa Greene's 1834 piece reprinted]; "A Literary Peter Funk," *Southern Literary Messenger* 32 (1861): 45–49; P. T. Barnum, *The Humbugs of the World* (New York: Carleton, 1866), pp. 167–75. Henry Louis Gates, Jr., reproduces a racist London broadside called "A Black Lecture on Language," published in 1846, which refers to "funk" as if it were black speech. The "joke" is to decline the verb ("we wer funked," "she was funked," "dey were funked"). It is difficult to tell from the broadside whether this is the word with the same meaning as the "funk" in "Peter Funk," but it is possible. See *The Signifying Monkey: A Theory of Afro-American Literary Criticism* (New York and Oxford: Oxford University Press, 1988), p. 93.

16. The definition of "Peter Funk" as a by-bidder in an auction (one who runs the price up for the auctioneer) is still in current unabridged dictionaries.

The *Dictionary of Americanisms on Historical Principles* takes its earliest citation from 1845, ten years after Greene's book. *A Dictionary of Slang, Jargon, and Cant*, compiled by Albert Barrère and Charles G. Leland (New York: Ballantine Press, 1889), gives the most helpful definition from a dictionary and makes it explicitly a New York word: "In New York, the word *funk* is connected with humbug, and 'Peter Funk' is a kind of mysterious spirit who inspires all kind of petty business tricks." Editor Leland is the same Leland who edited *Illustrated News* with P. T. Barnum in the early 1850s.

17. Cornelius Mathews, *False Pretenses; or, Both Sides of Good Society: A Comedy in Five Acts* (New York: Author, 1856).

18. The complete title continues: *Master of Arts, and Sometimes, Doctor of Medicine;—Alias, Dr. Hamilton, Col. Hamilton, Dr. Haynes, Col. Hayne, Dr. Porcher, Col. Singleton, Rev. Mr. Beman, Rev. Dr. Baker, Col. Allston, Maj. Parker, Col. Bention, Maj. Middleton, Lieut. Pringle, Capt. Rutledge, Col. Pinckney, Dr. Brandreth, Major Moore, &c &c &c in a Series of Letters to His Friends. Written by Himself* (New York: Bradley and Clark, 1840). Many of the pseudonyms are taken from respected South Carolina families. "Dr. Brandreth" comes from the "Dr. Brandreth's Pills" advertised in the *Herald*. All but five of the twenty-seven letters that make up the book are addressed to James Gordon Bennett. The copyright for the book was entered by a Thomas Hollis, so perhaps Hollis is the author.

19. Arthur Palmer Hudson's *Humor of the Old Deep South* (1936; reprint, Port Washington, N.Y.: Kennikat Press, 1970) contains a selection from Hines's *Life* that led me to the book as a whole. Hudson also reprints two articles about Hines from the *New Orleans Sun* of June 7 and 9, 1840 (pp. 342–53). Bennett's *Herald* for June 17, 1840, notes the first *Sun* article and continues: "Most of the large cities in the Union have suffered more or less from this fellow's rascalities. He has all the manners of a gentleman, an excellent education, is of good family, and his true history would be highly entertaining." Hines items also appear in the *Herald* for July 6 and October 15, 1840. Other newspaper items are: *Charleston Courier* (November 18 and 28, 1839); *New Orleans Daily Picayune* (June 6, 9, 10 and July 21, 1840); *New York Sun* (January 4 and 7, August 27, September 3, 1839; June 22, July 29, August 11, 18, 26, 28, September 4 and 24, 1840); *Brother Jonathan* (September 12, 1840). See also chapter 4 of "The Life and Adventures of Doctor D. T. Hines, the Notorious Bigamist, Jeremy Diddler, Confidence Man and Negro Thief" in *National Police Gazette* (December 1, 1860); subsequent and previous parts of this Life seem not to have survived.

20. *New York Herald*, February 28, 1837.

21. Jonathan Wild was a sophisticated eighteenth-century "thief-taker." He headed a London-wide organization that recovered stolen goods (often after having stolen them in the first place). There were many Wild pamphlets, but Fielding's *The Life of Mr. Jonathan Wild the Great* (1742) is the best-known

version. In that book the narrator seeks to establish the thief-taker as the best of men, as one of the "great." We know of course that he is one of the worst of men, cruelly manipulating tender souls. Fielding's satire is primarily political because it holds up to ridicule "the Great Man," Sir Robert Walpole, who controlled English politics during the era just before *Jonathan Wild* was published. The narrator says Wild is "great" in his field as others are in theirs—politics, for example.

22. Asa Greene, *A Glance at New York* (New York: Author, 1837), p. 67.

23. The liveliest account of the Heth hoax is in Barnum's own *The Life of P. T. Barnum; Written by Himself* (New York: Redfield, 1855), pp. 148–76. Barnum is hardly a reliable source, but then neither are the newspapers. Better is Neil Harris, *Humbug: The Art of P. T. Barnum* (Boston: Little, Brown & Co., 1973), pp. 20–26.

24. Charles Godfrey Leland, *Memoirs* (New York: D. Appleton, 1889), pp. 112–13.

25. Harris, *Humbug*, pp. 77–79.

26. "Barnum, you are the Self-Offered American Moral Sacrifice, and National Columbia Scape-Goat of the Century" *Vanity Fair* 2 (December 22, 1860), 306, as quoted in Frank Luther Mott, *A History of American Magazines, 1850–1865* (1938; reprint, Cambridge: Harvard University Press, 1966), 1:213.

27. Leland, *Memoirs*, p. 66.

28. Barnum, *Life*, p. 12.

29. *Harper's Monthly* 10 (1854–55): 551.

30. *New York Tribune* (July 8, 1854). Americans themselves were not necessarily unhappy that their highly finished rogues gave them notoriety. *Tricks and Traps of New York City*, despite its warnings to the public, is proud: "If the production of highly finished scoundrels ever becomes a matter of emulation among the nations of the earth, patriotism, a national pride in our country, and the undeniable facts in the case lead us to assert, that America need yield the palm to none; and should there ever be a great World Exhibition of Rogues, in which all nations shall vie with each other in producing fine assortments of scamps, we modestly claim in behalf of our beloved city of New York the very first place for its fine corps of swindlers" (Boston: C. H. Brainard, 1857), p. 5. *Tricks and Traps* was published in "Brainards Half-Dime Books," and a series of *Tricks and Traps* pamphlets followed. No authors are given.

31. The 1847 *Daily Globe* account is heretofore unrecorded, but the other details are from my article "The Original Confidence Man," *American Quarterly* 21 (1969): 560–77.

32. *New York Herald* (July 8, 1849).

33. *New York Herald* (July 11, 1849). The *Knickerbocker* praises the "widely circulated" and "trenchant satire" and attributes it to the *Herald's* congressional reporter Houston (*Knickerbocker* 34 [September 1849]: 279).

34. Several of Thompson's victims testified at his trial, and one cites

Thompson's use of a routine in which he claimed to be the son of Nicholas Biddle, thus connecting the 1849 Thompson to the 1847 swindler at least in his methods. The 1849 trial accounts are reported by Michael S. Reynolds in "The Prototype for Melville's Confidence Man," *PMLA* 86 (October 1971): 1009–13.

35. George W. Matsell, *Vocabulum; or, The Rogue's Lexicon* (New York: National Police Gazette, 1859), pp. 20–21.

Chapter 9 "We Golden Boys, the Moderns": *The Confidence-Man*

1. Herman Melville, *The Confidence-Man: His Masquerade*, ed. Harrison Hayford, Hershel Parker, and G. Thomas Tanselle (Evanston and Chicago: Northwestern University Press and the Newberry Library, 1984), p. 239. Subsequent citations will be in my text.

2. From the *Oxford English Dictionary*: "*Drummond light*, 1854. The lime-light or oxyhydrogen light (invented by Capt. T. Drummond, R. E. 1825), wherein a blow-pipe flame . . . impinges on a piece of pure lime, and renders it incandescent." The light was new in New York in the 1840s, and Barnum was noted for using it on top of his museum. George G. Foster gives it his usual overwriting: "Here we are at the American Museum, crowned with its Drummond Light, sending a livid, ghastly glare for a mile up the street, and pushing the shadows of the omnibuses well-nigh to Niblo's." A description of an assignation inside the museum follows. *New York by Gas-Light and Other Urban Sketches by George G. Foster,* ed. Stuart Blumin (Berkeley: University of California Press, 1990), p. 7.

3. As quoted by Donald Fanger, *Dostoevsky and Romantic Realism: A Study of Dostoevsky in Relation to Balzac, Dickens, and Gogol* (Cambridge: Harvard University Press, 1967), p. 35.

4. Cornelius Mathews, *A Pen-and-Ink Panorama of New York City* (New York: John S. Taylor, 1853), pp. 32–33.

5. Herman Melville, "Bartleby, the Scrivener," in *The Piazza Tales and Other Prose Pieces, 1839–1860*, ed. Harrison Hayford, Alma A. MacDougall, and G. Thomas Tanselle (Evanston and Chicago: Northwestern University Press and the Newberry Library, 1987), p. 28.

6. The Mississippi was often in the 1850s the image for a kind of confidence in American progress and unity, a confidence that Melville found spectacularly foolish. Here is the historian George Bancroft in an 1854 speech called "The Necessity, the Reality, and the Promise of the Progress of the Human Race": "The course of civilization flows on like a mighty river through a boundless valley, calling to the streams from every side to swell its current, which is always growing wider, and deeper, and clearer, as it rolls along. Let us trust ourselves upon its bosom without fear; nay, rather with confidence and joy. Since the progress of the race appears to be the great

purpose of Providence, it becomes us all to venerate the future. . . . Everything is in movement, and for the better" (*Literary and Historical Miscellanies* [New York: Harper's, 1855]).

7. Lydia Maria Child, *Letters from New York* (New York: C. S. Francis, 1844), p. 13; Elizabeth Oakes Smith, *The Newsboy* (New York: J. C. Derby, 1854), p. 192. There is no reason to think the blind African Americans Child and Smith describe are the same man. Samuel Iraneus Prime does describe the same man Child wrote about. He is leaning against a building where an elegant dinner is taking place. See *Life in New York* (New York: Robert Carter, 1847), pp. 87–100.

8. *Westminster Review* (July 1857) as quoted in the "Historical Note" to *The Confidence-Man*, p. 318; H. Bruce Franklin, *The Wake of the Gods: Melville's Mythology* (Stanford, Calif.: Stanford University Press, 1963), p. 153; Fitz-James O'Brien, "Our Young Authors—Melville," *Putnam's Monthly* 1 (February 1853): 164.

9. The Curtis letter to Dix is quoted in the "Historical Note" to the Northwestern-Newberry edition of *The Confidence-Man*, p. 278.

10. My source for the details of publication of *The Confidence-Man* is the "Historical Note" to the Northwestern-Newberry edition, pp. 278–79.

11. Helen Trimpi identifies this character unambiguously as Mose. She points out as well that Lewis Cass was caricatured in political cartoons as a "b'hoy" (*Melville's Confidence Men and American Politics in the 1850s* [Hamden, Conn.: Archon Books, 1987], p. 143).

12. See Ted N. Weissbuch, "A Note on the Confidence-Man's Counterfeit Detector," *ESQ* 19 (1960): 16–18.

13. Cornelius Mathews, *The Career of Puffer Hopkins* (New York: D. Appleton & Co., 1842), p. 272.

14. Elizabeth S. Foster, thanking Jay Leyda, records the title of the Springfield *Daily Republican* article in her edition of *The Confidence-Man* (New York: Hendricks House, 1954), "Notes," p. 299. The Albany item and its connection to the late 1840s swindler is explained at greater length in my "The Original Confidence Man," *American Quarterly* 21 (1969): 560–77.

15. *Newark Daily Advertiser* (May 23, 1857), as quoted in Hugh W. Hetherington, *Melville's Reviewers: British and American 1846–1891* (Chapel Hill: University of North Carolina Press, 1961), p. 257. *Boston Evening Transcript* (April 10, 1857). Other praise came from a writer of an inexpensive pamphlet. Following a definition of "Confidence Man," *Tricks and Traps of Chicago* (New York: n.p., 1859) adds: "Whoever has read Hermann [*sic*] Melville's "Confidence Man" will have formed a very clear and accurate idea of this species of the genus homo, as exhibited in many of his chameleon-like phases" (p. 51).

16. O'Brien, "Melville and Curtis," p. 391. The "Historical Note" of the Northwestern-Newberry edition of *The Confidence-Man* also identifies the editor O'Brien refers to as Greeley (p. 321).

17. Erik S. Lunde quotes from John G. Shortall's "Horace Greeley" in the Horace Greeley collection in the Library of Congress: "Sitting at a desk as high as his chin, with his back toward you as you entered, you might have seen [Greeley], his long flaxen hair, curling a little at the ends very thinly covering his large shapely head, the floor about his feet thickly strewn with exchanges, and nothing audible but the scratch, scratch, of that busy pen . . . his gold framed spectacles well upon his forehead, and his chin almost touching the large, white, well-formed hand with which he wrote his almost undecipherable 'Copy,' sheet after sheet of which he would throw upon the floor beside him, or hold upon his knees. When he turned toward you, however, the curiously shrewd, yet child-like face, cleanshaven, with its sweet smile, and the combination of directness, earnestness, honesty, visible in it, when once well seen, could never be forgotten." *Horace Greeley* (Boston: Twayne, 1981), p. 21. See also George Ripley's description in "Horace Greeley," *Putnam's Magazine* 6 (July 1855): 76–85. All descriptions concentrate on *whiteness*.

18. William M. Ramsey, "Audiences of *The Confidence-Man*: Consensus vs. Interpretive Communities," *Melville Society Extracts* 72 (February 1988): 9–12. See also John Bryant's "*The Confidence-Man*," in his *A Companion to Melville Studies* (New York: Greenwood Press, 1986), pp. 315–50, and the "Historical Note" in the Northwestern-Newberry *The Confidence-Man*, pp. 255–357.

19. John Bryant identifies a "cosmopolitan" type in American culture and in Melville's *The Confidence-Man*. See *Melville and Repose: The Rhetoric of Humor in the American Renaissance* (New York: Oxford University Press, 1993), pp. 109–28, 244–67, passim. Many New York literary men of the period fancied themselves sophisticated versions of cosmopolitans—including particularly *Tribune* writers George William Curtis and Bayard Taylor.

20. Since for Helen Trimpi the Philosophical Intelligence Officer is unambiguously Horace Greeley, for her the mute cannot be Greeley. He is a combination of the Quakers John Woolman and Benjamin Lundy. Other Trimpi identifications are the barber as Stephen A. Douglas, the episcopal clergyman as Dudley Tyng, the Methodist minister as William Brownlow, Henry Roberts as David Wilmot, the man in gray as Theodore Parker, the charitable lady as Lydia M. Sigourney, John Truman as Thurlow Weed, the miser as Francis Preston Blair, the herb doctor as Charles Sumner, the Titan as either John C. Calhoun or Preston Brooks, Pitch as Thomas Hart Benton, and Frank Goodman as Henry Ward Beecher. Even the Irish voice in the last chapter is identified as an allusion to Mike Walsh, the Bowery b'hoy politician. All of these identifications and counter-identifications are well summarized in the "Historical Note" to the Northwestern-Newberry edition and in John Bryant, "*The Confidence-Man*," in his *Companion*. The "Historical Note" says: "a critic deficient in confidence might even declare that except for Emerson not one of the public figures canvassed . . . was beyond reasonable doubt used as a

model by Melville—or, if in part so used, meant to be recognized" (p. 292). And Bryant says, "*The Confidence-Man* is far from being a *Fable for Critics*; its satiric butts, if they exist at all, are deeply submerged" (p. 330).

21. Hershel Parker's annotations to his edition of *The Confidence-Man* are an excellent guide to finding the Devil in the text (New York: W. W. Norton, 1971), passim. The "Historical Note" to the Northwestern-Newberry edition of the novel has other fascinating readings and suggestions. It notes that in 1849 Melville jotted into his Shakespeare the phrase "Devil as a Quaker" and some notes indicating that the Devil was to appear at the Astor House hotel in New York, go to a party, talk about archangels, and address a group of the "principal" devils with "arguments to persuade." There seems to be no published story with this theme, although the group of ideas in Melville's mind may have worked their way into the writing of *The Confidence-Man* some six years later (p. 305). For my purposes it is important that Melville was imagining the Devil in New York.

22. Jean-Christophe Agnew writes, "The novel abounds with references to the popular events and figures of the day, but these commonplaces undergo a radical defamiliarization in Melville's hands. Nothing is what it seems in the placeless market and theater of the *Fidèle*" (*Worlds Apart: The Market and the Theater in Anglo-American Thought, 1550–1750* [Cambridge: Cambridge University Press, 1986], p. 199).

23. "On the Genius of Charles Dickens," *Putnam's Monthly* 5 (1855): 262–72. George W. Curtis repeatedly gave a lecture with the same title. See Gordon Milne, *George William Curtis and the Genteel Tradition* (Bloomington: Indiana University Press, 1956), "Bibliography," p. 266.

24. *Philadelphia North American* (April 4, 1857). O'Brien quoted in the "Historical Note" to the Northwestern-Newberry edition of *The Confidence-Man*, p. 319.

25. Edgar A. Dryden writes about the conflation of the divine and the human in *The Confidence-Man*. See his *Melville's Thematics of Form: The Great Art of Telling the Truth* (Baltimore: Johns Hopkins University Press, 1968), pp. 150–95.

26. The quotation is from "Hawthorne and His Mosses," *Piazza Tales and Other Prose Pieces*, p. 244.

27. Bryant, *Melville and Repose*, p. 261. Subsequent citations will be in my text.

28. Elizabeth S. Foster, in her edition of *The Confidence-Man*, first suggested the meanings of the symbols (New York: Hendricks House, 1954), p. xvi.

29. Dryden relates the boy to Hermes in his *Melville's Thematics of Form*, pp. 192–95. R.W.B. Lewis associates Hermes with the confidence man but not with the peddler boy (*Trials of the Word* [New Haven: Yale University Press, 1965], p. 69).

INDEX